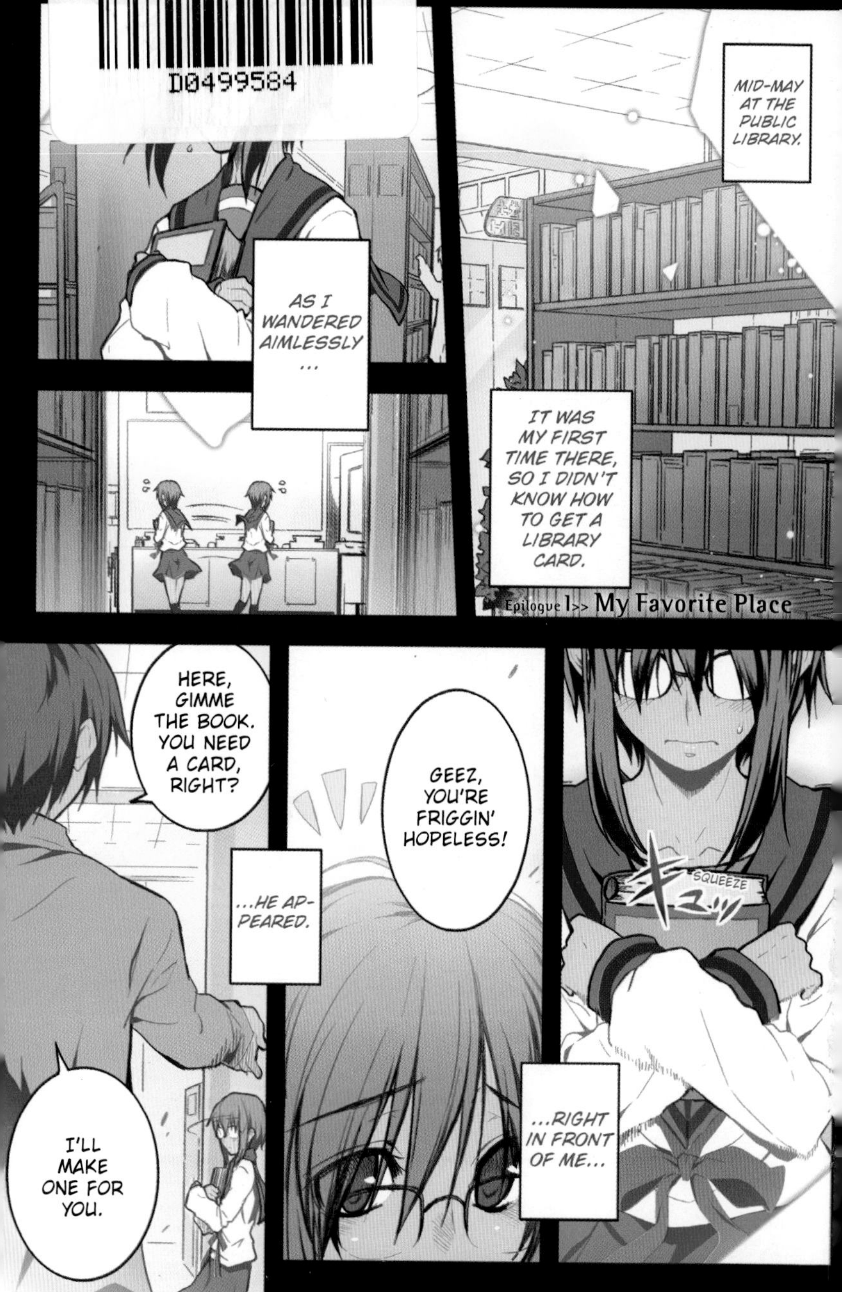
MID-MAY AT THE PUBLIC LIBRARY.
IT WAS MY FIRST TIME THERE, SO I DIDN'T KNOW HOW TO GET A LIBRARY CARD.
Epilogue 1>> My Favorite Place
AS I WANDERED AIMLESSLY...
SQUEEZE
...RIGHT IN FRONT OF ME...
GEEZ, YOU'RE FRIGGIN' HOPELESS!
...HE AP-PEARED.
HERE, GIMME THE BOOK. YOU NEED A CARD, RIGHT?
I'LL MAKE ONE FOR YOU.

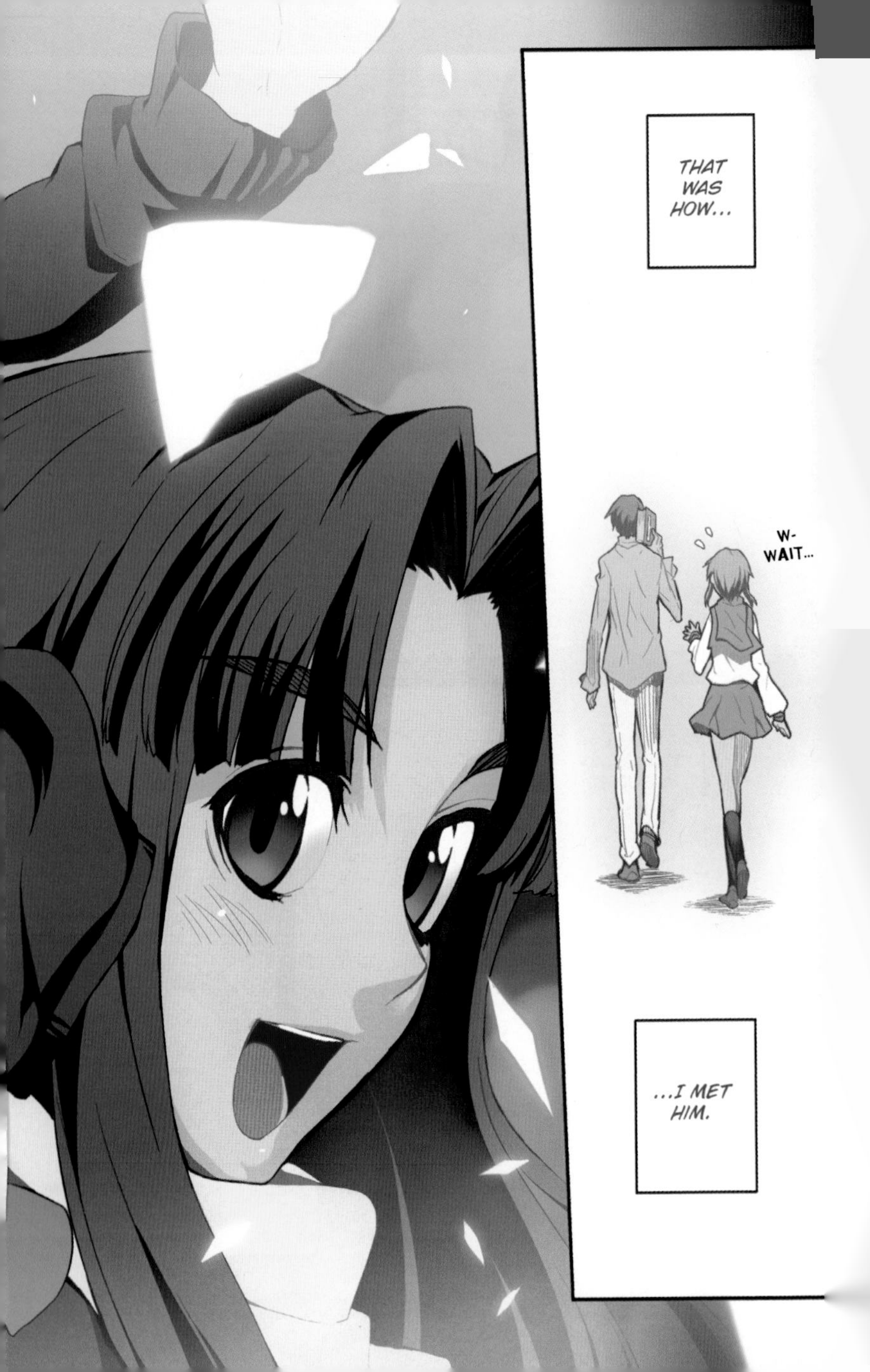
THAT WAS HOW...
W-WAIT...
...I MET HIM.

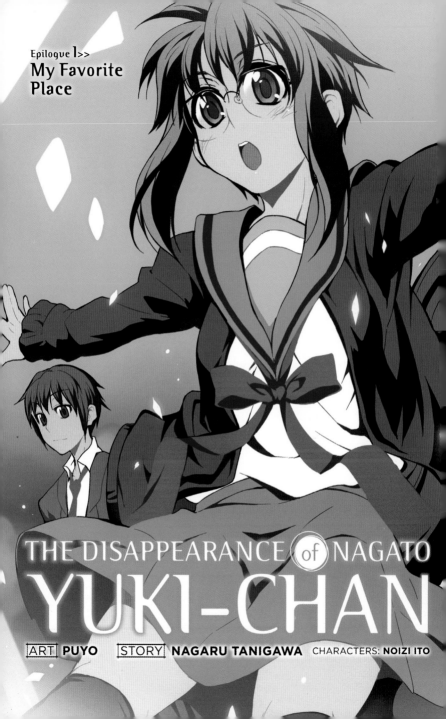

Epilogue 1>>
My Favorite
Place

THE DISAPPEARANCE of NAGATO
YUKI-CHAN

ART PUYO   STORY NAGARU TANIGAWA   CHARACTERS: NOIZI ITO

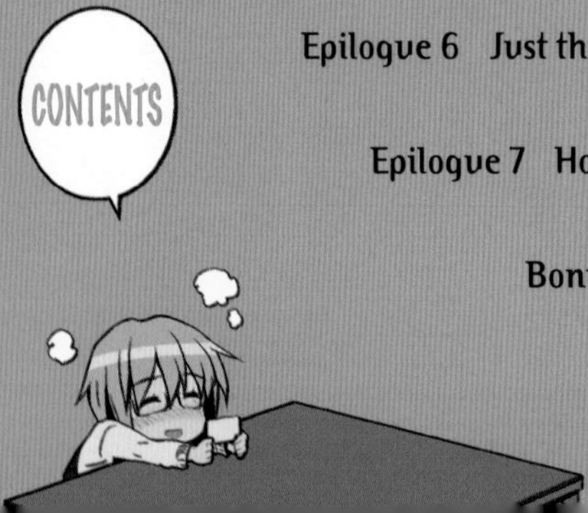
CONTENTS

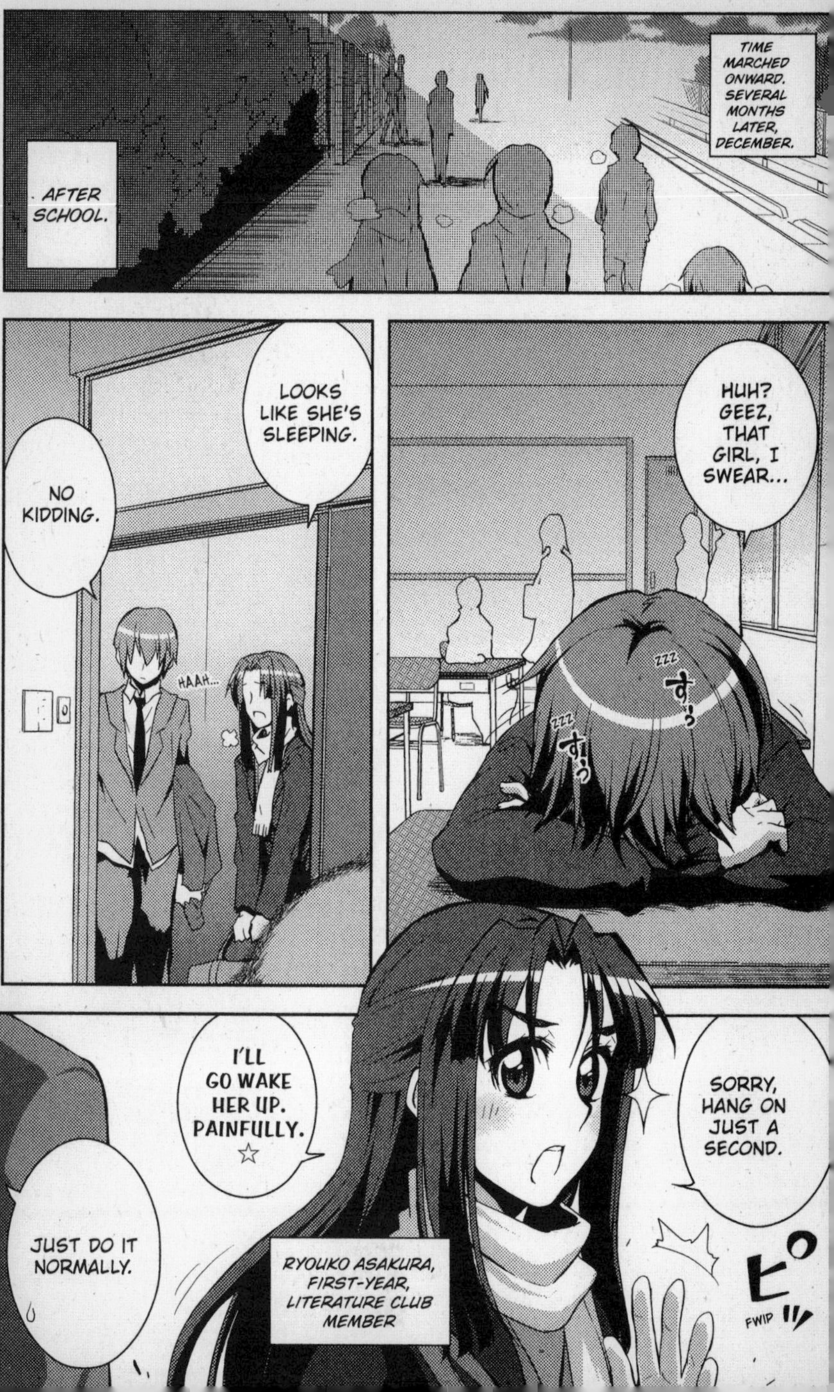
TIME MARCHED ONWARD. SEVERAL MONTHS LATER, DECEMBER.
AFTER SCHOOL.
HUH? GEEZ, THAT GIRL, I SWEAR...
ZZZ すぅ
ZZZ すぅ
LOOKS LIKE SHE'S SLEEPING.
NO KIDDING.
HAAAH...
SORRY, HANG ON JUST A SECOND.
I'LL GO WAKE HER UP. PAINFULLY. ☆
RYOUKO ASAKURA, FIRST-YEAR, LITERATURE CLUB MEMBER
ピ FWIP
JUST DO IT NORMALLY.

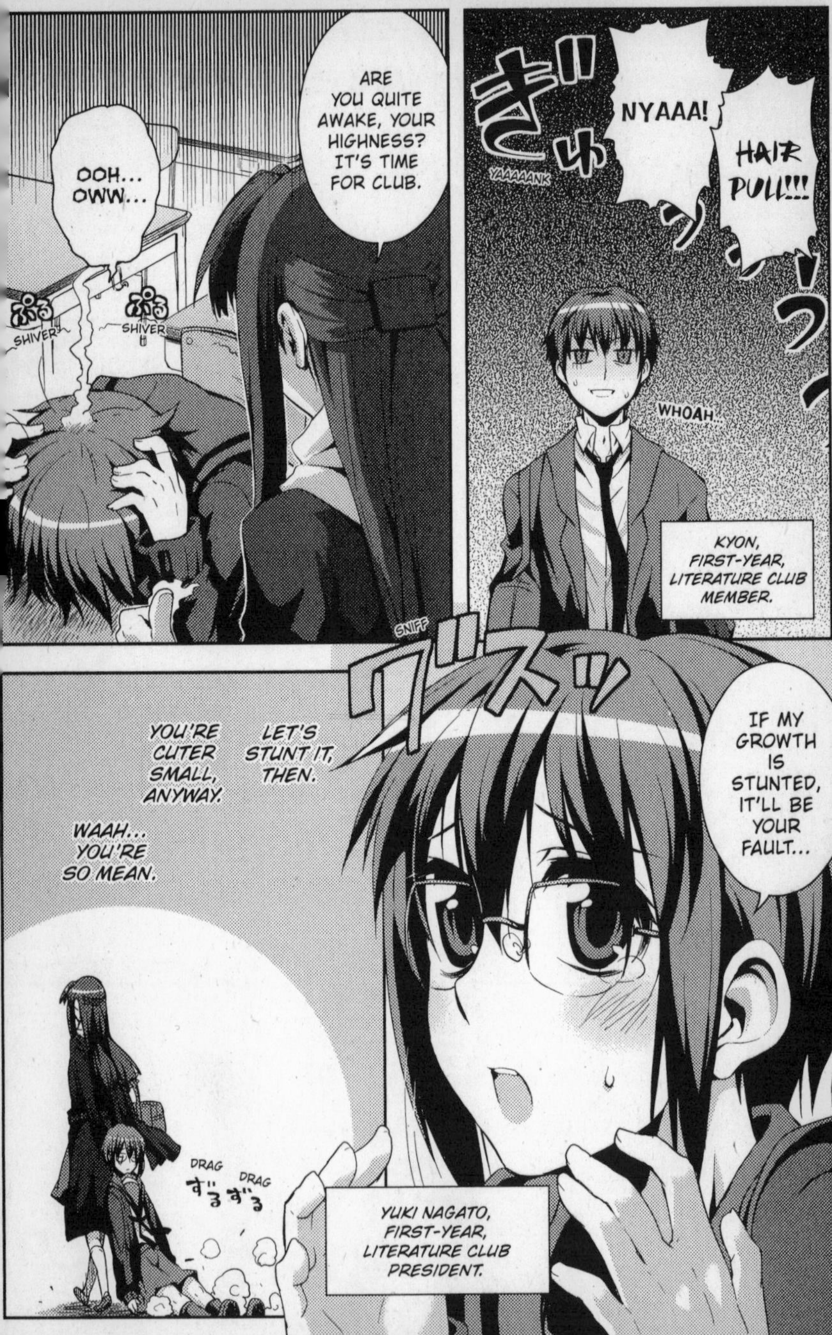
ぎゅ
YAAAAANK
NYAAA!
HAIR PULL!!!
WHOAH...
KYON, FIRST-YEAR, LITERATURE CLUB MEMBER.
ARE YOU QUITE AWAKE, YOUR HIGHNESS? IT'S TIME FOR CLUB.
OOH... OWW...
ぷる
SHIVER
ぷる
SHIVER
グズッ
SNIFF
IF MY GROWTH IS STUNTED, IT'LL BE YOUR FAULT...
LET'S STUNT IT, THEN.
YOU'RE CUTER SMALL, ANYWAY.
WAAH... YOU'RE SO MEAN.
ずるずる
DRAG DRAG
YUKI NAGATO, FIRST-YEAR, LITERATURE CLUB PRESIDENT.

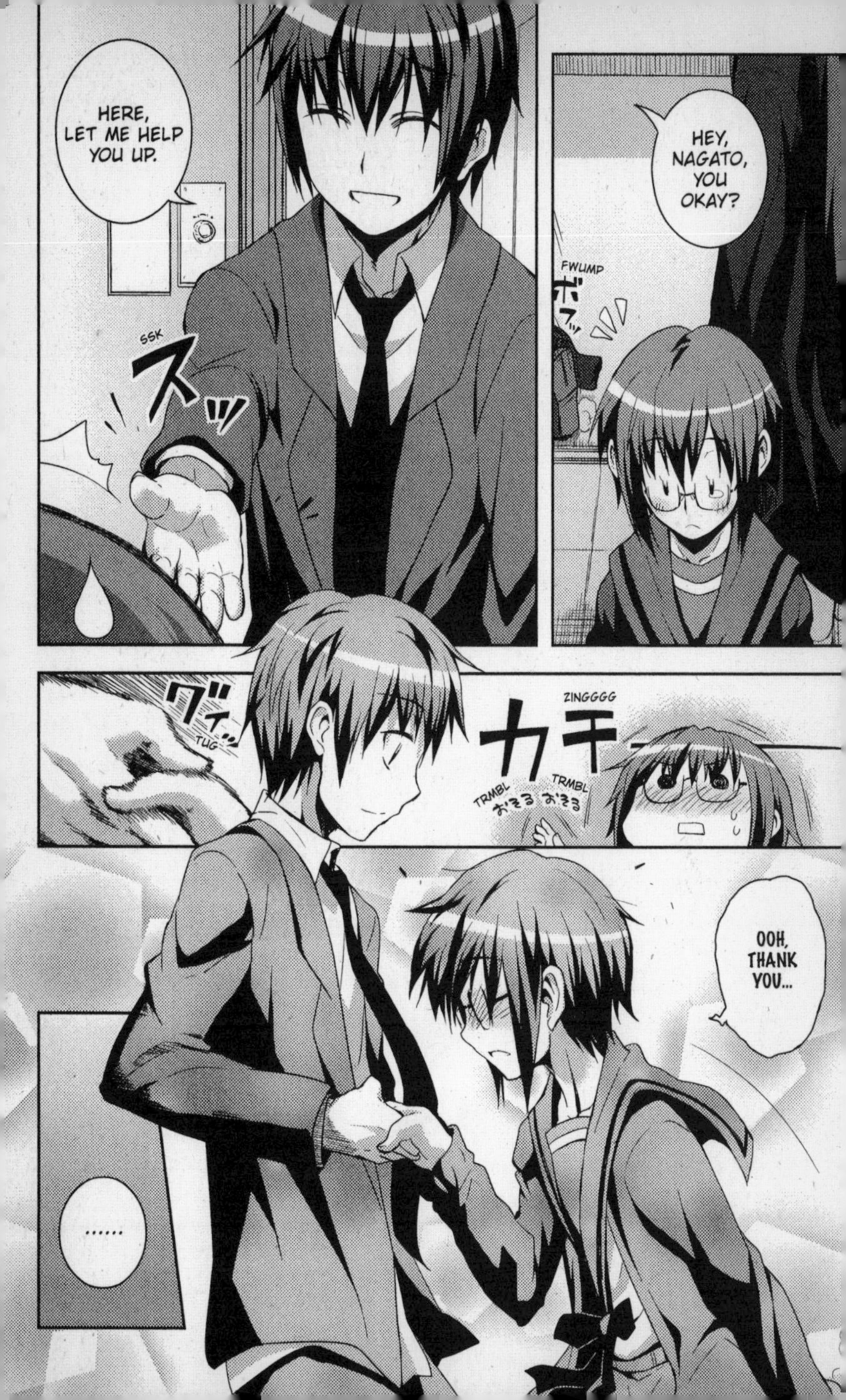
HEY, NAGATO, YOU OKAY?
FWUMP
ボフッ
HERE, LET ME HELP YOU UP.
SSK
スッ
ZINGGGG
カチー
TRMBL
TRMBL
おそる おそる
TUG
グイ
OOH, THANK YOU...
......

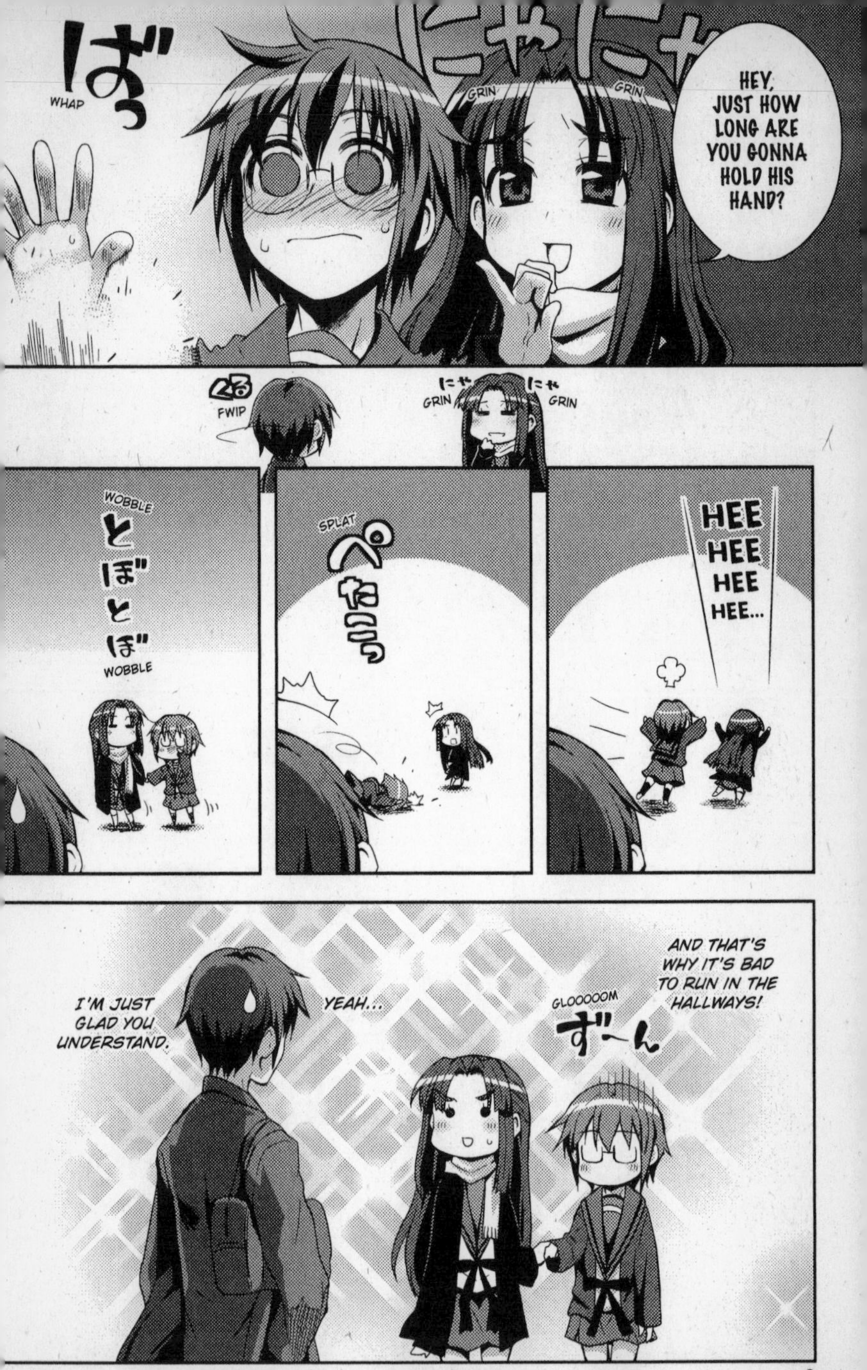
HEY, JUST HOW LONG ARE YOU GONNA HOLD HIS HAND?
GRIN
GRIN
ぱっ
WHAP
にや
GRIN
にや
GRIN
くる
FWIP
HEE HEE HEE HEE...
SPLAT
ぺたっ
WOBBLE
とぼとぼ
WOBBLE
AND THAT'S WHY IT'S BAD TO RUN IN THE HALLWAYS!
GLOOOOOM
ず～ん
YEAH...
I'M JUST GLAD YOU UNDERSTAND.

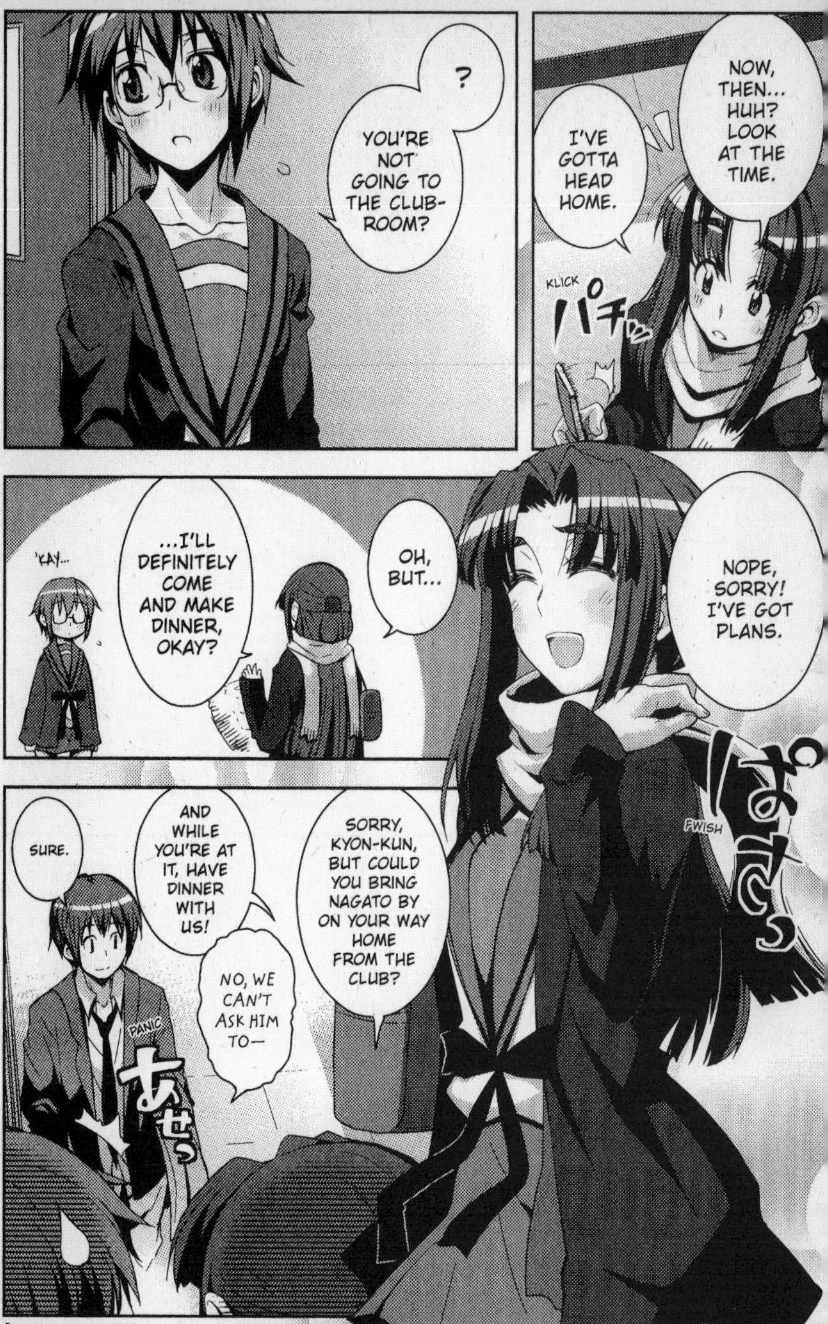
NOW, THEN... HUH? LOOK AT THE TIME.
I'VE GOTTA HEAD HOME.
KLICK
?
YOU'RE NOT GOING TO THE CLUB-ROOM?
NOPE, SORRY! I'VE GOT PLANS.
FWISH
OH, BUT...
...I'LL DEFINITELY COME AND MAKE DINNER, OKAY?
'KAY...
SORRY, KYON-KUN, BUT COULD YOU BRING NAGATO BY ON YOUR WAY HOME FROM THE CLUB?
AND WHILE YOU'RE AT IT, HAVE DINNER WITH US!
NO, WE CAN'T ASK HIM TO—
SURE.
PANIC

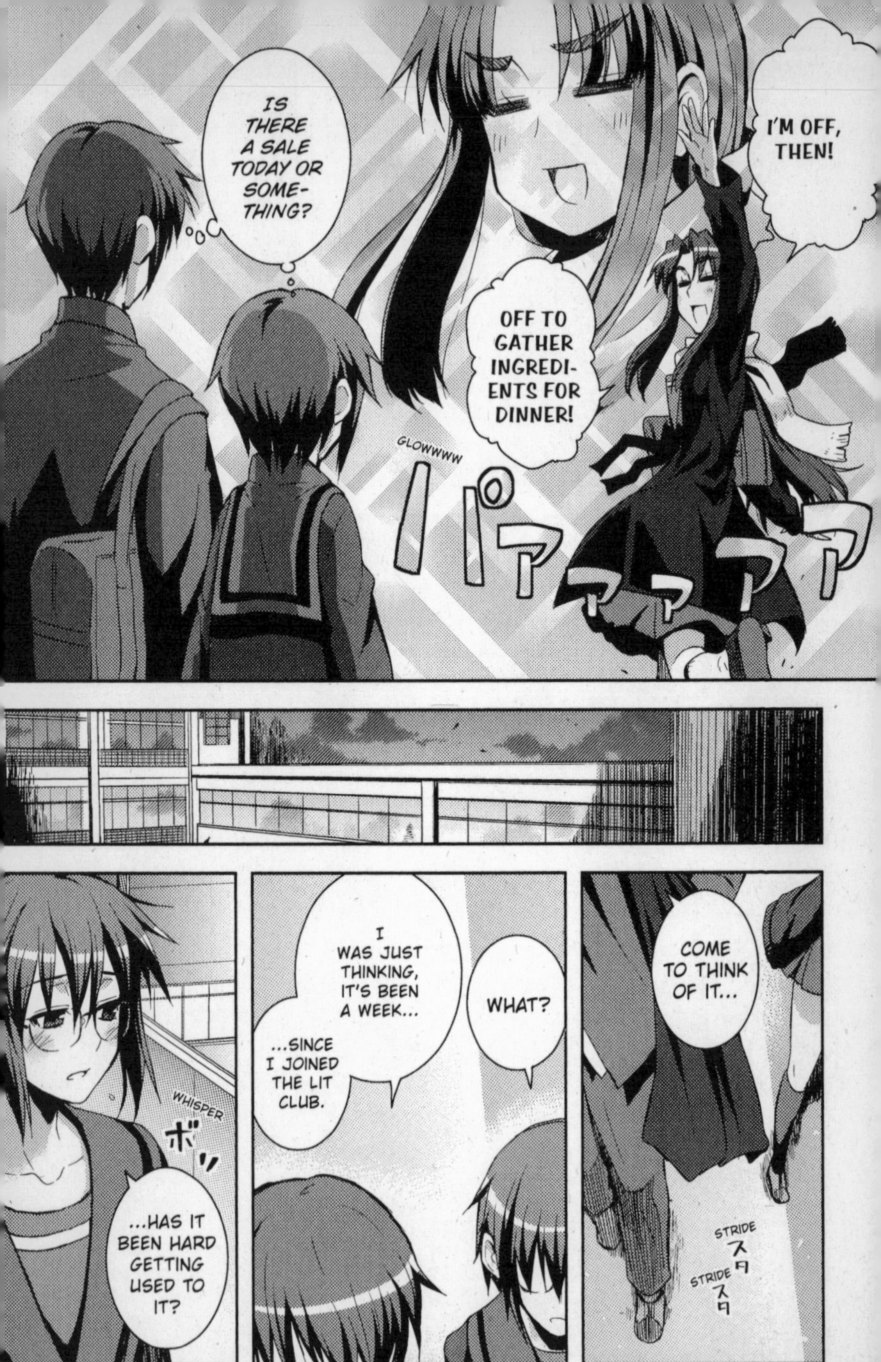
I'M OFF, THEN!
OFF TO GATHER INGREDIENTS FOR DINNER!
GLOWWWW
パァァァァ
IS THERE A SALE TODAY OR SOMETHING?
COME TO THINK OF IT...
STRIDE
スタ
STRIDE
スタ
WHAT?
I WAS JUST THINKING, IT'S BEEN A WEEK...
...SINCE I JOINED THE LIT CLUB.
WHISPER
ボソ
...HAS IT BEEN HARD GETTING USED TO IT?

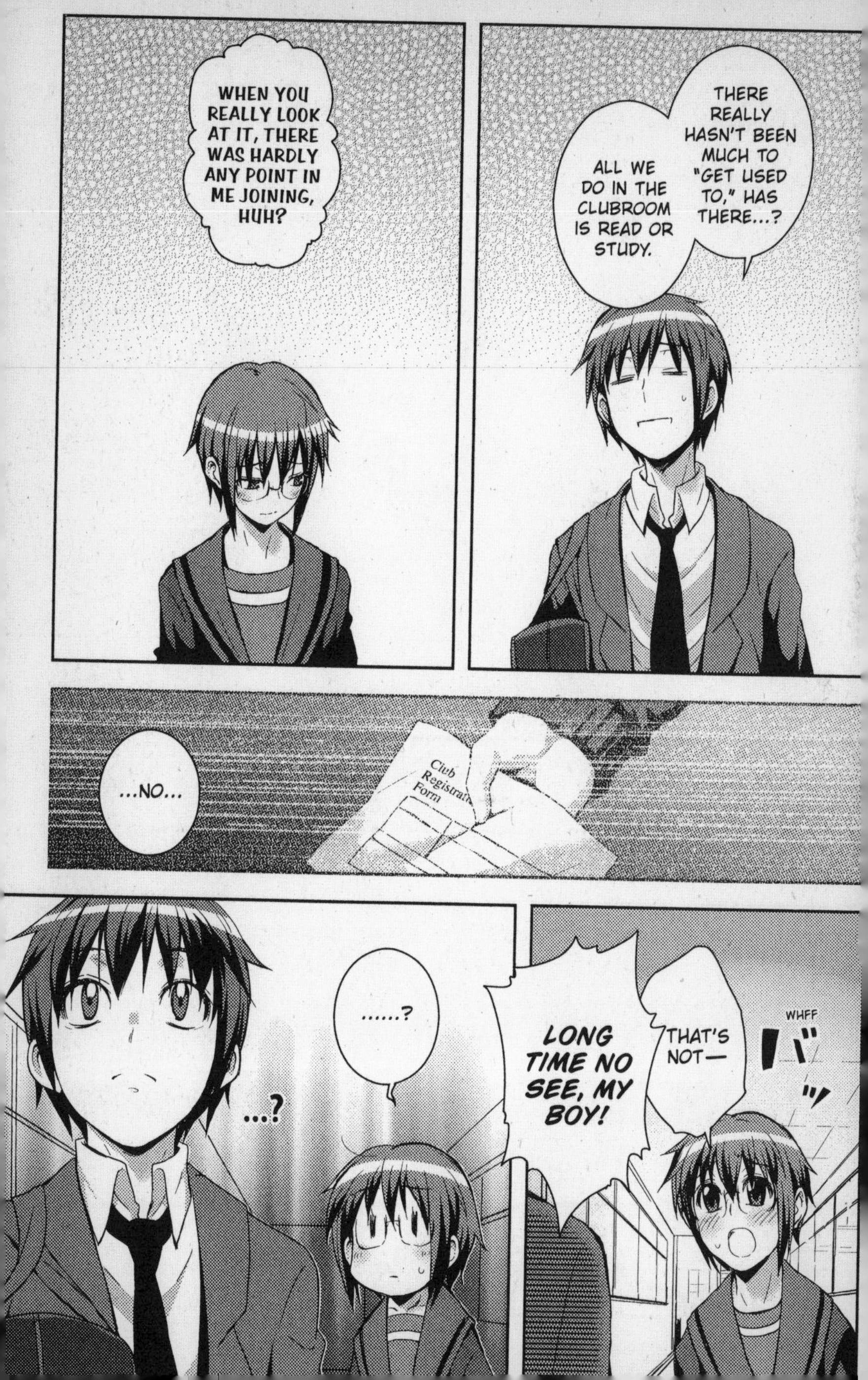
THERE REALLY HASN'T BEEN MUCH TO "GET USED TO," HAS THERE...?
ALL WE DO IN THE CLUBROOM IS READ OR STUDY.
WHEN YOU REALLY LOOK AT IT, THERE WAS HARDLY ANY POINT IN ME JOINING, HUH?
Club Registrat Form
...NO...
WHFF
バッ
THAT'S NOT—
LONG TIME NO SEE, MY BOY!
......?
...?

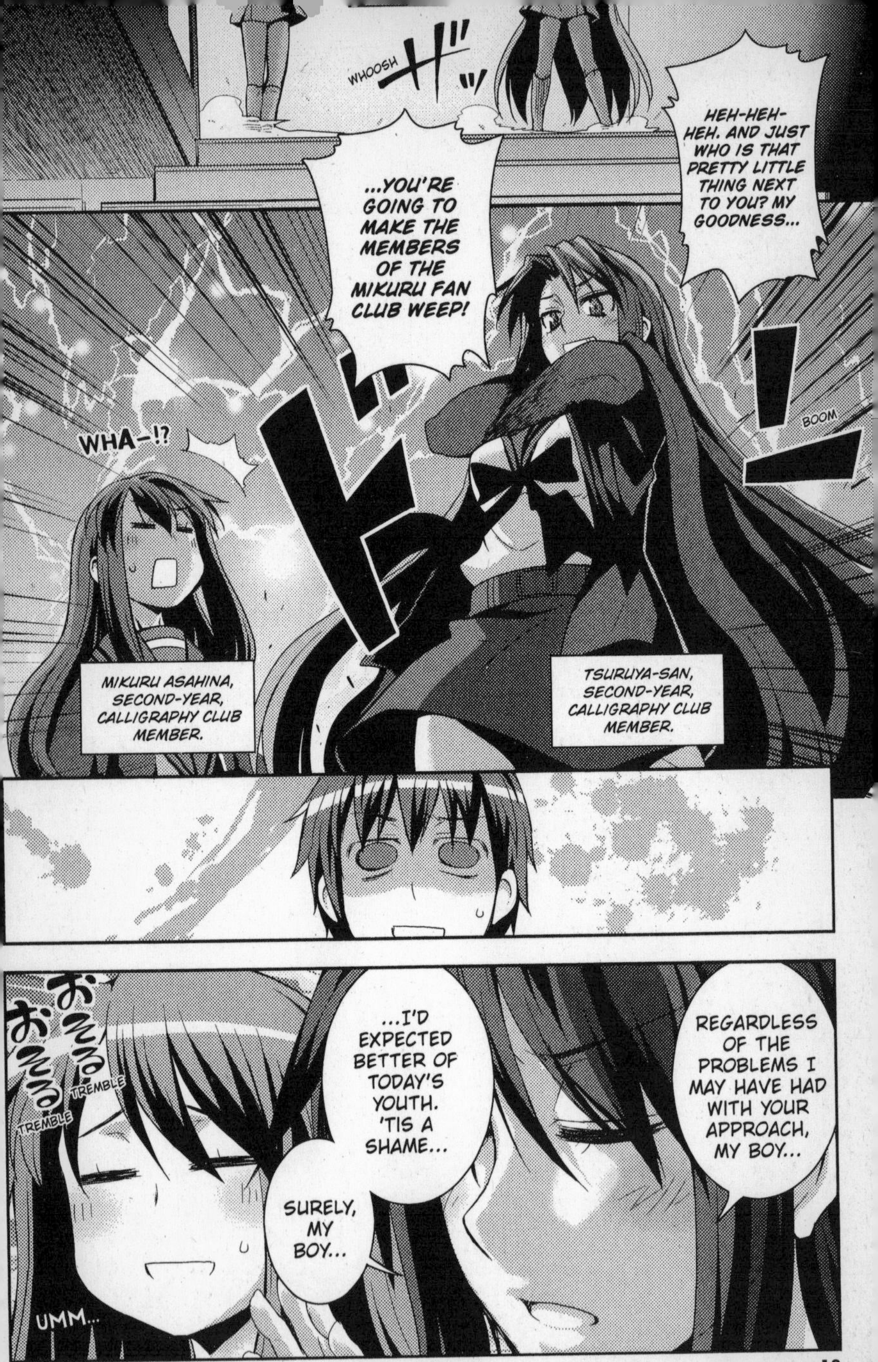
WHOOSH
HEH-HEH-HEH. AND JUST WHO IS THAT PRETTY LITTLE THING NEXT TO YOU? MY GOODNESS...
...YOU'RE GOING TO MAKE THE MEMBERS OF THE MIKURU FAN CLUB WEEP!
BOOM
WHA-!?
TSURUYA-SAN, SECOND-YEAR, CALLIGRAPHY CLUB MEMBER.
MIKURU ASAHINA, SECOND-YEAR, CALLIGRAPHY CLUB MEMBER.
REGARDLESS OF THE PROBLEMS I MAY HAVE HAD WITH YOUR APPROACH, MY BOY...
...I'D EXPECTED BETTER OF TODAY'S YOUTH. 'TIS A SHAME...
SURELY, MY BOY...
おそるおそる
TREMBLE
TREMBLE
UMM...

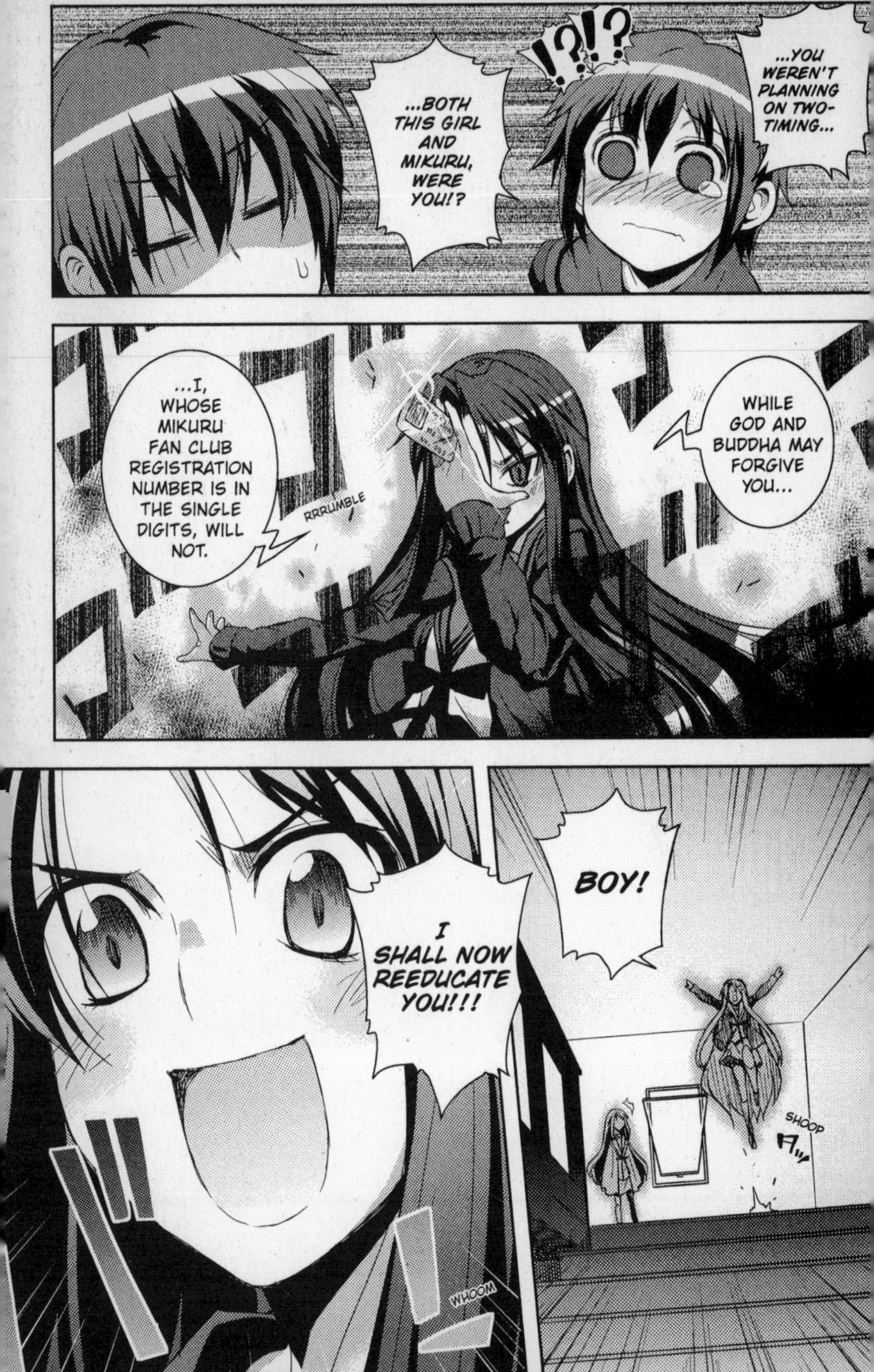
...YOU WEREN'T PLANNING ON TWO-TIMING...
!?!?
...BOTH THIS GIRL AND MIKURU, WERE YOU!?
WHILE GOD AND BUDDHA MAY FORGIVE YOU...
RRRUMBLE
...I, WHOSE MIKURU FAN CLUB REGISTRATION NUMBER IS IN THE SINGLE DIGITS, WILL NOT.
BOY!
SHOOP
I SHALL NOW REEDUCATE YOU!!!
WHOOM

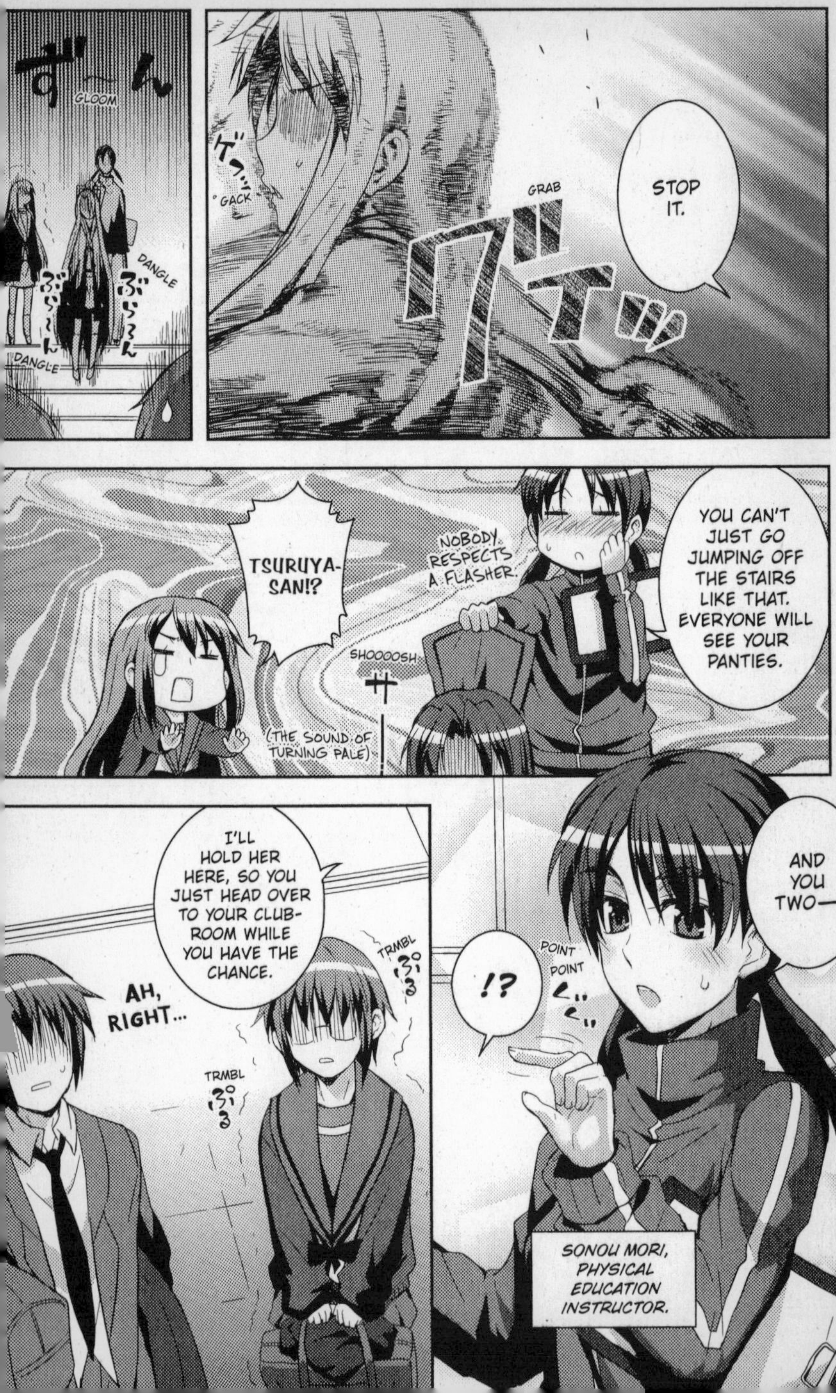
STOP IT.
GRAB
ガッ
ゲフッ
GACK
ず〜ん
GLOOM
ぶら〜ん
DANGLE
ぶら〜ん
DANGLE
YOU CAN'T JUST GO JUMPING OFF THE STAIRS LIKE THAT. EVERYONE WILL SEE YOUR PANTIES.
NOBODY RESPECTS A FLASHER.
TSURUYA-SAN!?
SHOOOOSH
サ
(THE SOUND OF TURNING PALE)
AND YOU TWO—
POINT
POINT
く
く
!?
TRMBL
ぷる
I'LL HOLD HER HERE, SO YOU JUST HEAD OVER TO YOUR CLUB-ROOM WHILE YOU HAVE THE CHANCE.
AH, RIGHT...
TRMBL
ぷる
SONOU MORI, PHYSICAL EDUCATION INSTRUCTOR.

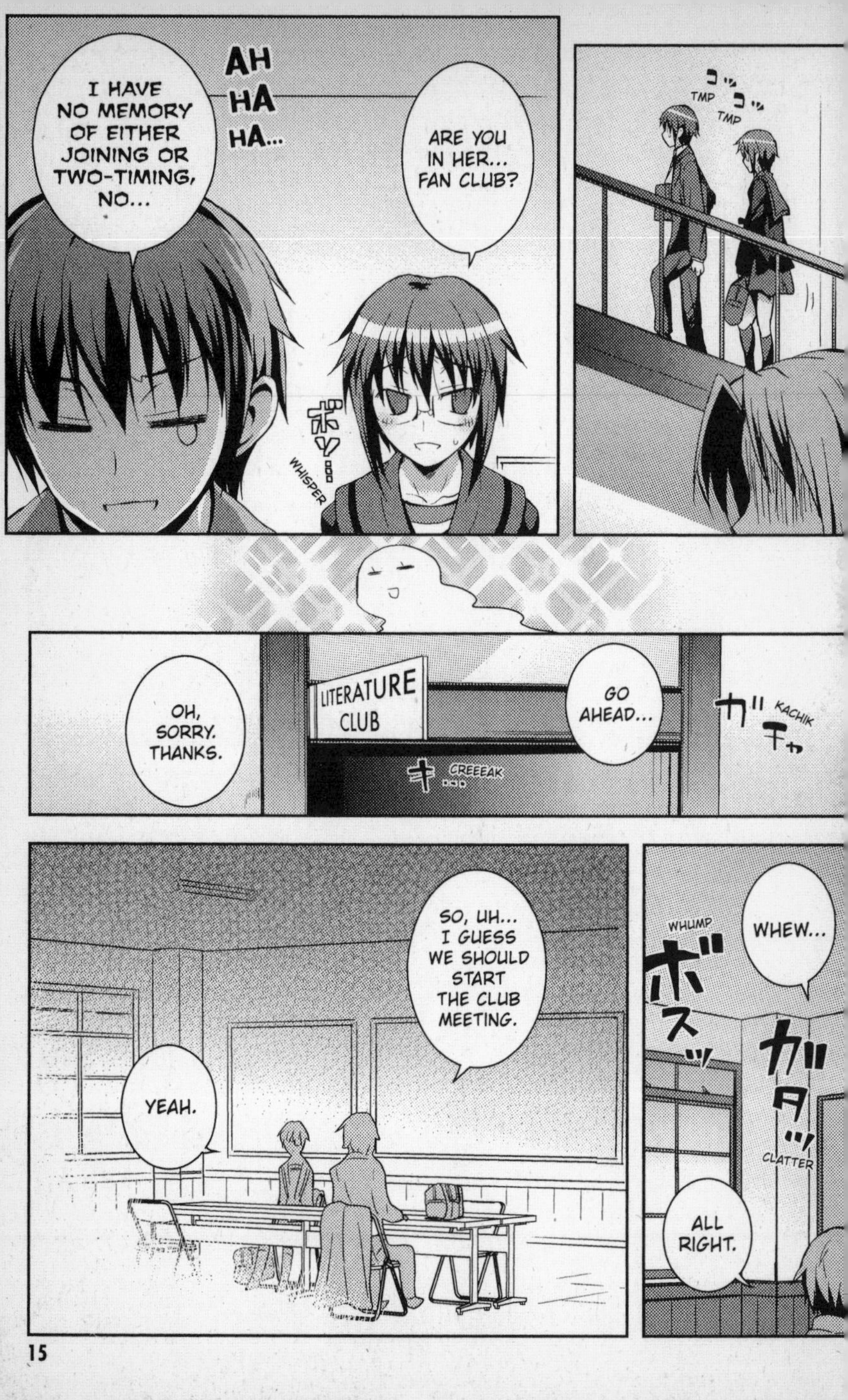
TMP
TMP
ARE YOU IN HER... FAN CLUB?
AH HA HA...
I HAVE NO MEMORY OF EITHER JOINING OR TWO-TIMING, NO...
WHISPER
KACHIK
GO AHEAD...
LITERATURE CLUB
CREEEAK
OH, SORRY. THANKS.
WHEW...
WHUMP
CLATTER
ALL RIGHT.
SO, UH... I GUESS WE SHOULD START THE CLUB MEETING.
YEAH.

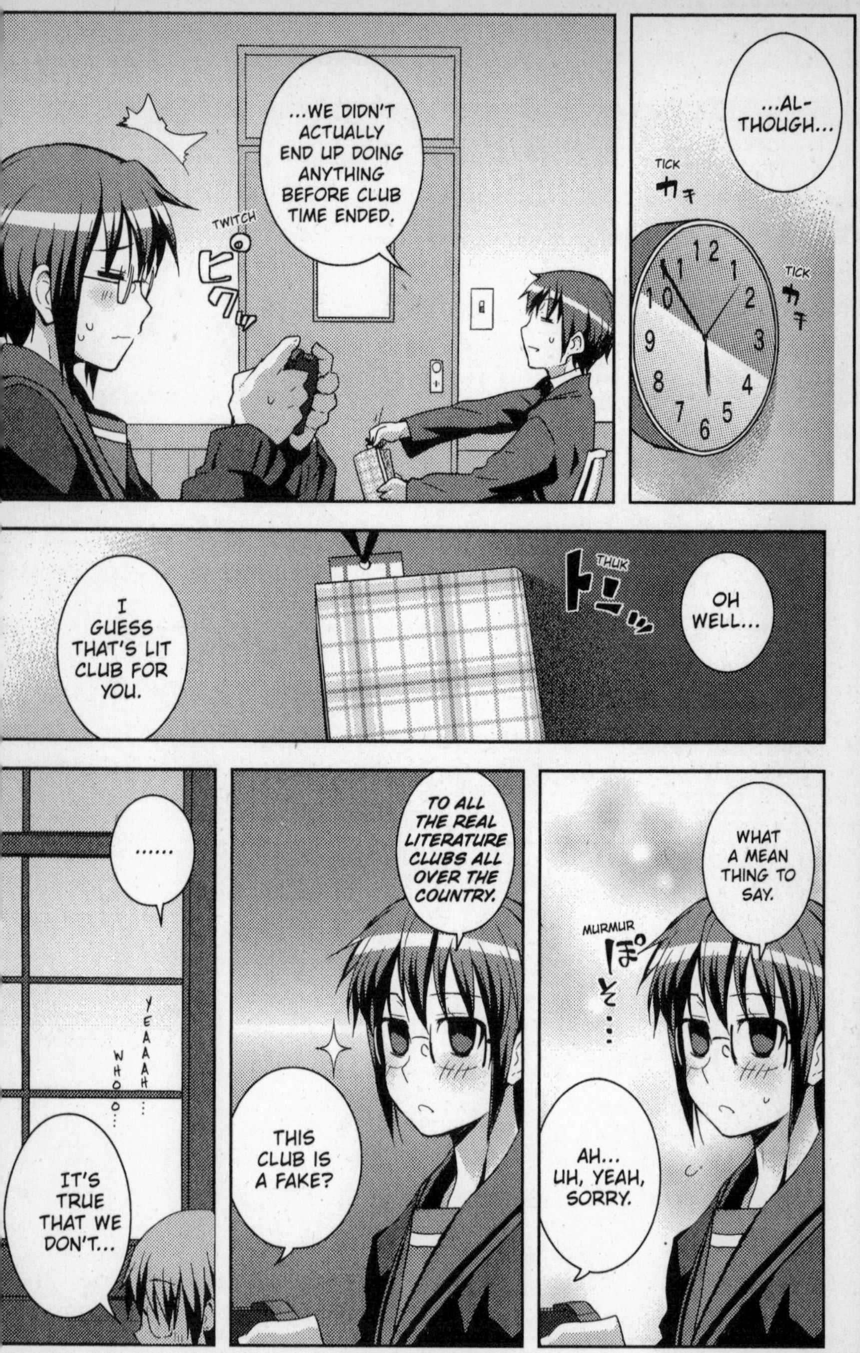
...AL-THOUGH...
TICK
カチ
TICK
カチ
...WE DIDN'T ACTUALLY END UP DOING ANYTHING BEFORE CLUB TIME ENDED.
TWITCH
ピクッ
OH WELL...
THUK
トンッ
I GUESS THAT'S LIT CLUB FOR YOU.
WHAT A MEAN THING TO SAY.
MURMUR
ぽそ...
AH... UH, YEAH, SORRY.
TO ALL THE REAL LITERATURE CLUBS ALL OVER THE COUNTRY.
THIS CLUB IS A FAKE?
......
YEAAAH...
WHOO...
IT'S TRUE THAT WE DON'T...

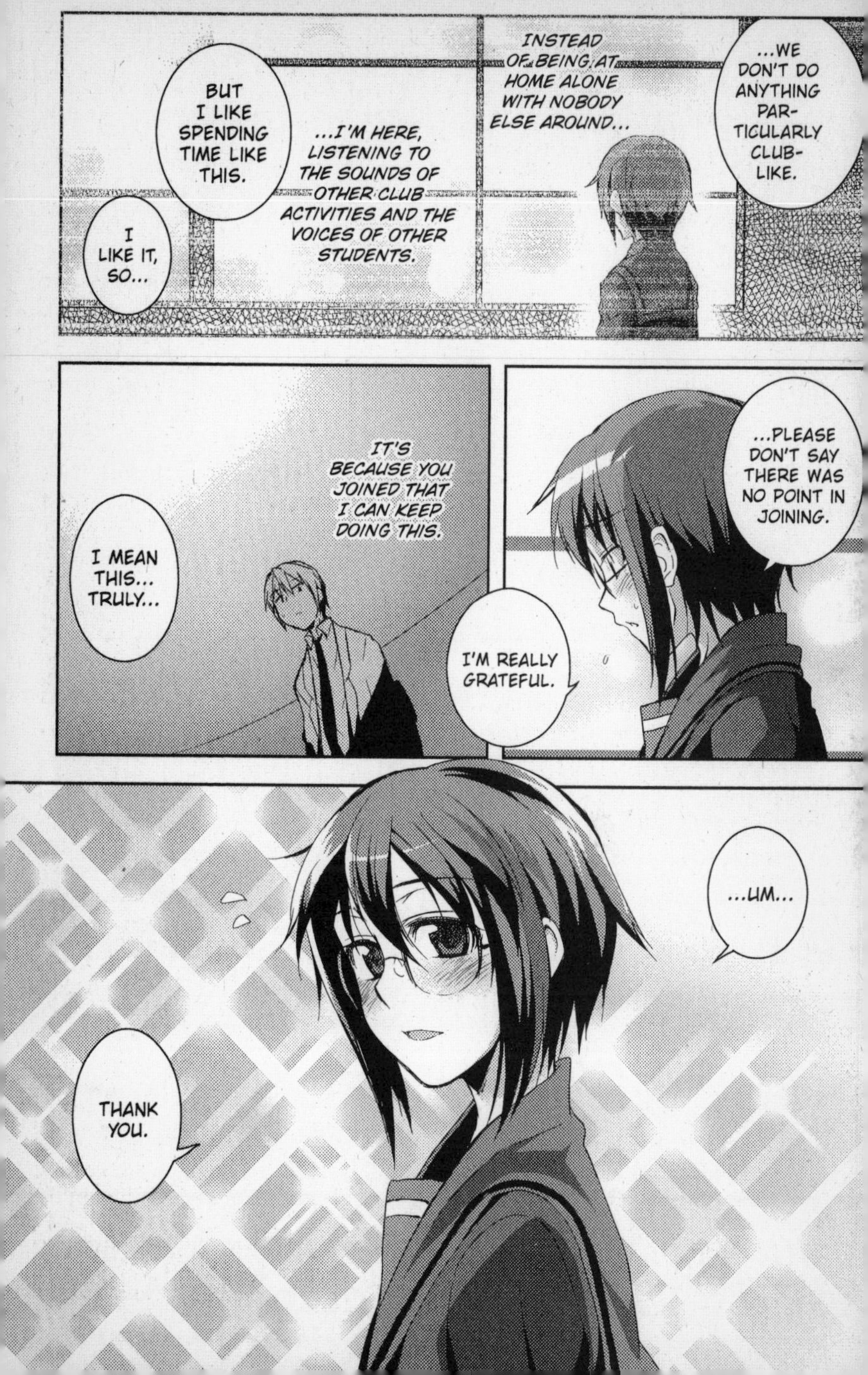
...WE DON'T DO ANYTHING PAR-TICULARLY CLUB-LIKE.
INSTEAD OF BEING AT HOME ALONE WITH NOBODY ELSE AROUND...
...I'M HERE, LISTENING TO THE SOUNDS OF OTHER CLUB ACTIVITIES AND THE VOICES OF OTHER STUDENTS.
BUT I LIKE SPENDING TIME LIKE THIS.
I LIKE IT, SO...
...PLEASE DON'T SAY THERE WAS NO POINT IN JOINING.
I'M REALLY GRATEFUL.
IT'S BECAUSE YOU JOINED THAT I CAN KEEP DOING THIS.
I MEAN THIS... TRULY...
...UM...
THANK YOU.

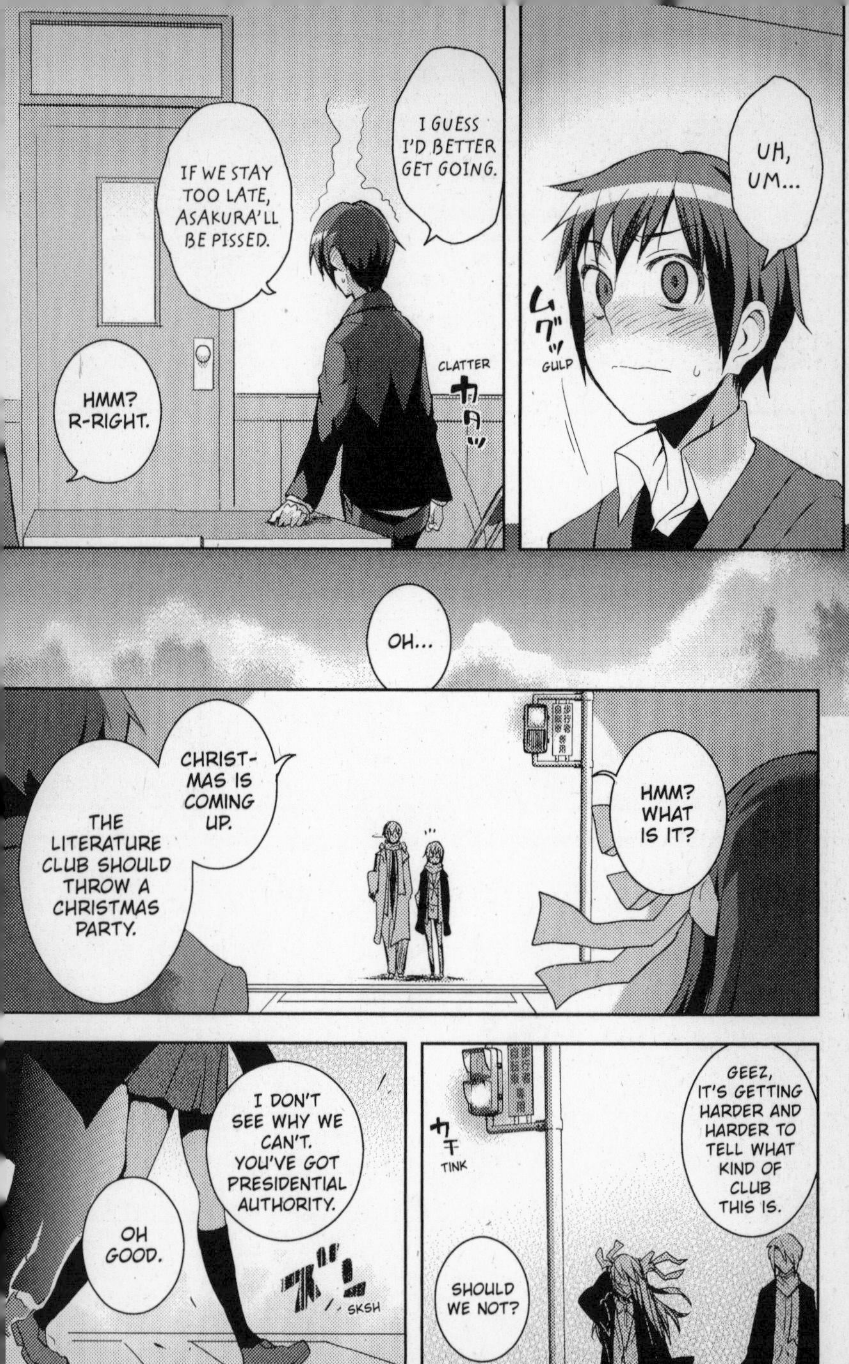
UH, UM...
ムグッ
GULP
I GUESS I'D BETTER GET GOING.
IF WE STAY TOO LATE, ASAKURA'LL BE PISSED.
CLATTER
カタッ
HMM? R-RIGHT.
OH...
HMM? WHAT IS IT?
CHRIST-MAS IS COMING UP.
THE LITERATURE CLUB SHOULD THROW A CHRISTMAS PARTY.
GEEZ, IT'S GETTING HARDER AND HARDER TO TELL WHAT KIND OF CLUB THIS IS.
カチ
TINK
SHOULD WE NOT?
I DON'T SEE WHY WE CAN'T. YOU'VE GOT PRESIDENTIAL AUTHORITY.
OH GOOD.
SKSH

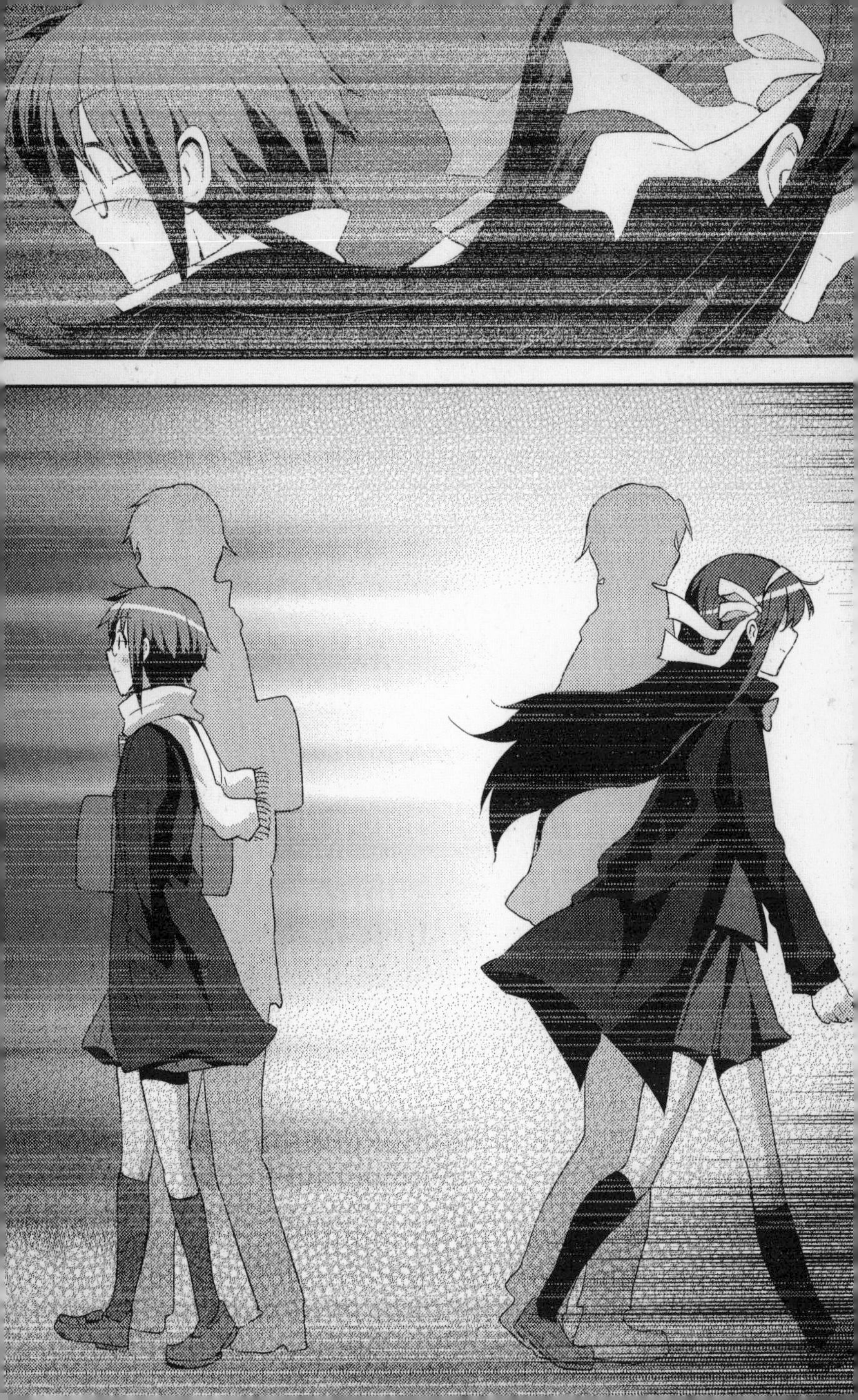

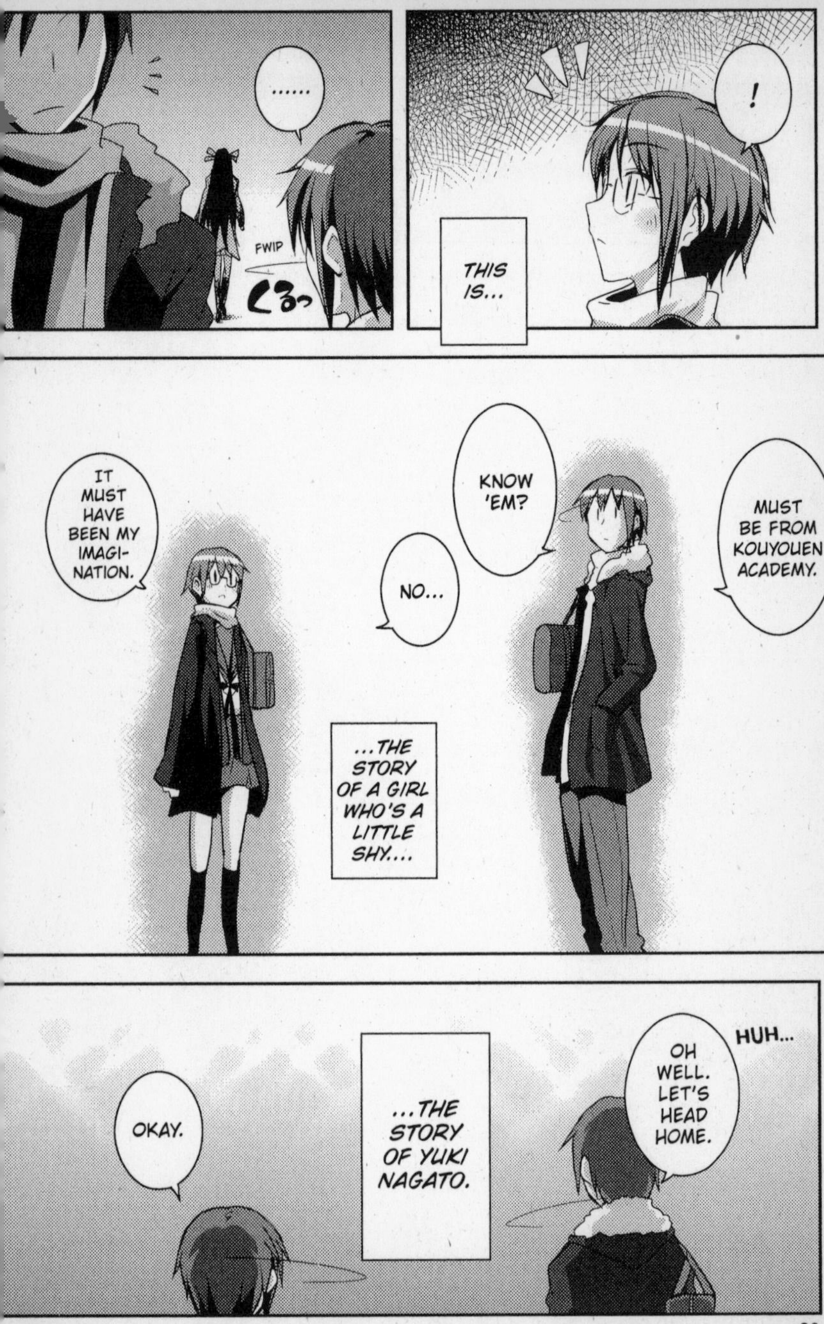
!
THIS IS...
......
FWIP
くるっ
MUST BE FROM KOUYOUEN ACADEMY.
KNOW 'EM?
NO...
IT MUST HAVE BEEN MY IMAGINATION.
...THE STORY OF A GIRL WHO'S A LITTLE SHY....
HUH...
OH WELL. LET'S HEAD HOME.
...THE STORY OF YUKI NAGATO.
OKAY.

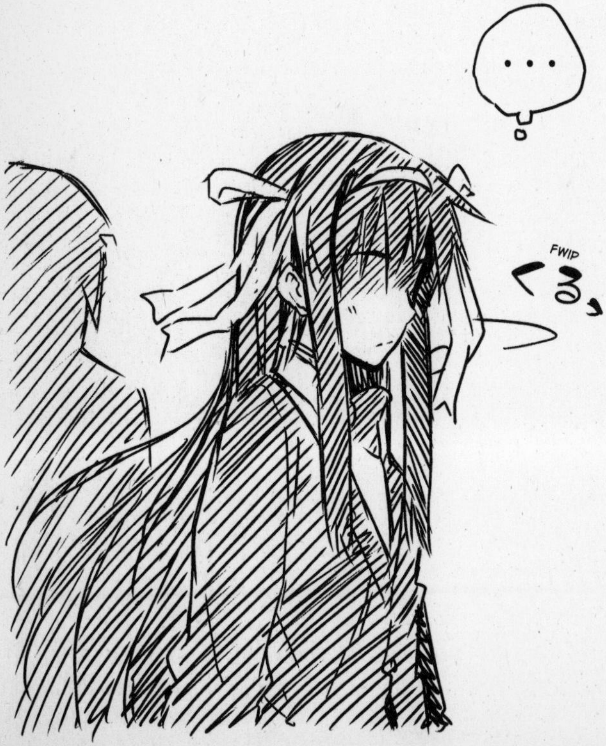
...
FWIP
くるっ

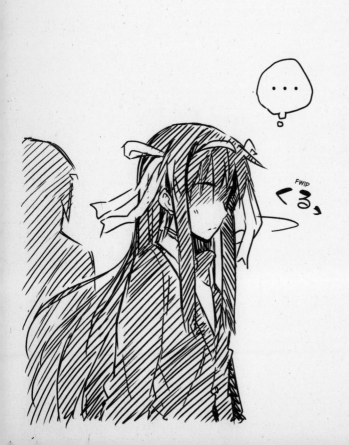

Look at all the stuff I bought... ♡

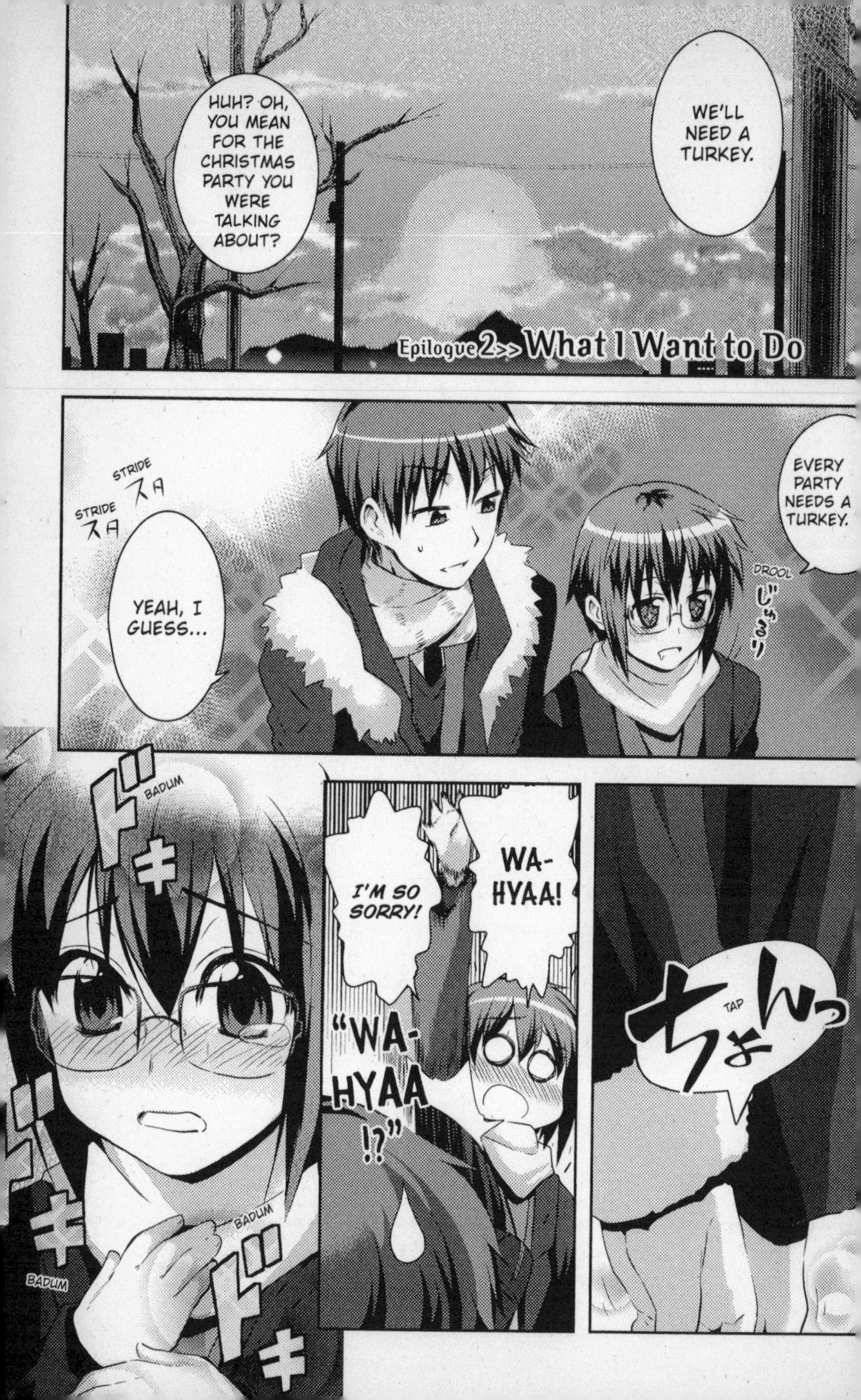
WE'LL NEED A TURKEY.
HUH? OH, YOU MEAN FOR THE CHRISTMAS PARTY YOU WERE TALKING ABOUT?
Epilogue 2>> What I Want to Do
EVERY PARTY NEEDS A TURKEY.
DROOL
じゅるり
STRIDE
スタ
STRIDE
スタ
YEAH, I GUESS...
TAP
ちょんっ
WA-HYAA!
I'M SO SORRY!
"WA-HYAA!?"
BADUM
ドキ
BADUM
BADUM
ドキドキ

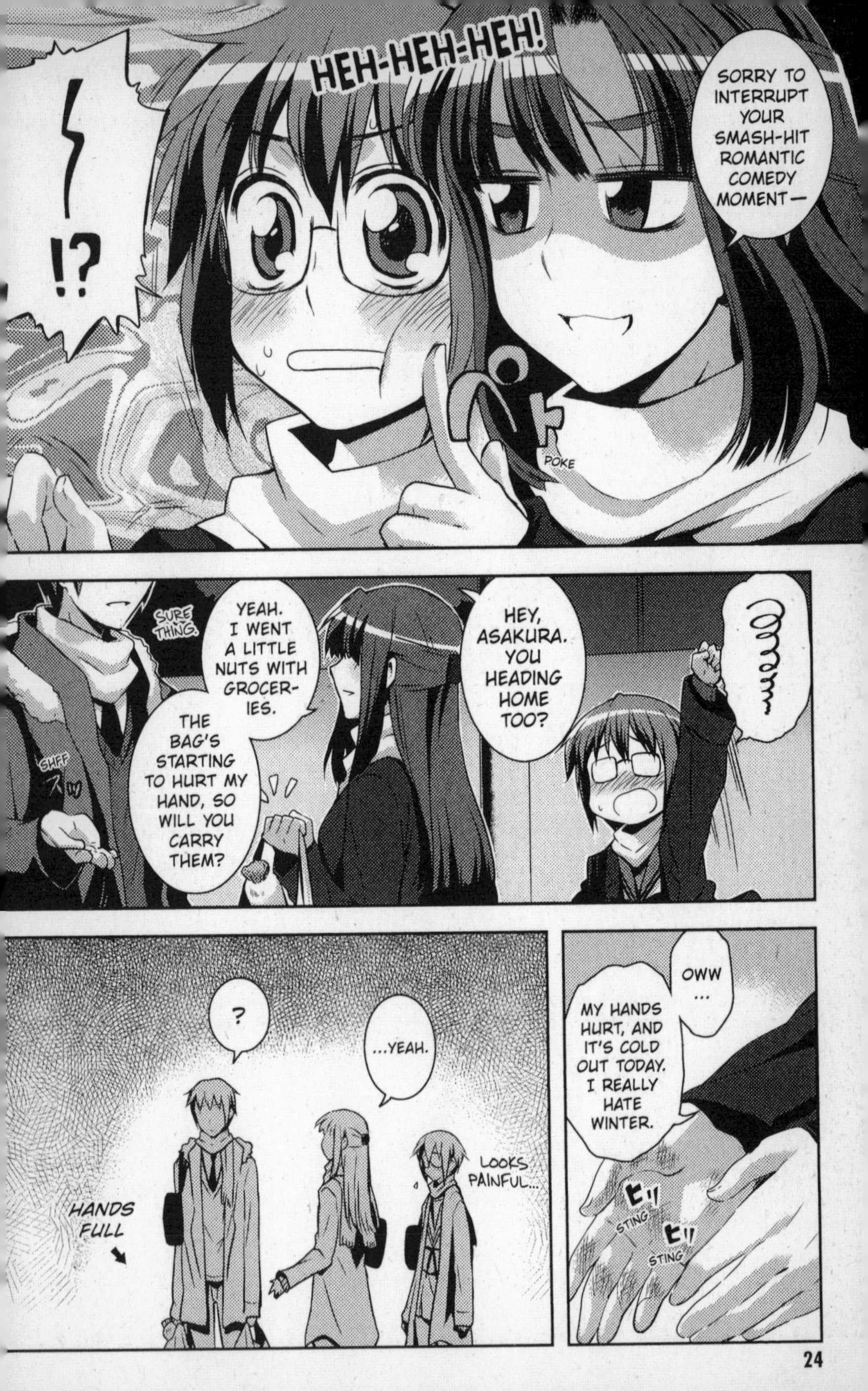
SORRY TO INTERRUPT YOUR SMASH-HIT ROMANTIC COMEDY MOMENT—
HEH-HEH-HEH!
!?
POKE
HEY, ASAKURA. YOU HEADING HOME TOO?
YEAH. I WENT A LITTLE NUTS WITH GROCER-IES.
THE BAG'S STARTING TO HURT MY HAND, SO WILL YOU CARRY THEM?
SURE THING.
SHFF
OWW ...
MY HANDS HURT, AND IT'S COLD OUT TODAY. I REALLY HATE WINTER.
STING
STING
...YEAH.
?
LOOKS PAINFUL...
HANDS FULL

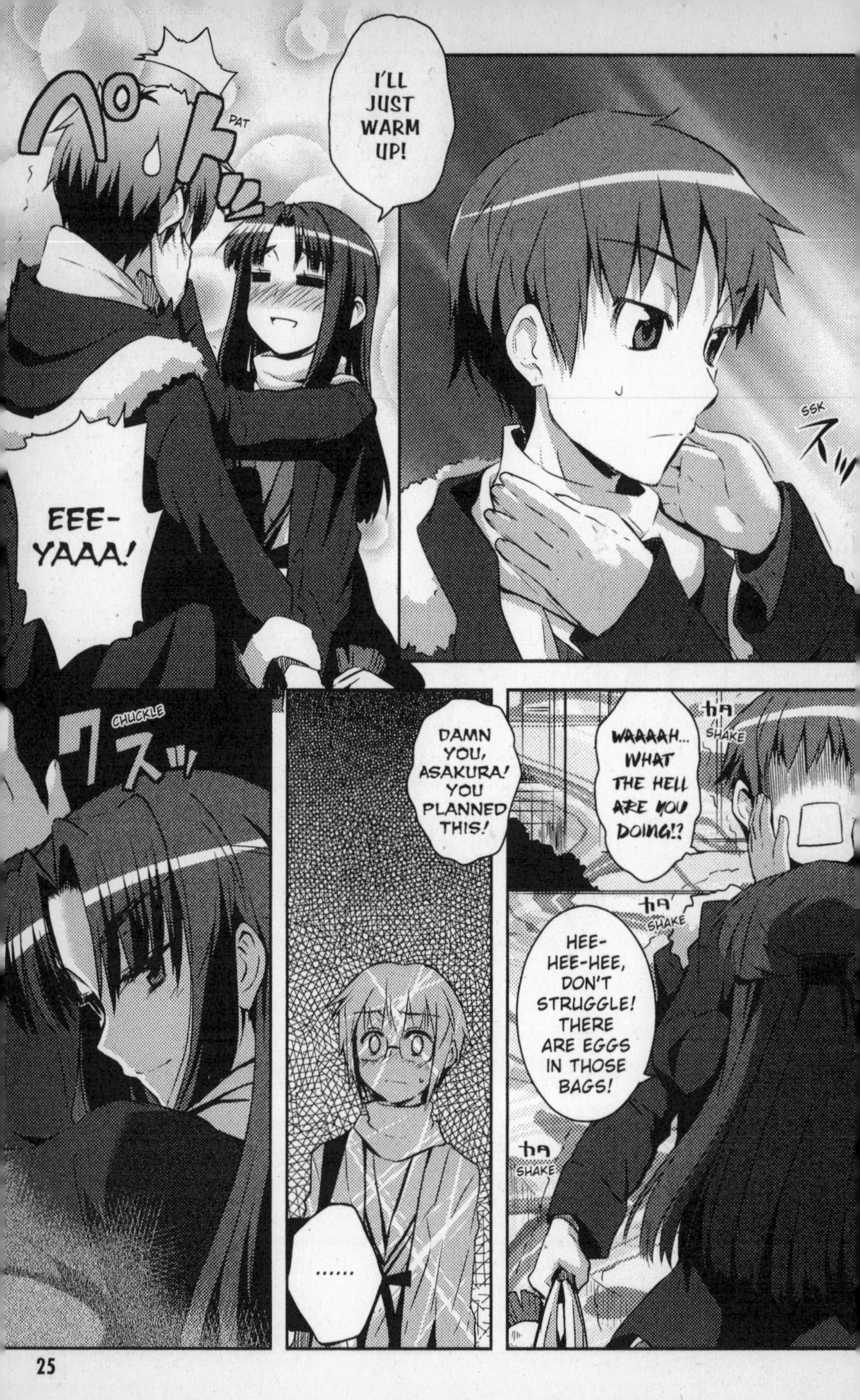
SSK
I'LL JUST WARM UP!
PAT
EEE-YAAA!
SHAKE
WAAAAH... WHAT THE HELL ARE YOU DOING!?
SHAKE
HEE-HEE-HEE, DON'T STRUGGLE! THERE ARE EGGS IN THOSE BAGS!
SHAKE
DAMN YOU, ASAKURA! YOU PLANNED THIS!
......
CHUCKLE

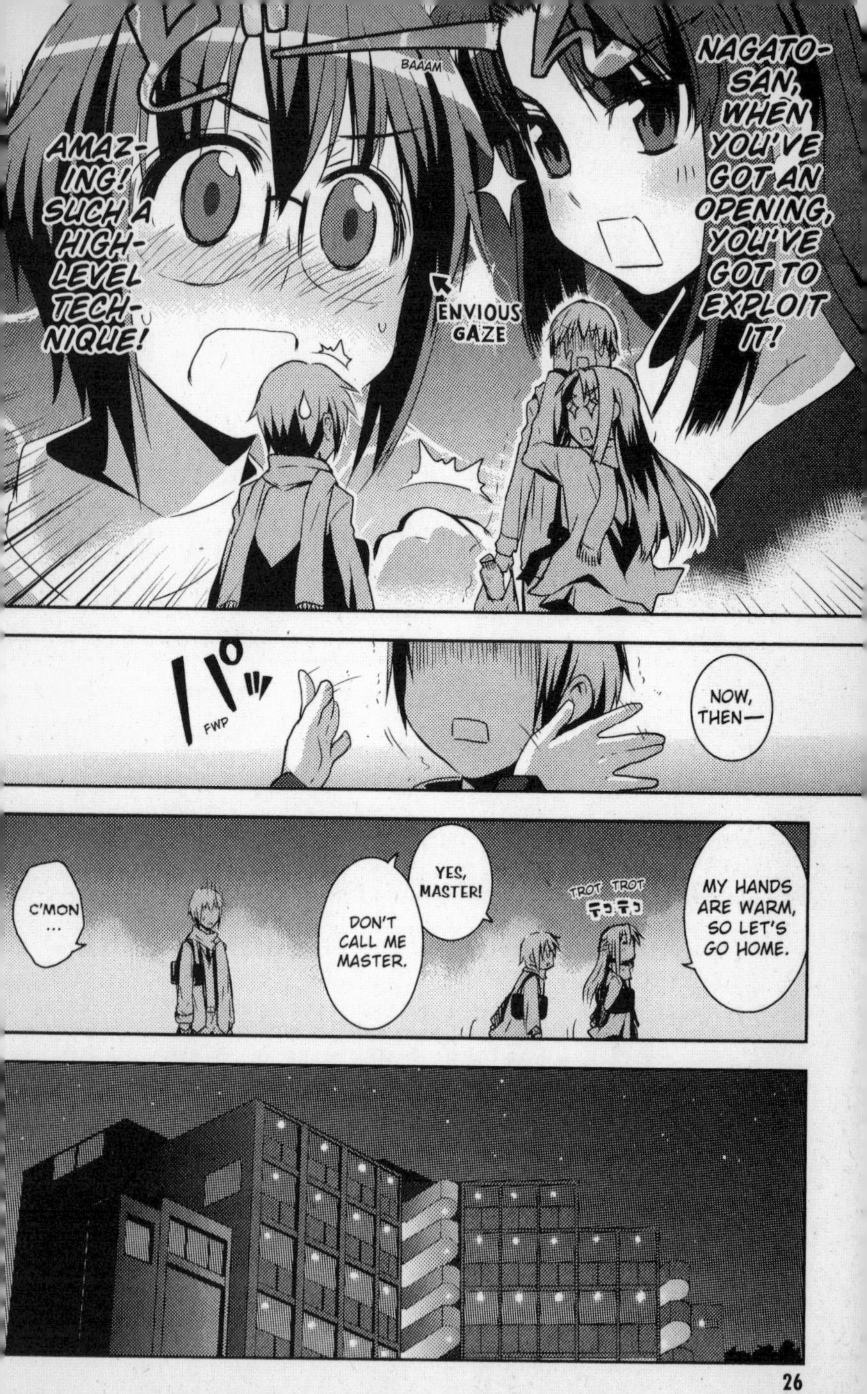
NAGATO-SAN, WHEN YOU'VE GOT AN OPENING, YOU'VE GOT TO EXPLOIT IT!
BAAAM
AMAZING! SUCH A HIGH-LEVEL TECHNIQUE!
ENVIOUS GAZE
NOW, THEN—
パッ
FWP
MY HANDS ARE WARM, SO LET'S GO HOME.
TROT TROT
テコテコ
YES, MASTER!
DON'T CALL ME MASTER.
C'MON...

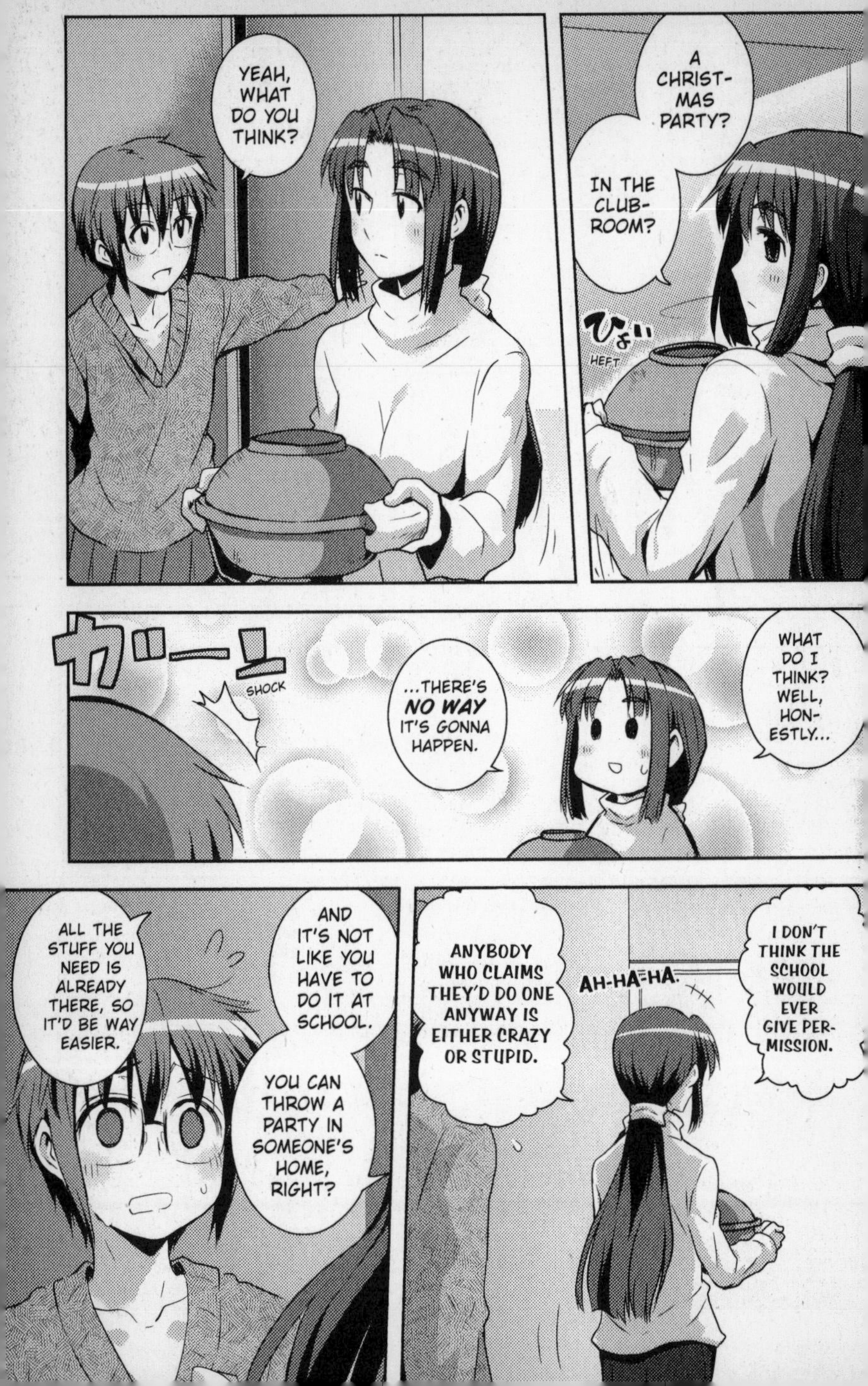
A CHRIST-MAS PARTY?
IN THE CLUB-ROOM?
ひょい
HEFT
YEAH, WHAT DO YOU THINK?
WHAT DO I THINK? WELL, HON-ESTLY...
...THERE'S **NO WAY** IT'S GONNA HAPPEN.
ガーン
SHOCK
I DON'T THINK THE SCHOOL WOULD EVER GIVE PER-MISSION.
AH-HA-HA.
ANYBODY WHO CLAIMS THEY'D DO ONE ANYWAY IS EITHER CRAZY OR STUPID.
AND IT'S NOT LIKE YOU HAVE TO DO IT AT SCHOOL.
ALL THE STUFF YOU NEED IS ALREADY THERE, SO IT'D BE WAY EASIER.
YOU CAN THROW A PARTY IN SOMEONE'S HOME, RIGHT?

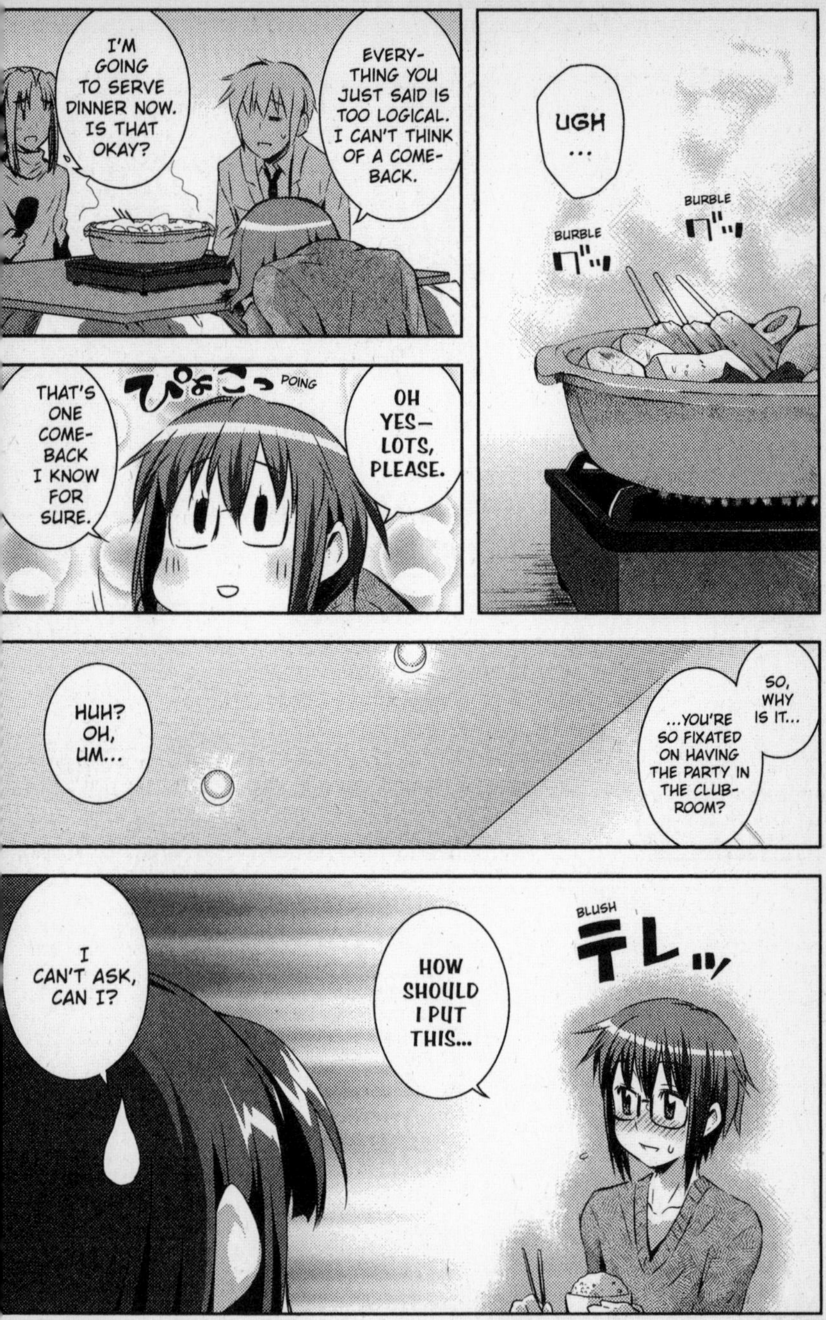
UGH ...
BURBLE
BURBLE
EVERYTHING YOU JUST SAID IS TOO LOGICAL. I CAN'T THINK OF A COMEBACK.
I'M GOING TO SERVE DINNER NOW. IS THAT OKAY?
OH YES— LOTS, PLEASE.
ぴょこっ POING
THAT'S ONE COMEBACK I KNOW FOR SURE.
SO, WHY IS IT...
...YOU'RE SO FIXATED ON HAVING THE PARTY IN THE CLUBROOM?
HUH? OH, UM...
テレッ BLUSH
HOW SHOULD I PUT THIS...
I CAN'T ASK, CAN I?

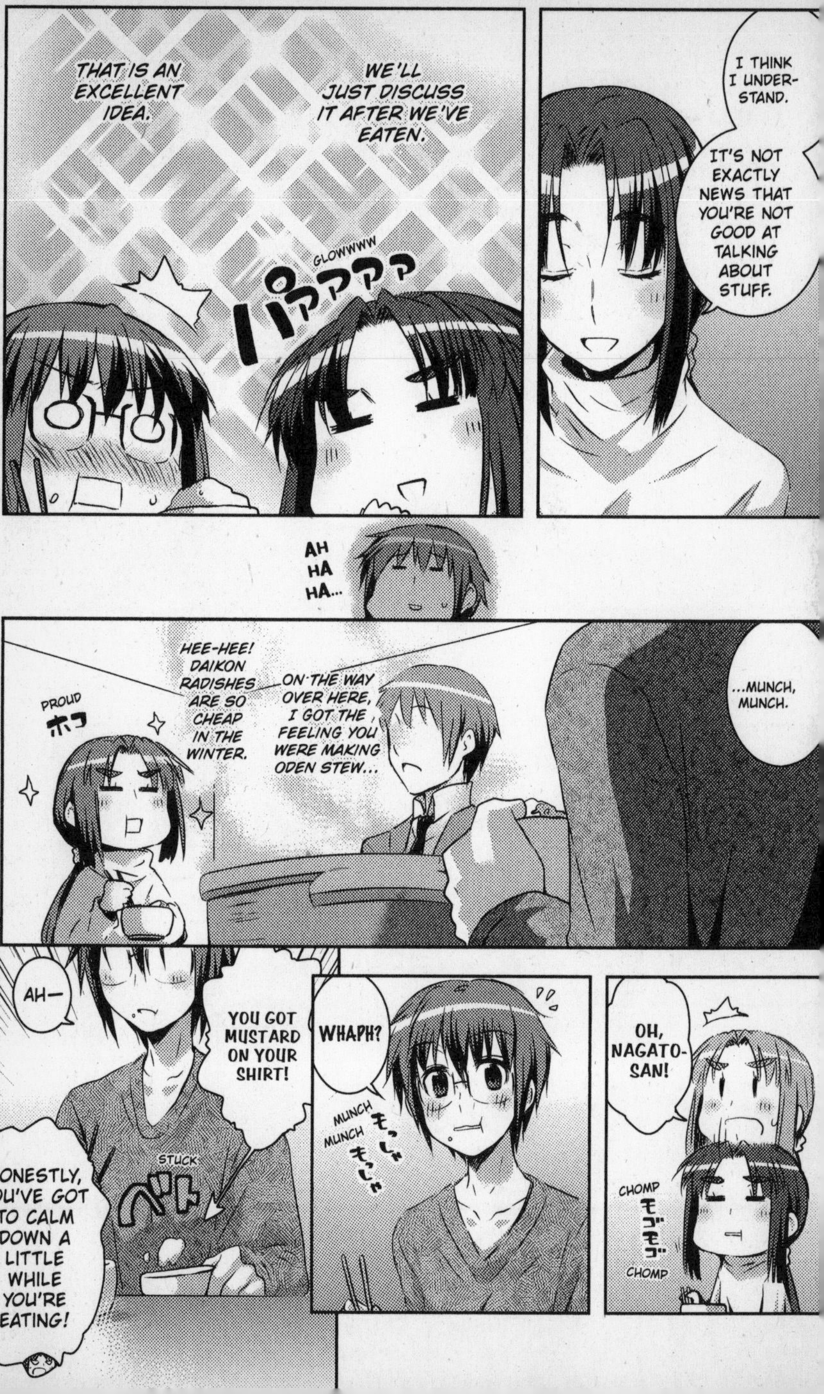
I THINK I UNDER-STAND.
IT'S NOT EXACTLY NEWS THAT YOU'RE NOT GOOD AT TALKING ABOUT STUFF.
WE'LL JUST DISCUSS IT AFTER WE'VE EATEN.
THAT IS AN EXCELLENT IDEA.
GLOWWWW
パァァァァ
AH HA HA...
...MUNCH, MUNCH.
ON THE WAY OVER HERE, I GOT THE FEELING YOU WERE MAKING ODEN STEW...
HEE-HEE! DAIKON RADISHES ARE SO CHEAP IN THE WINTER.
PROUD
ホコ
OH, NAGATO-SAN!
CHOMP
モゴモゴ
CHOMP
WHAPH?
MUNCH
MUNCH
もっしゃもっしゃ
AH—
YOU GOT MUSTARD ON YOUR SHIRT!
STUCK
ベト
HONESTLY, YOU'VE GOT TO CALM DOWN A LITTLE WHILE YOU'RE EATING!

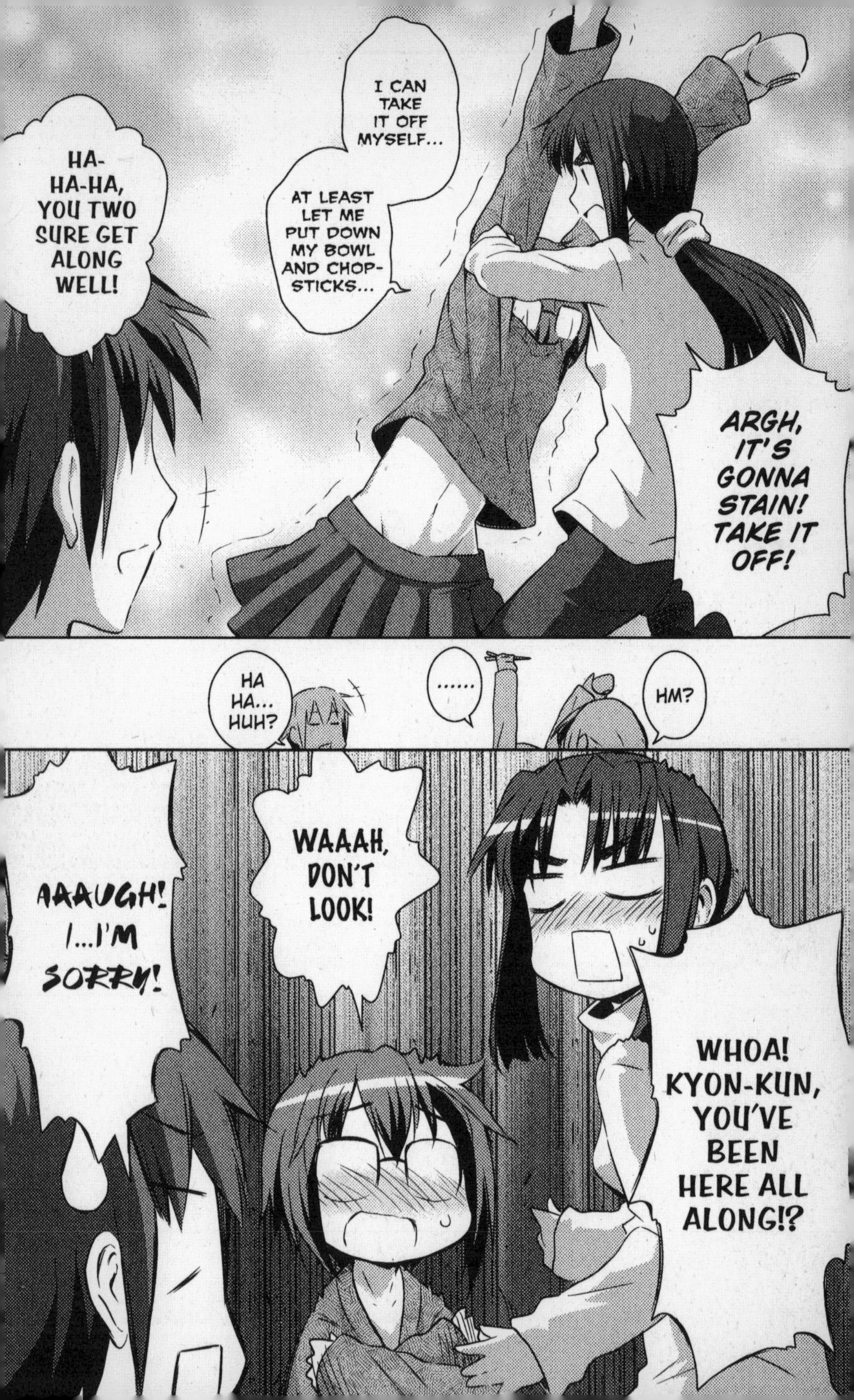

ARGH, IT'S GONNA STAIN! TAKE IT OFF!
I CAN TAKE IT OFF MYSELF...
AT LEAST LET ME PUT DOWN MY BOWL AND CHOP-STICKS...
HA-HA-HA, YOU TWO SURE GET ALONG WELL!
HM?
......
HA HA... HUH?
WHOA! KYON-KUN, YOU'VE BEEN HERE ALL ALONG!?
WAAAH, DON'T LOOK!
AAAUGH! I...I'M SORRY!

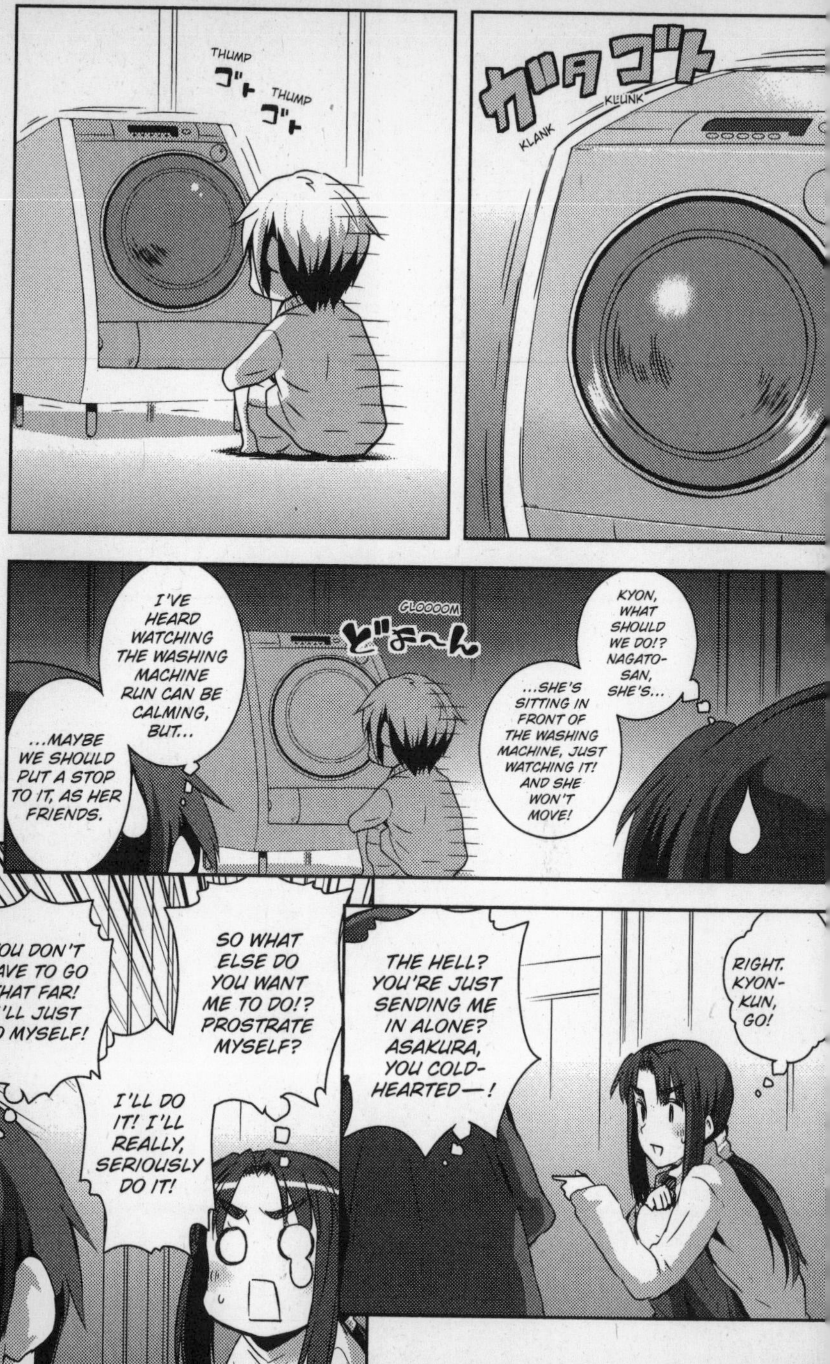
ガタゴト
KLANK
KLUNK
THUMP
ゴト
THUMP
ゴト
KYON, WHAT SHOULD WE DO!? NAGATO-SAN, SHE'S...
...SHE'S SITTING IN FRONT OF THE WASHING MACHINE, JUST WATCHING IT! AND SHE WON'T MOVE!
GLOOOOM
どよ～ん
I'VE HEARD WATCHING THE WASHING MACHINE RUN CAN BE CALMING, BUT...
...MAYBE WE SHOULD PUT A STOP TO IT, AS HER FRIENDS.
RIGHT. KYON-KUN, GO!
THE HELL? YOU'RE JUST SENDING ME IN ALONE? ASAKURA, YOU COLD-HEARTED—!
SO WHAT ELSE DO YOU WANT ME TO DO!? PROSTRATE MYSELF?
I'LL DO IT! I'LL REALLY, SERIOUSLY DO IT!
YOU DON'T HAVE TO GO THAT FAR! I'LL JUST GO MYSELF!

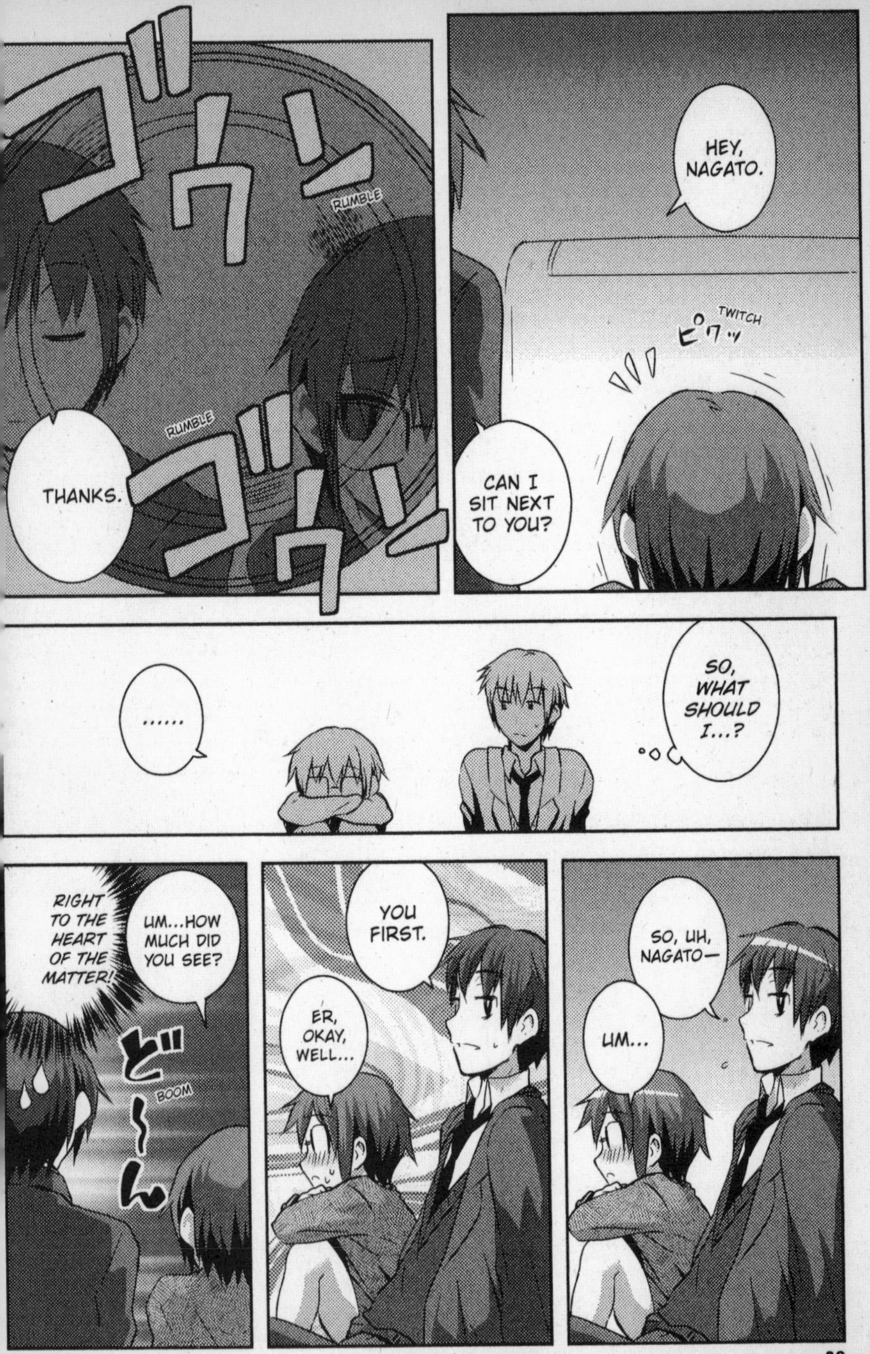
HEY, NAGATO.
TWITCH
ピクッ
CAN I SIT NEXT TO YOU?
RUMBLE
RUMBLE
THANKS.
SO, WHAT SHOULD I...?
......
SO, UH, NAGATO—
UM...
YOU FIRST.
ER, OKAY, WELL...
UM...HOW MUCH DID YOU SEE?
RIGHT TO THE HEART OF THE MATTER!
どーん
BOOM

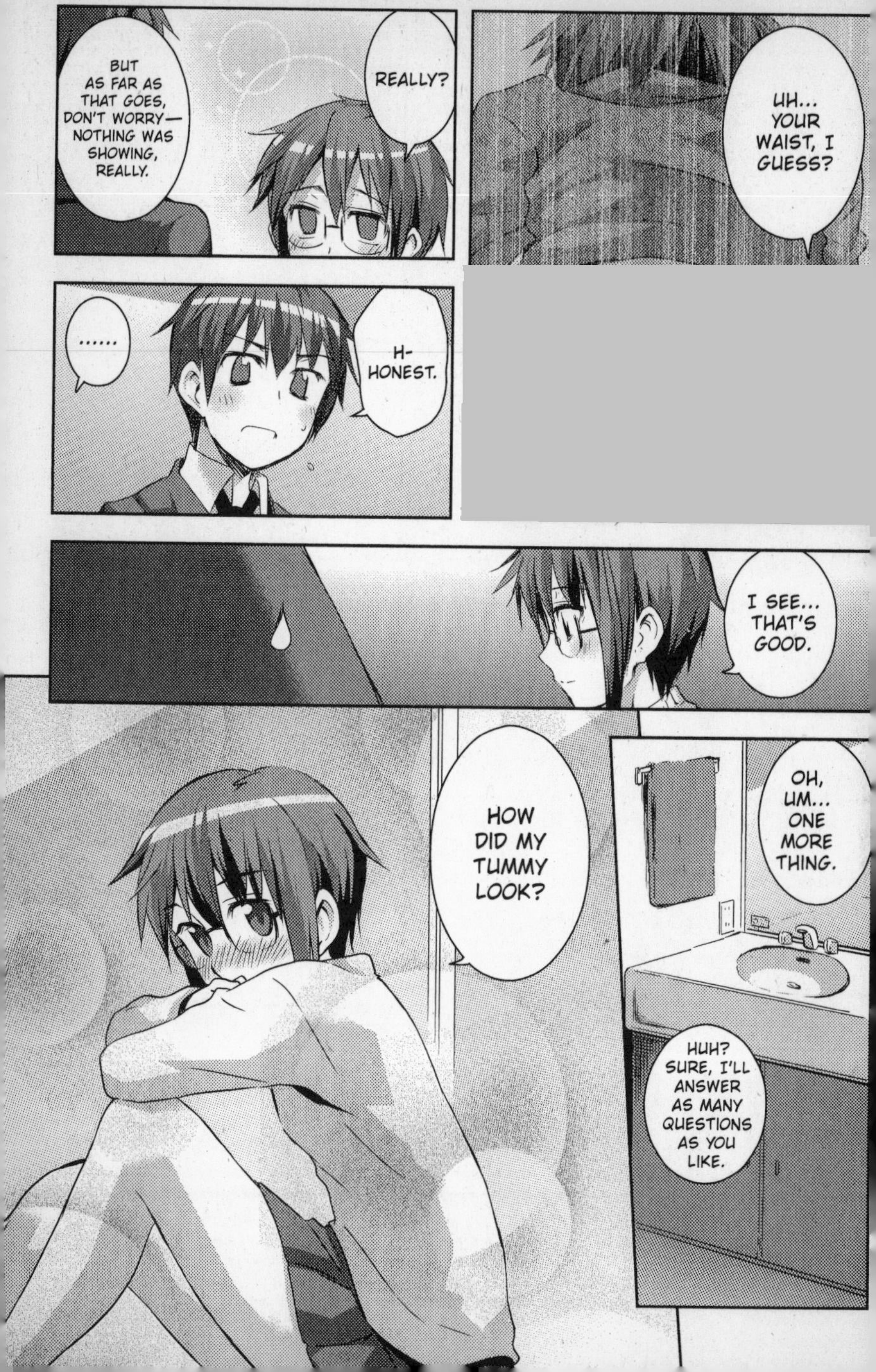
UH... YOUR WAIST, I GUESS?
REALLY?
BUT AS FAR AS THAT GOES, DON'T WORRY—NOTHING WAS SHOWING, REALLY.
H-HONEST.
......
I SEE... THAT'S GOOD.
OH, UM... ONE MORE THING.
HUH? SURE, I'LL ANSWER AS MANY QUESTIONS AS YOU LIKE.
HOW DID MY TUMMY LOOK?

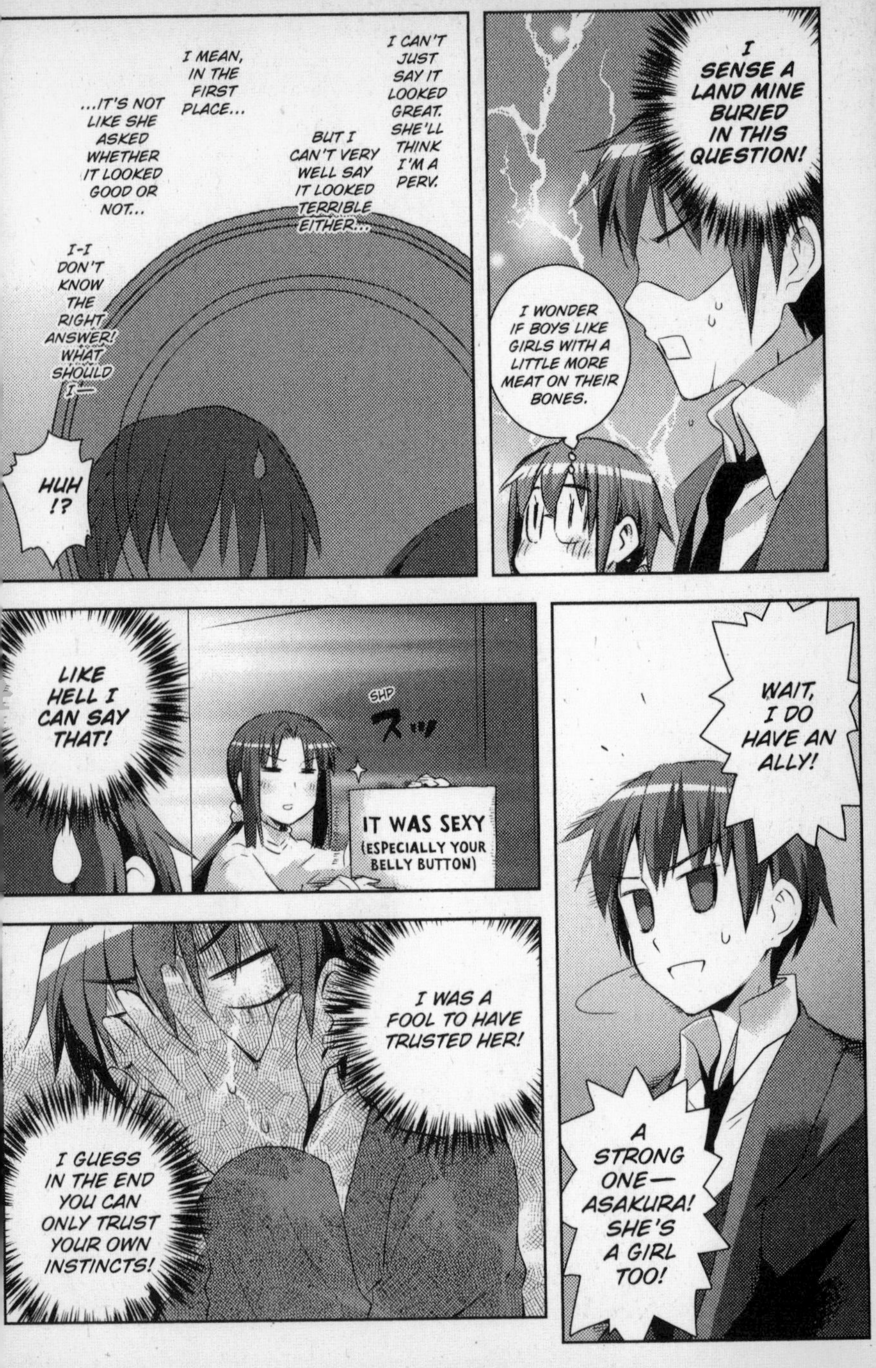

I SENSE A LAND MINE BURIED IN THIS QUESTION!
I WONDER IF BOYS LIKE GIRLS WITH A LITTLE MORE MEAT ON THEIR BONES.
I CAN'T JUST SAY IT LOOKED GREAT. SHE'LL THINK I'M A PERV.
BUT I CAN'T VERY WELL SAY IT LOOKED TERRIBLE EITHER...
I MEAN, IN THE FIRST PLACE...
...IT'S NOT LIKE SHE ASKED WHETHER IT LOOKED GOOD OR NOT...
I-I DON'T KNOW THE RIGHT ANSWER! WHAT SHOULD I—
HUH!?
WAIT, I DO HAVE AN ALLY!
A STRONG ONE—ASAKURA! SHE'S A GIRL TOO!
SHP
IT WAS SEXY (ESPECIALLY YOUR BELLY BUTTON)
LIKE HELL I CAN SAY THAT!
I WAS A FOOL TO HAVE TRUSTED HER!
I GUESS IN THE END YOU CAN ONLY TRUST YOUR OWN INSTINCTS!

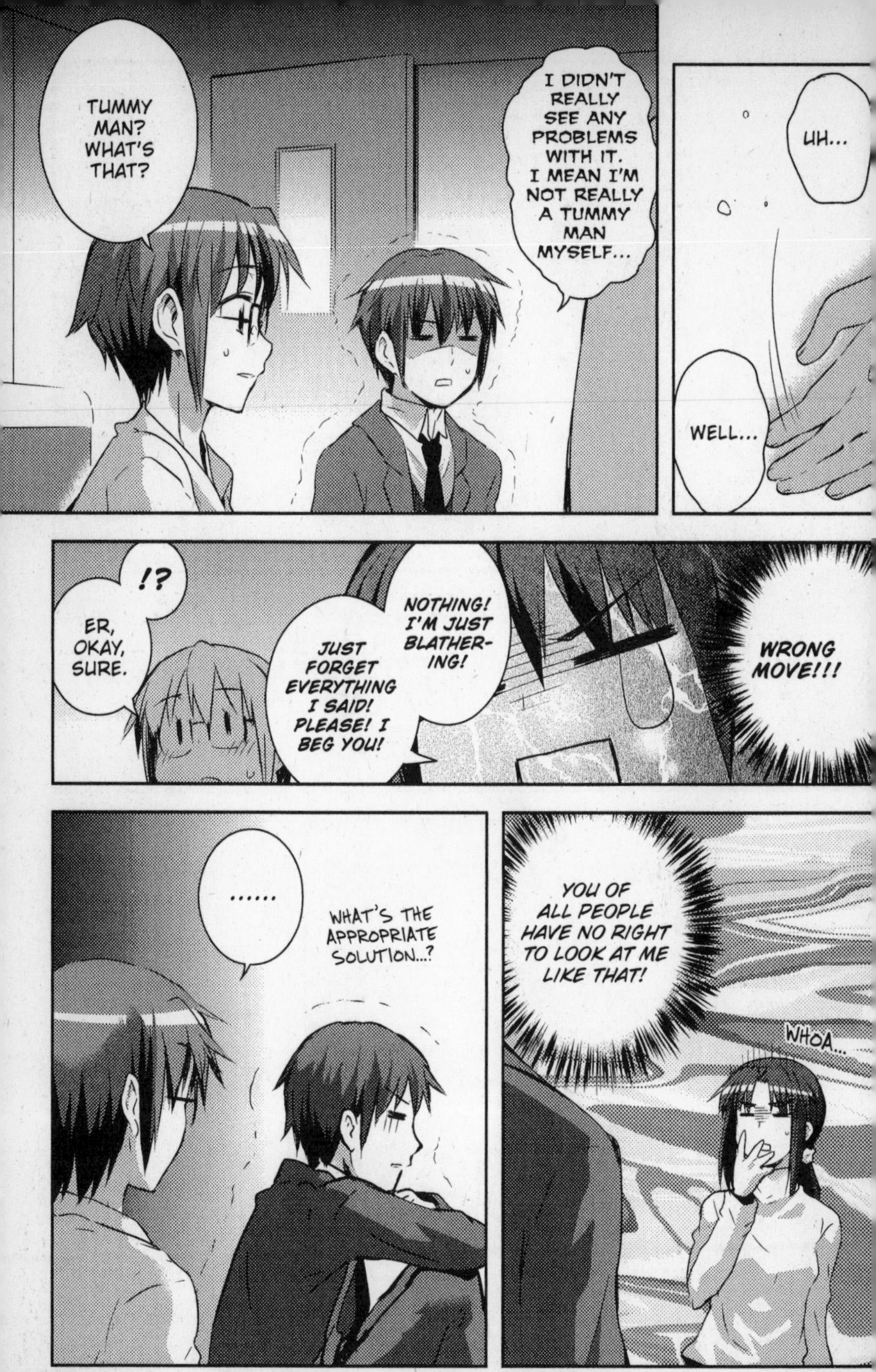
UH...
WELL...
I DIDN'T REALLY SEE ANY PROBLEMS WITH IT. I MEAN I'M NOT REALLY A TUMMY MAN MYSELF...
TUMMY MAN? WHAT'S THAT?
WRONG MOVE!!!
NOTHING! I'M JUST BLATHER-ING!
JUST FORGET EVERYTHING I SAID! PLEASE! I BEG YOU!
!?
ER, OKAY, SURE.
YOU OF ALL PEOPLE HAVE NO RIGHT TO LOOK AT ME LIKE THAT!
WHOA...
......
WHAT'S THE APPROPRIATE SOLUTION...?

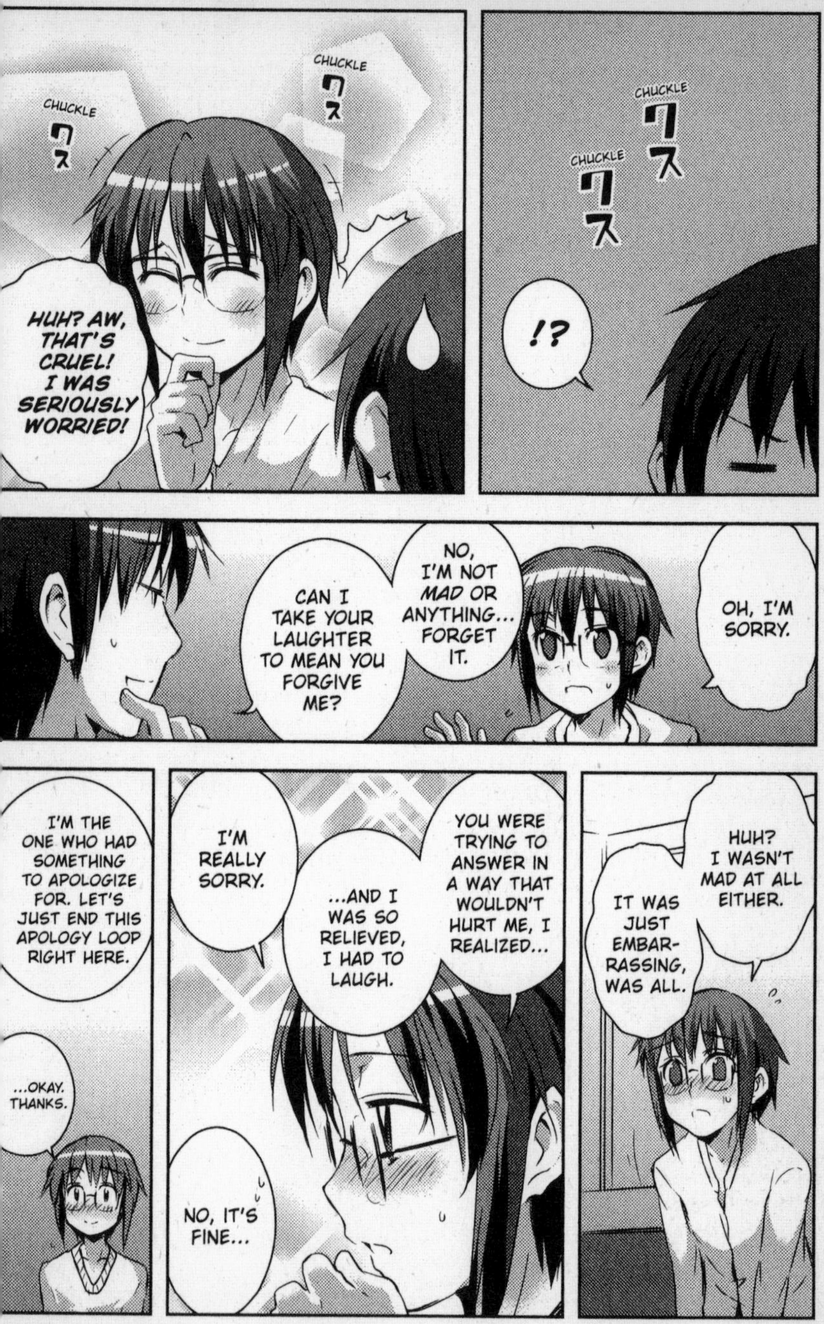
CHUCKLE
クス
CHUCKLE
クス
!?
CHUCKLE
クス
CHUCKLE
クス
HUH? AW, THAT'S CRUEL! I WAS SERIOUSLY WORRIED!
OH, I'M SORRY.
NO, I'M NOT MAD OR ANYTHING... FORGET IT.
CAN I TAKE YOUR LAUGHTER TO MEAN YOU FORGIVE ME?
HUH? I WASN'T MAD AT ALL EITHER.
IT WAS JUST EMBARRASSING, WAS ALL.
YOU WERE TRYING TO ANSWER IN A WAY THAT WOULDN'T HURT ME, I REALIZED...
...AND I WAS SO RELIEVED, I HAD TO LAUGH.
I'M REALLY SORRY.
NO, IT'S FINE...
I'M THE ONE WHO HAD SOMETHING TO APOLOGIZE FOR. LET'S JUST END THIS APOLOGY LOOP RIGHT HERE.
...OKAY. THANKS.

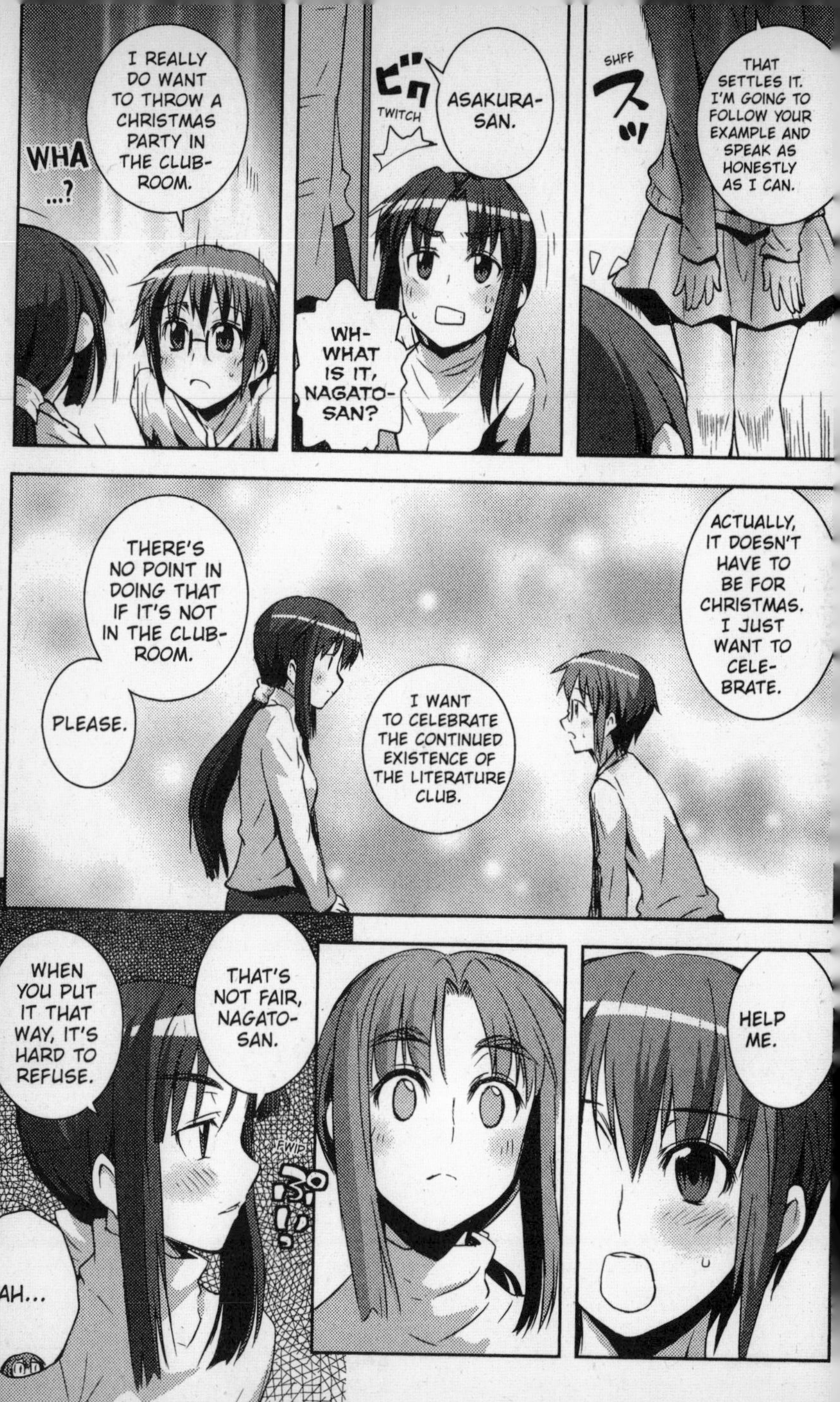
SHFF
スッ
THAT SETTLES IT. I'M GOING TO FOLLOW YOUR EXAMPLE AND SPEAK AS HONESTLY AS I CAN.
ビクッ
TWITCH
ASAKURA-SAN.
WH-WHAT IS IT, NAGATO-SAN?
I REALLY DO WANT TO THROW A CHRISTMAS PARTY IN THE CLUB-ROOM.
WHA ...?
ACTUALLY, IT DOESN'T HAVE TO BE FOR CHRISTMAS. I JUST WANT TO CELEBRATE.
I WANT TO CELEBRATE THE CONTINUED EXISTENCE OF THE LITERATURE CLUB.
THERE'S NO POINT IN DOING THAT IF IT'S NOT IN THE CLUB-ROOM.
PLEASE.
HELP ME.
FWIP
THAT'S NOT FAIR, NAGATO-SAN.
WHEN YOU PUT IT THAT WAY, IT'S HARD TO REFUSE.
AH...

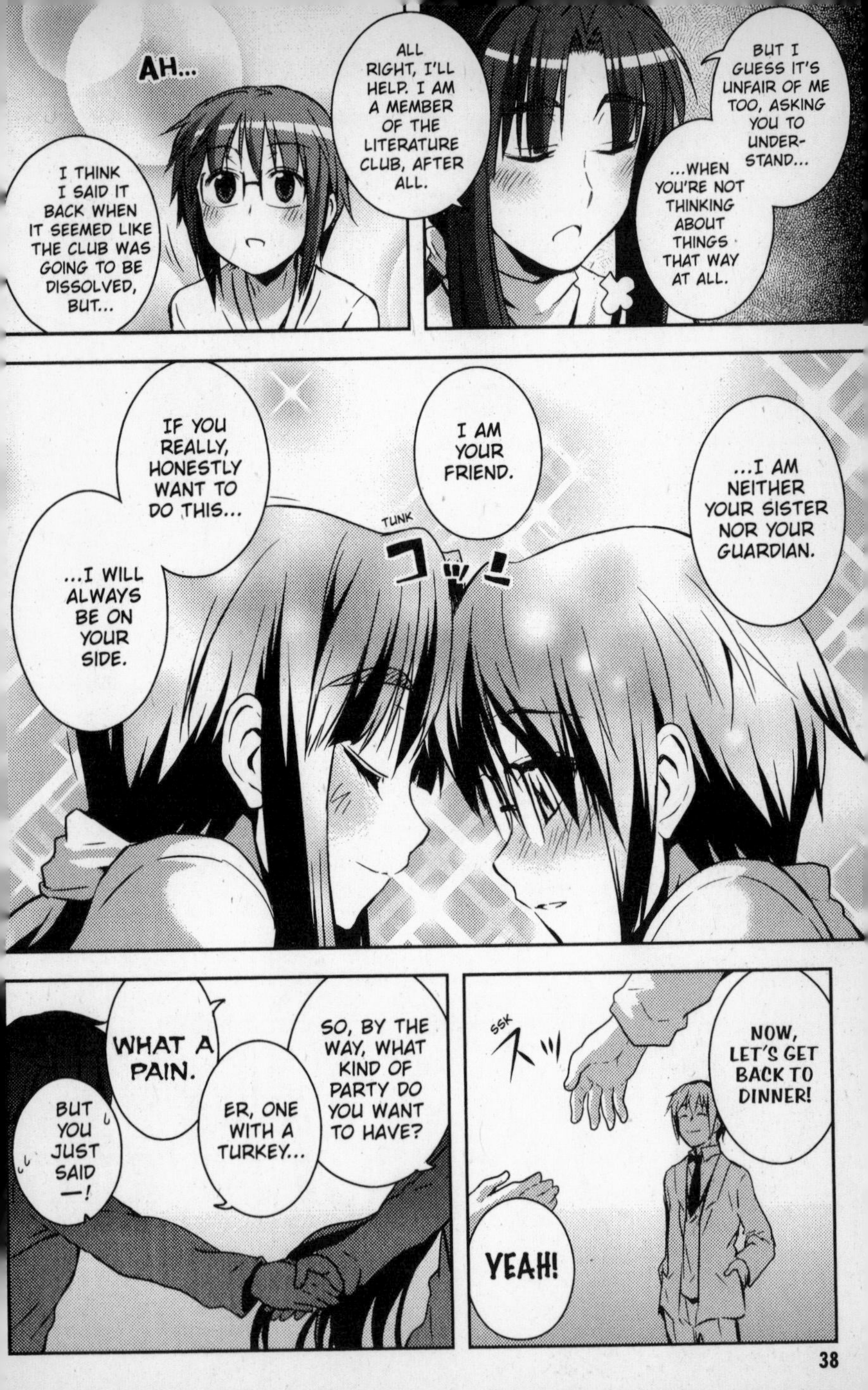
BUT I GUESS IT'S UNFAIR OF ME TOO, ASKING YOU TO UNDER-STAND...
...WHEN YOU'RE NOT THINKING ABOUT THINGS THAT WAY AT ALL.
ALL RIGHT, I'LL HELP. I AM A MEMBER OF THE LITERATURE CLUB, AFTER ALL.
AH...
I THINK I SAID IT BACK WHEN IT SEEMED LIKE THE CLUB WAS GOING TO BE DISSOLVED, BUT...
...I AM NEITHER YOUR SISTER NOR YOUR GUARDIAN.
I AM YOUR FRIEND.
TUNK
IF YOU REALLY, HONESTLY WANT TO DO THIS...
...I WILL ALWAYS BE ON YOUR SIDE.
NOW, LET'S GET BACK TO DINNER!
SSK
YEAH!
SO, BY THE WAY, WHAT KIND OF PARTY DO YOU WANT TO HAVE?
WHAT A PAIN.
ER, ONE WITH A TURKEY...
BUT YOU JUST SAID—!

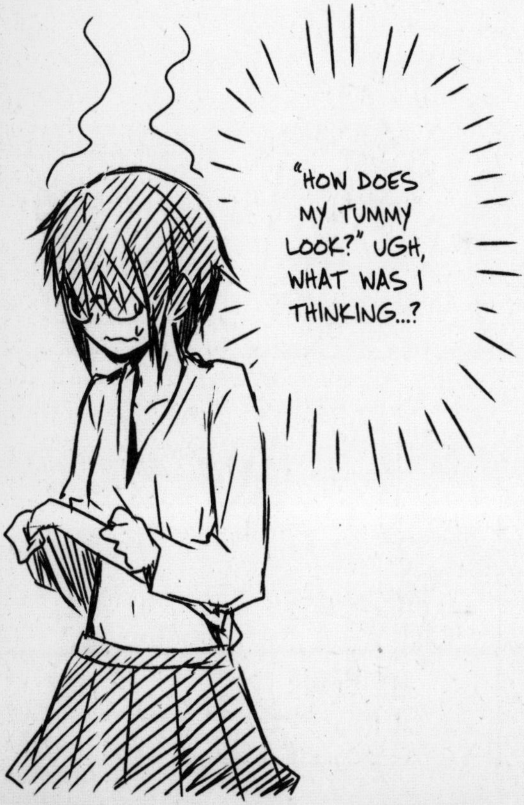
"HOW DOES MY TUMMY LOOK?" UGH, WHAT WAS I THINKING...?

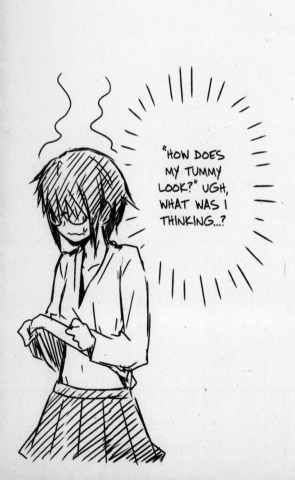

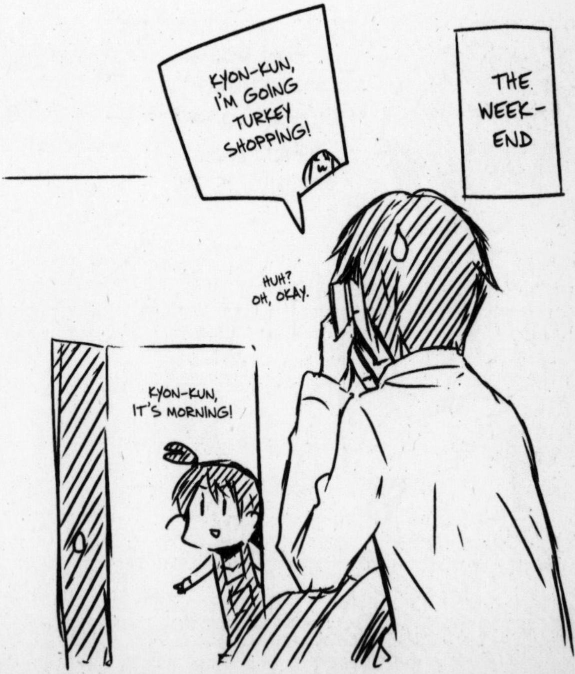
THE WEEK-END
KYON-KUN, I'M GOING TURKEY SHOPPING!
HUH? OH, OKAY.
KYON-KUN, IT'S MORNING!

Epilogue 3>> Shopping Scenery

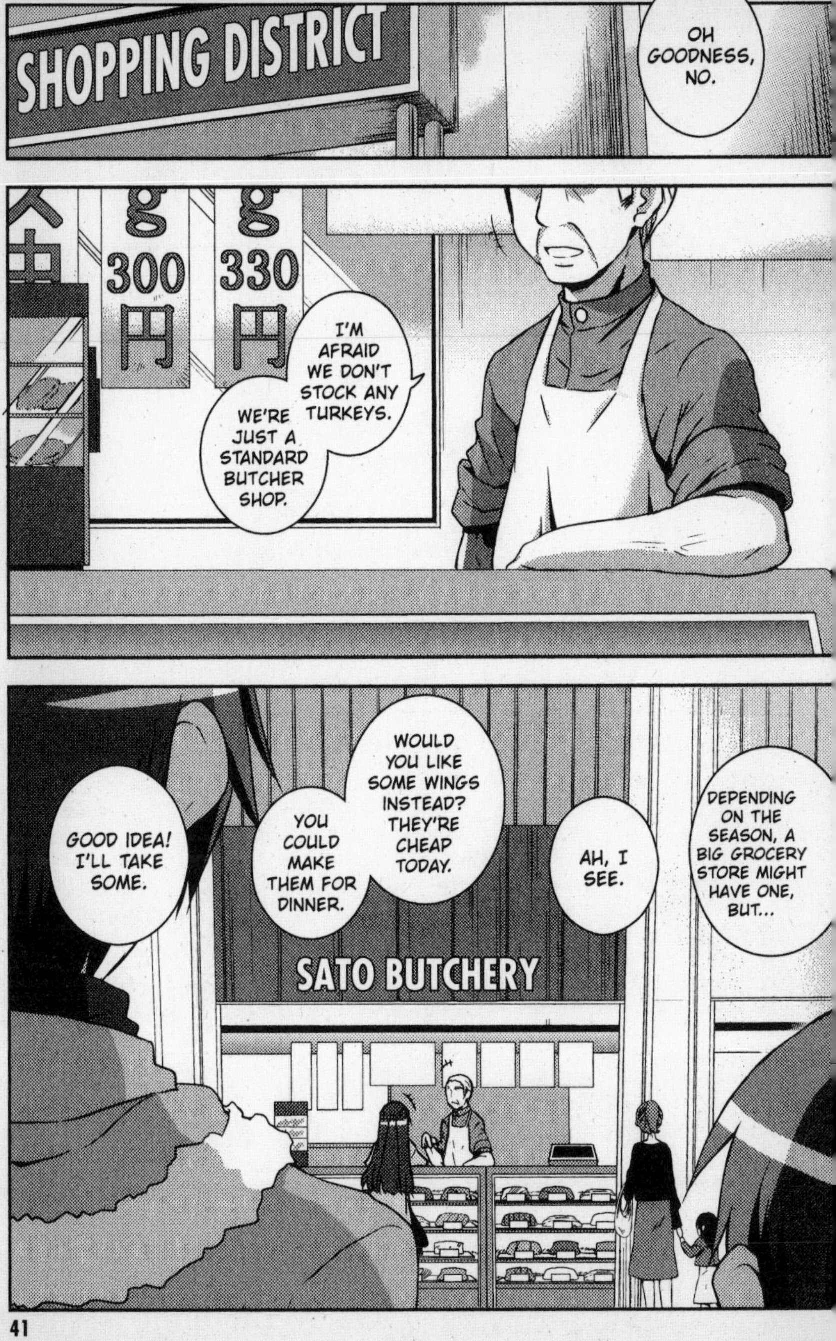
OH GOODNESS, NO.
SHOPPING DISTRICT
I'M AFRAID WE DON'T STOCK ANY TURKEYS.
WE'RE JUST A STANDARD BUTCHER SHOP.
330円
300円
DEPENDING ON THE SEASON, A BIG GROCERY STORE MIGHT HAVE ONE, BUT...
AH, I SEE.
WOULD YOU LIKE SOME WINGS INSTEAD? THEY'RE CHEAP TODAY.
YOU COULD MAKE THEM FOR DINNER.
GOOD IDEA! I'LL TAKE SOME.
SATO BUTCHERY

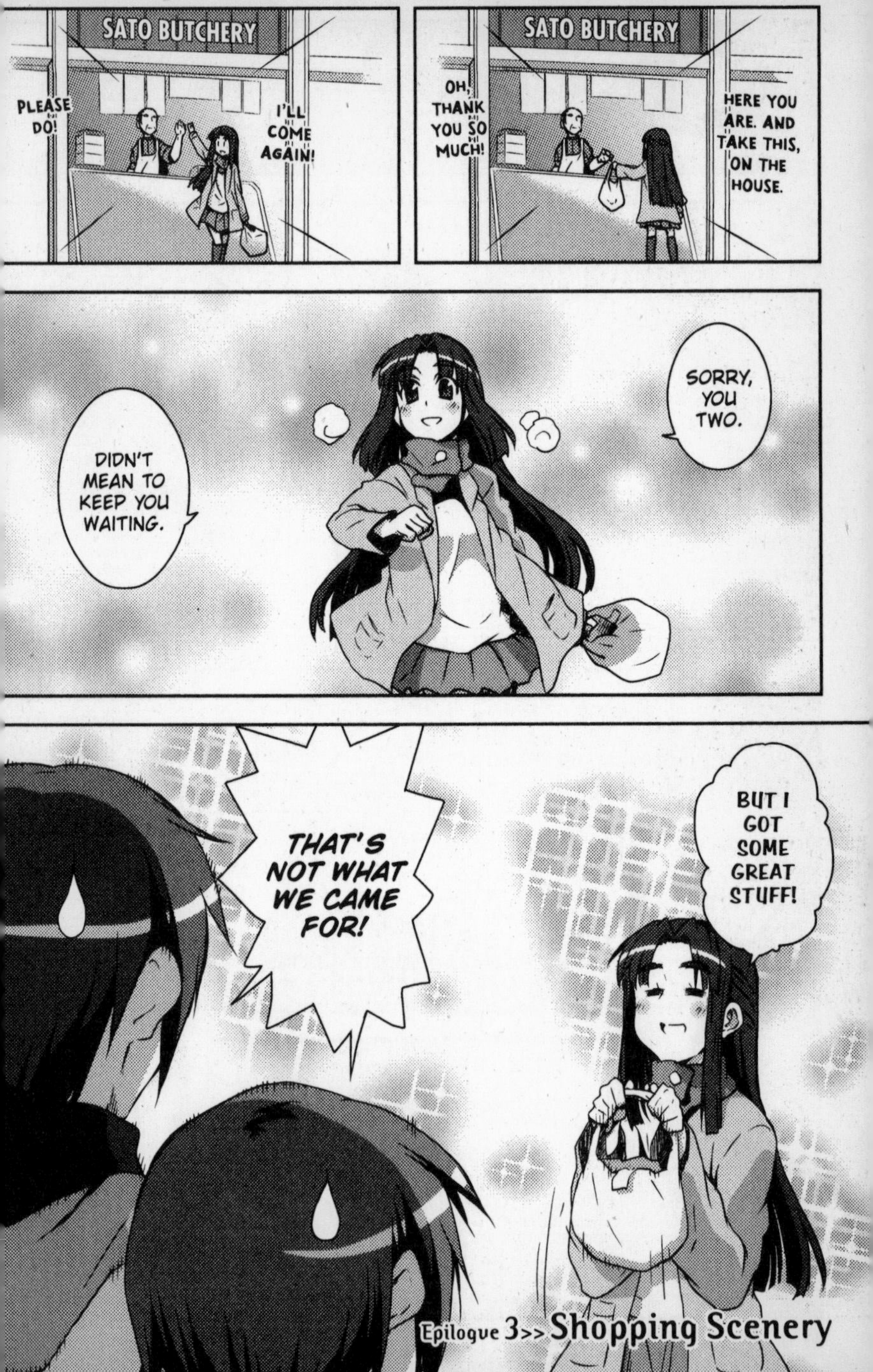
SATO BUTCHERY
HERE YOU ARE. AND TAKE THIS, ON THE HOUSE.
OH, THANK YOU SO MUCH!
SATO BUTCHERY
I'LL COME AGAIN!
PLEASE DO!
SORRY, YOU TWO.
DIDN'T MEAN TO KEEP YOU WAITING.
BUT I GOT SOME GREAT STUFF!
THAT'S NOT WHAT WE CAME FOR!
Epilogue 3>> Shopping Scenery

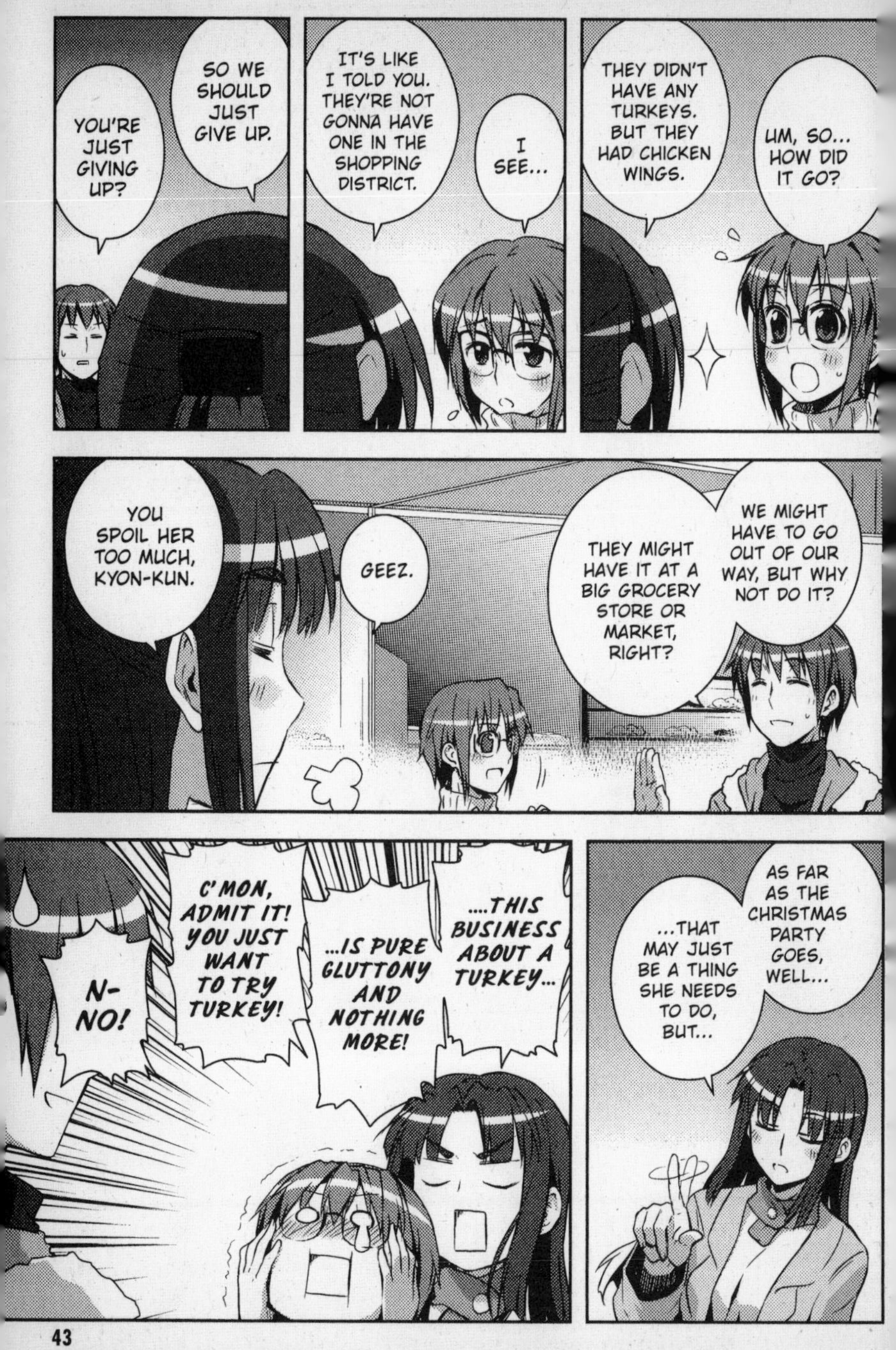
UM, SO... HOW DID IT GO?
THEY DIDN'T HAVE ANY TURKEYS. BUT THEY HAD CHICKEN WINGS.
I SEE...
IT'S LIKE I TOLD YOU. THEY'RE NOT GONNA HAVE ONE IN THE SHOPPING DISTRICT.
SO WE SHOULD JUST GIVE UP.
YOU'RE JUST GIVING UP?
WE MIGHT HAVE TO GO OUT OF OUR WAY, BUT WHY NOT DO IT?
THEY MIGHT HAVE IT AT A BIG GROCERY STORE OR MARKET, RIGHT?
GEEZ.
YOU SPOIL HER TOO MUCH, KYON-KUN.
AS FAR AS THE CHRISTMAS PARTY GOES, WELL...
...THAT MAY JUST BE A THING SHE NEEDS TO DO, BUT...
....THIS BUSINESS ABOUT A TURKEY...
...IS PURE GLUTTONY AND NOTHING MORE!
C'MON, ADMIT IT! YOU JUST WANT TO TRY TURKEY!
N-NO!

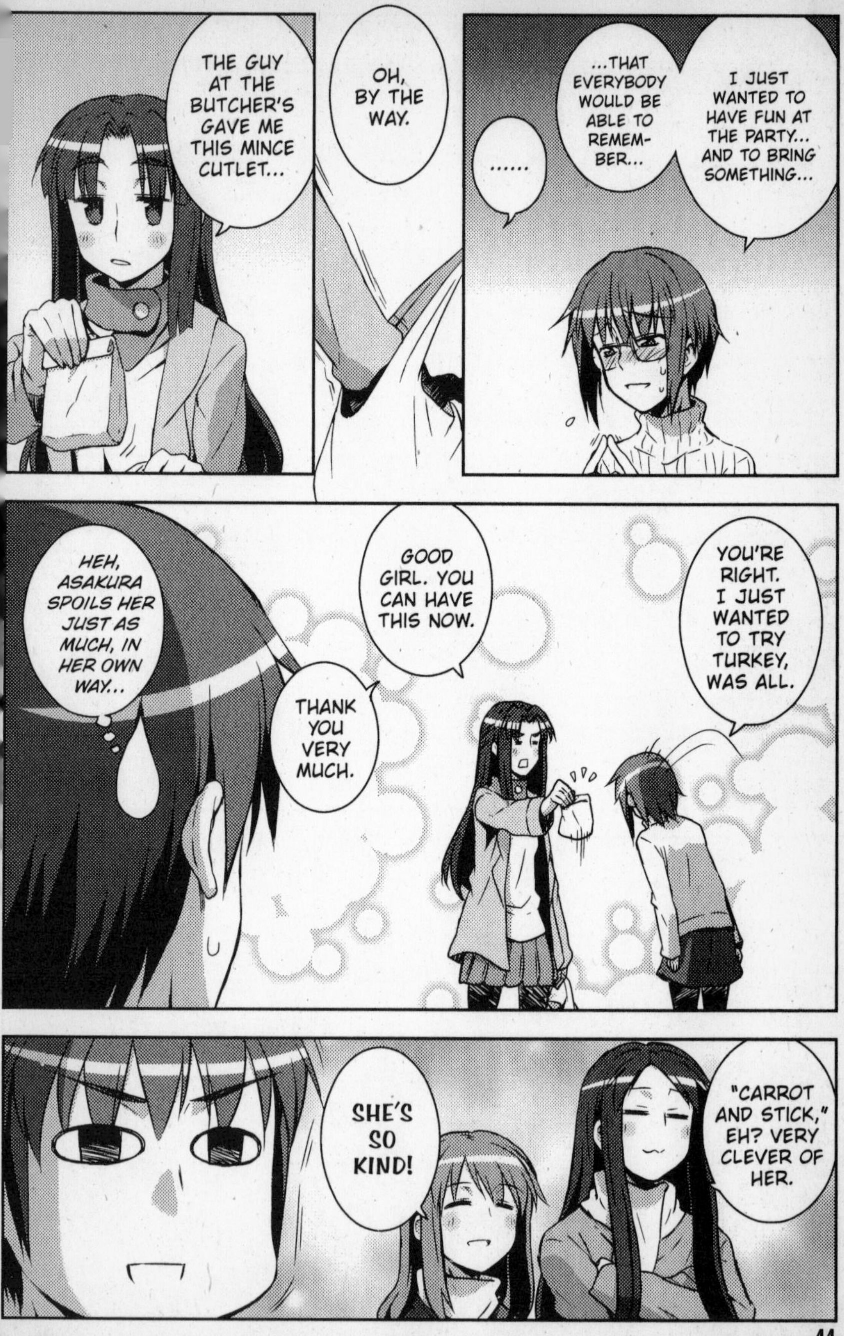
I JUST WANTED TO HAVE FUN AT THE PARTY... AND TO BRING SOMETHING...
...THAT EVERYBODY WOULD BE ABLE TO REMEMBER...
......
OH, BY THE WAY.
THE GUY AT THE BUTCHER'S GAVE ME THIS MINCE CUTLET...
YOU'RE RIGHT. I JUST WANTED TO TRY TURKEY, WAS ALL.
GOOD GIRL. YOU CAN HAVE THIS NOW.
THANK YOU VERY MUCH.
HEH, ASAKURA SPOILS HER JUST AS MUCH, IN HER OWN WAY...
"CARROT AND STICK," EH? VERY CLEVER OF HER.
SHE'S SO KIND!

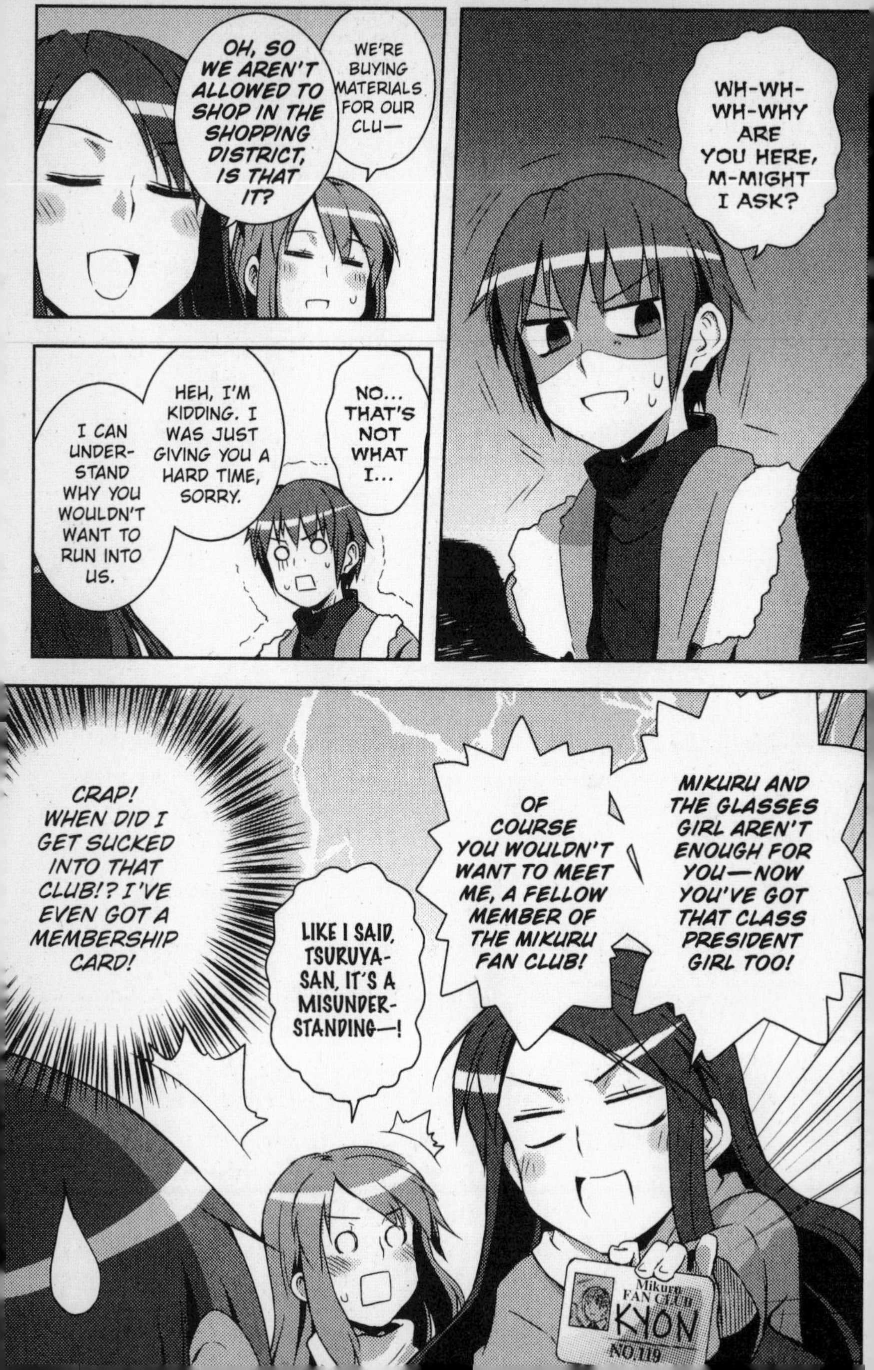
WH-WH-WH-WHY ARE YOU HERE, M-MIGHT I ASK?
WE'RE BUYING MATERIALS FOR OUR CLU—
OH, SO WE AREN'T ALLOWED TO SHOP IN THE SHOPPING DISTRICT, IS THAT IT?
NO... THAT'S NOT WHAT I...
HEH, I'M KIDDING. I WAS JUST GIVING YOU A HARD TIME, SORRY.
I CAN UNDER-STAND WHY YOU WOULDN'T WANT TO RUN INTO US.
MIKURU AND THE GLASSES GIRL AREN'T ENOUGH FOR YOU—NOW YOU'VE GOT THAT CLASS PRESIDENT GIRL TOO!
OF COURSE YOU WOULDN'T WANT TO MEET ME, A FELLOW MEMBER OF THE MIKURU FAN CLUB!
LIKE I SAID, TSURUYA-SAN, IT'S A MISUNDER-STANDING—!
CRAP! WHEN DID I GET SUCKED INTO THAT CLUB!? I'VE EVEN GOT A MEMBERSHIP CARD!
Mikuru FAN CLUB
KYON
NO.119

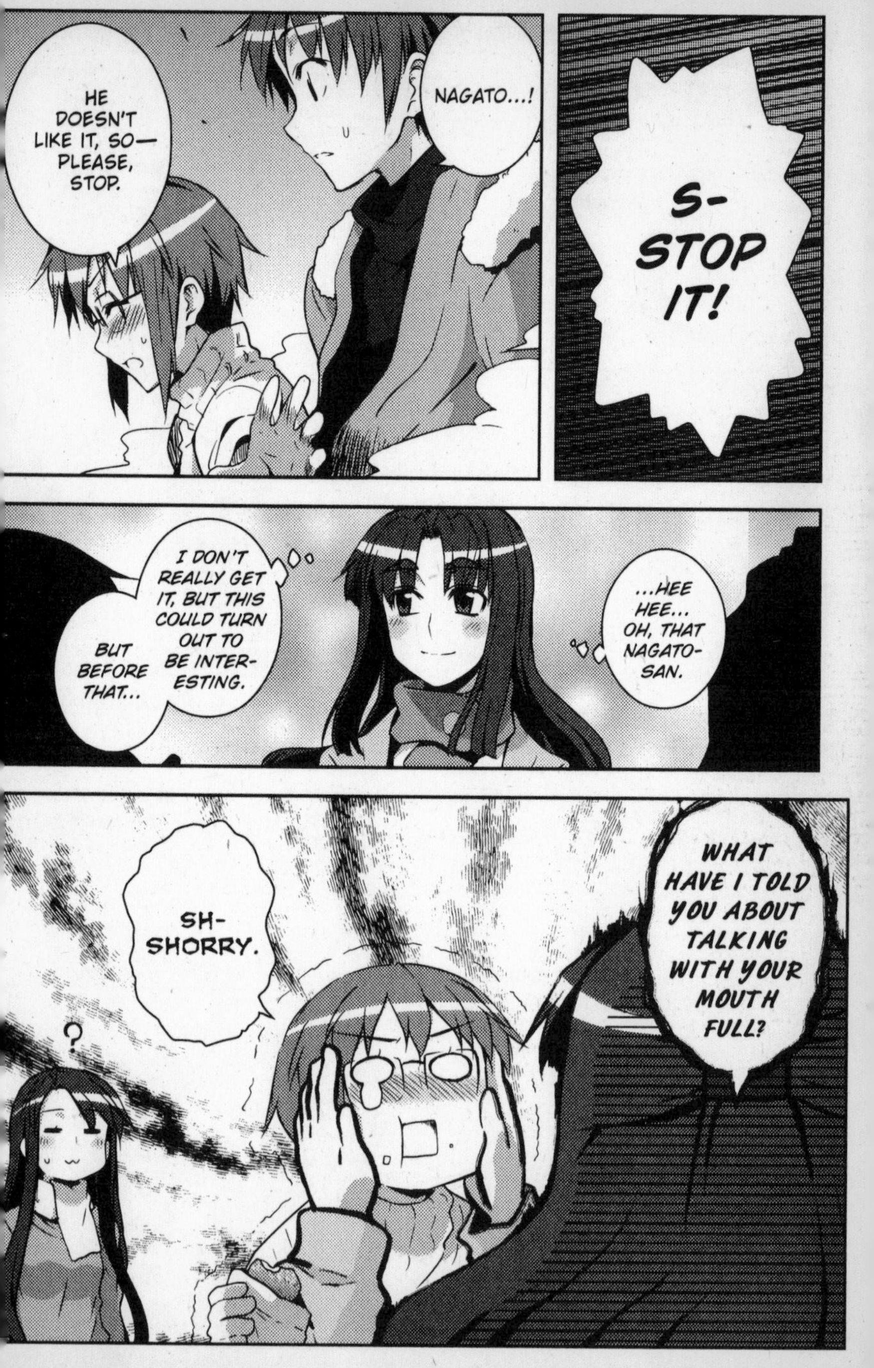
S-STOP IT!
NAGATO...!
HE DOESN'T LIKE IT, SO— PLEASE, STOP.
...HEE HEE... OH, THAT NAGATO-SAN.
I DON'T REALLY GET IT, BUT THIS COULD TURN OUT TO BE INTERESTING.
BUT BEFORE THAT...
WHAT HAVE I TOLD YOU ABOUT TALKING WITH YOUR MOUTH FULL?
SH-SHORRY.
?

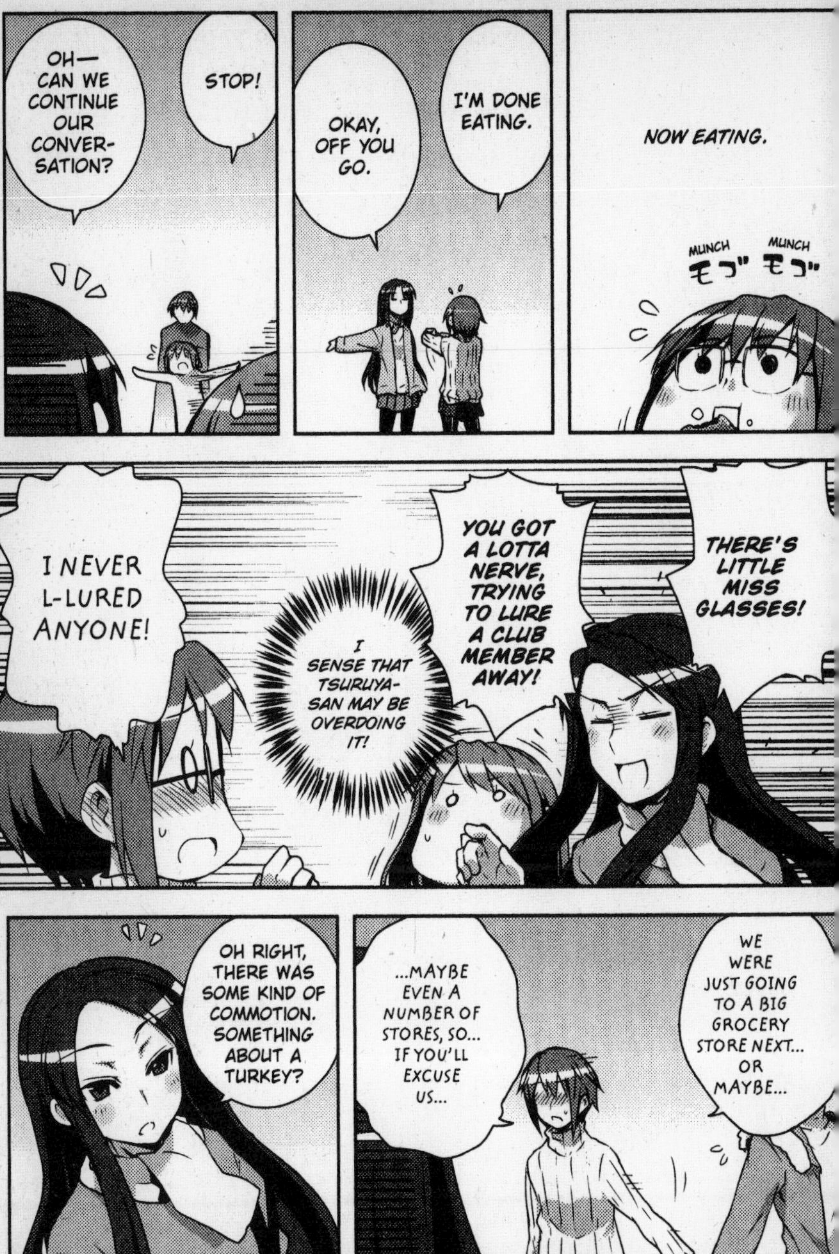
NOW EATING.
MUNCH MUNCH
モゴ モゴ
I'M DONE EATING.
OKAY, OFF YOU GO.
STOP!
OH— CAN WE CONTINUE OUR CONVERSATION?
THERE'S LITTLE MISS GLASSES!
YOU GOT A LOTTA NERVE, TRYING TO LURE A CLUB MEMBER AWAY!
I SENSE THAT TSURUYA-SAN MAY BE OVERDOING IT!
I NEVER L-LURED ANYONE!
WE WERE JUST GOING TO A BIG GROCERY STORE NEXT... OR MAYBE...
...MAYBE EVEN A NUMBER OF STORES, SO... IF YOU'LL EXCUSE US...
OH RIGHT, THERE WAS SOME KIND OF COMMOTION. SOMETHING ABOUT A TURKEY?

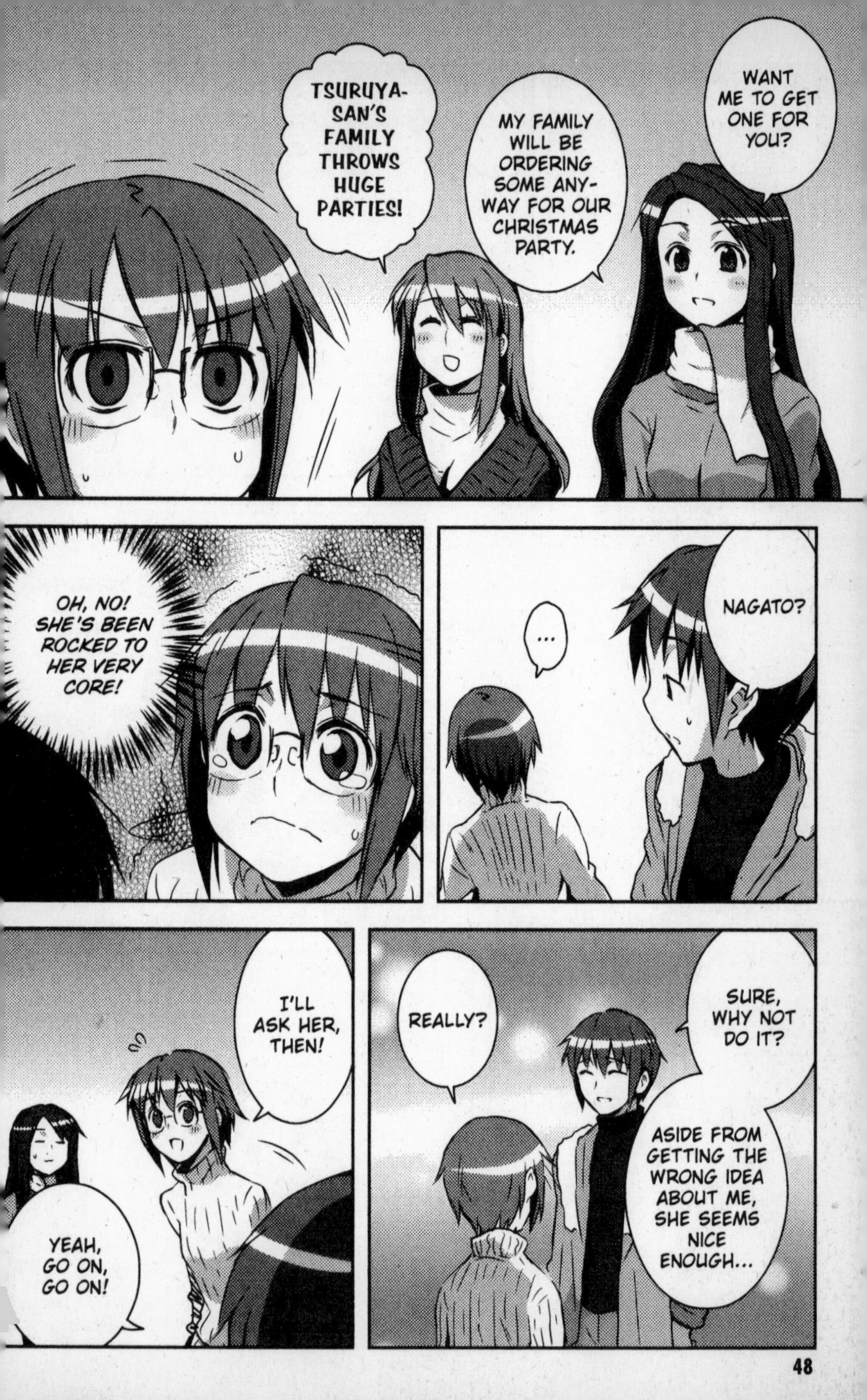
WANT ME TO GET ONE FOR YOU?
MY FAMILY WILL BE ORDERING SOME ANY-WAY FOR OUR CHRISTMAS PARTY.
TSURUYA-SAN'S FAMILY THROWS HUGE PARTIES!
NAGATO?
...
OH, NO! SHE'S BEEN ROCKED TO HER VERY CORE!
SURE, WHY NOT DO IT?
REALLY?
ASIDE FROM GETTING THE WRONG IDEA ABOUT ME, SHE SEEMS NICE ENOUGH...
I'LL ASK HER, THEN!
YEAH, GO ON, GO ON!

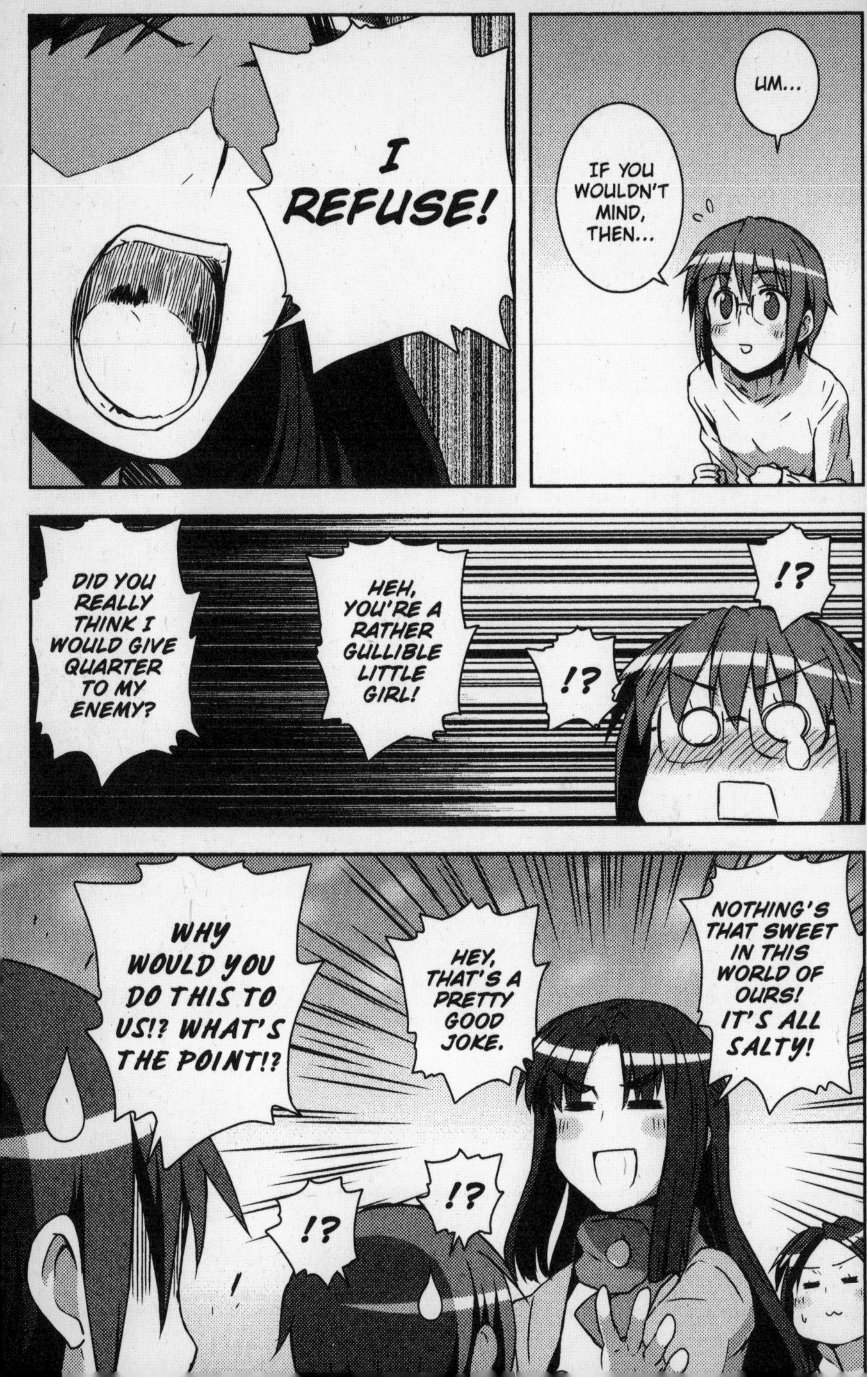
UM...
IF YOU WOULDN'T MIND, THEN...
I REFUSE!
!?
!?
HEH, YOU'RE A RATHER GULLIBLE LITTLE GIRL!
DID YOU REALLY THINK I WOULD GIVE QUARTER TO MY ENEMY?
NOTHING'S THAT SWEET IN THIS WORLD OF OURS! IT'S ALL SALTY!
HEY, THAT'S A PRETTY GOOD JOKE.
WHY WOULD YOU DO THIS TO US!? WHAT'S THE POINT!?
!?
!?

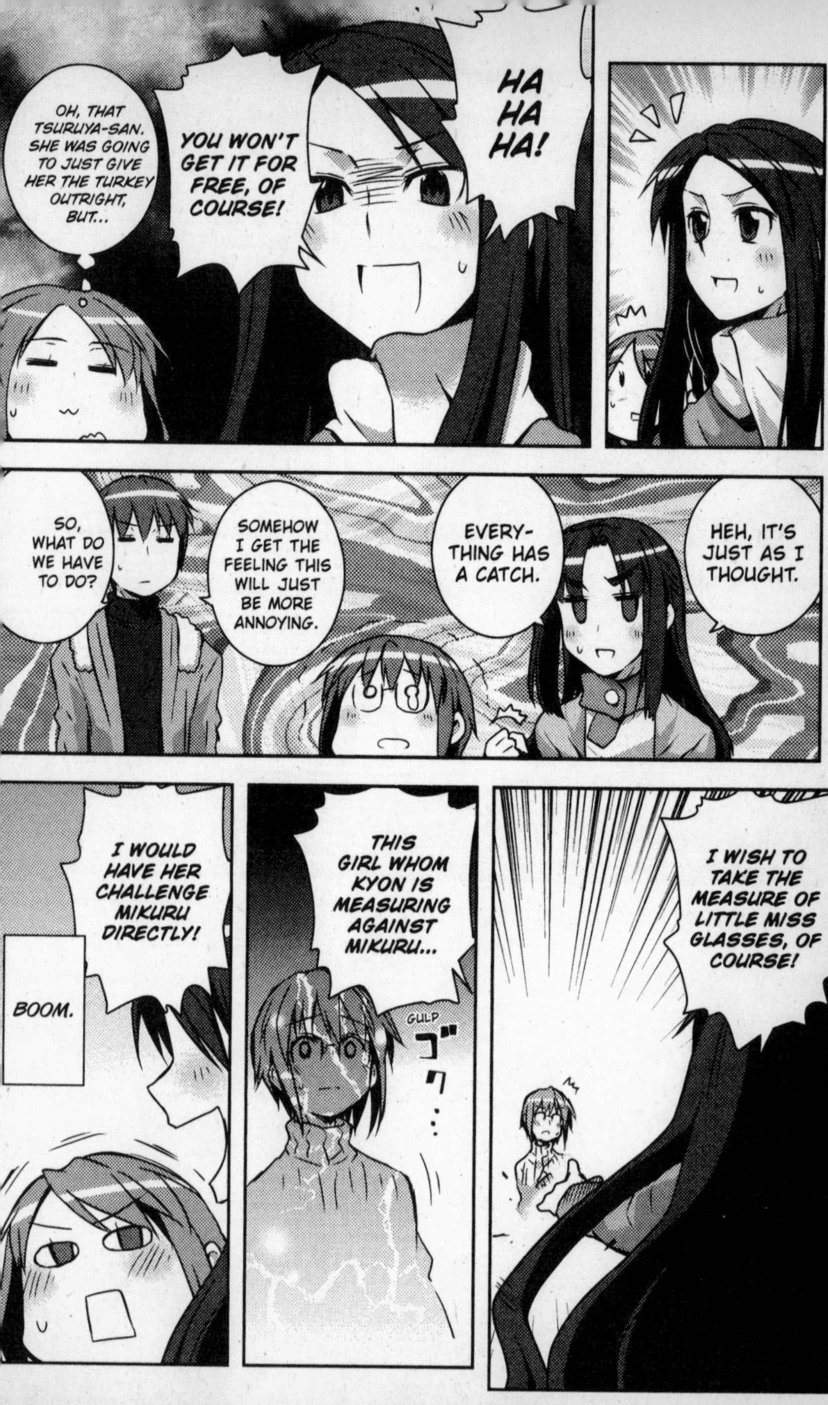
HA HA HA!
YOU WON'T GET IT FOR FREE, OF COURSE!
OH, THAT TSURUYA-SAN. SHE WAS GOING TO JUST GIVE HER THE TURKEY OUTRIGHT, BUT...
HEH, IT'S JUST AS I THOUGHT.
EVERY-THING HAS A CATCH.
SOMEHOW I GET THE FEELING THIS WILL JUST BE MORE ANNOYING.
SO, WHAT DO WE HAVE TO DO?
I WISH TO TAKE THE MEASURE OF LITTLE MISS GLASSES, OF COURSE!
THIS GIRL WHOM KYON IS MEASURING AGAINST MIKURU...
GULP
I WOULD HAVE HER CHALLENGE MIKURU DIRECTLY!
BOOM.

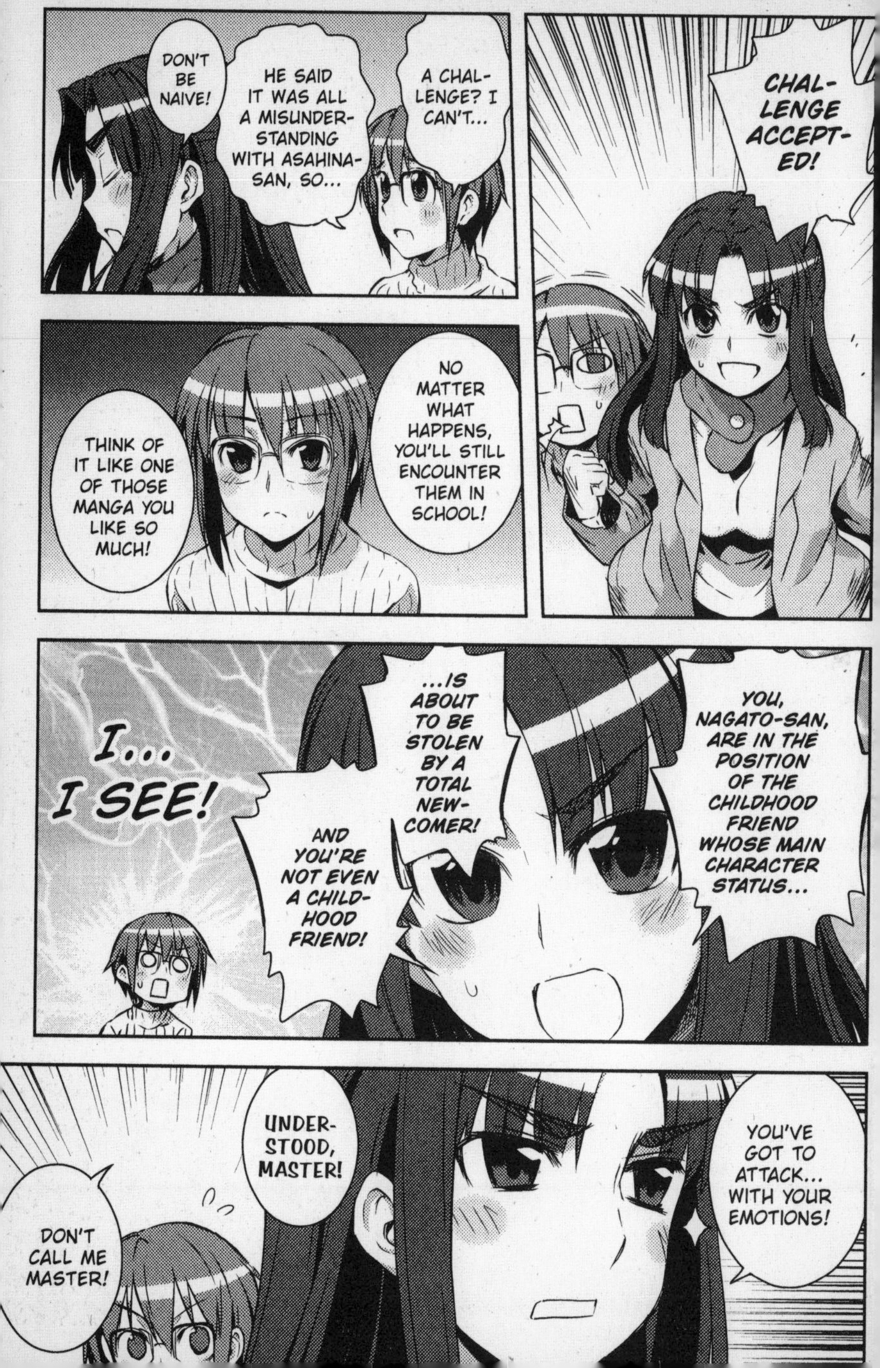

CHAL-LENGE ACCEPT-ED!
A CHAL-LENGE? I CAN'T...
HE SAID IT WAS ALL A MISUNDER-STANDING WITH ASAHINA-SAN, SO...
DON'T BE NAIVE!
NO MATTER WHAT HAPPENS, YOU'LL STILL ENCOUNTER THEM IN SCHOOL!
THINK OF IT LIKE ONE OF THOSE MANGA YOU LIKE SO MUCH!
YOU, NAGATO-SAN, ARE IN THE POSITION OF THE CHILDHOOD FRIEND WHOSE MAIN CHARACTER STATUS...
...IS ABOUT TO BE STOLEN BY A TOTAL NEW-COMER!
AND YOU'RE NOT EVEN A CHILD-HOOD FRIEND!
I... I SEE!
YOU'VE GOT TO ATTACK... WITH YOUR EMOTIONS!
UNDER-STOOD, MASTER!
DON'T CALL ME MASTER!

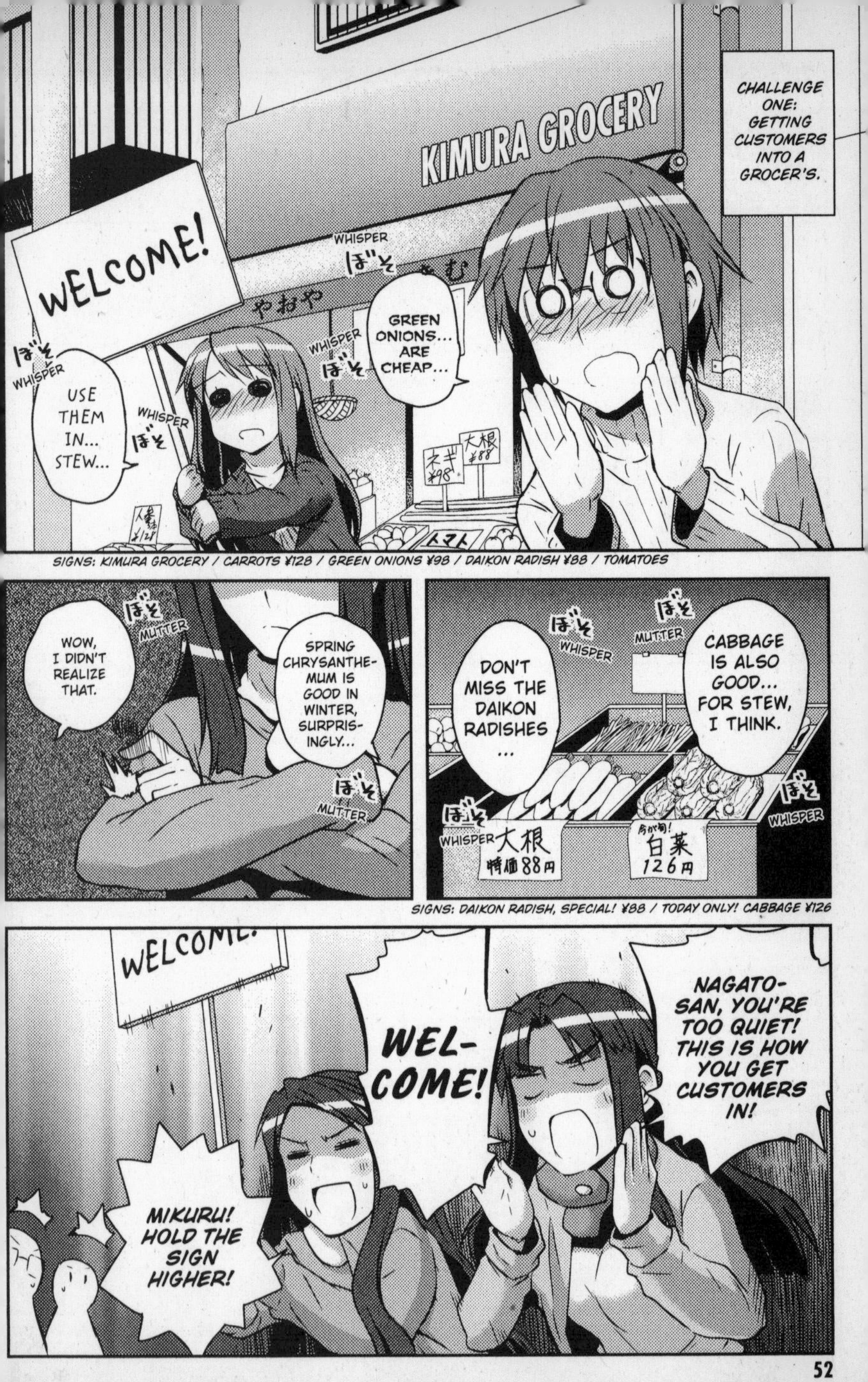
CHALLENGE ONE: GETTING CUSTOMERS INTO A GROCER'S.
KIMURA GROCERY
WHISPER
ぼそ
WHISPER
ぼそ
GREEN ONIONS... ARE CHEAP...
大根 ¥88
ネギ ¥98
トマト
WELCOME!
WHISPER
ぼそ
USE THEM IN... STEW...
ぼそ
WHISPER
やおや
SIGNS: KIMURA GROCERY / CARROTS ¥128 / GREEN ONIONS ¥98 / DAIKON RADISH ¥88 / TOMATOES
ぼそ
MUTTER
CABBAGE IS ALSO GOOD... FOR STEW, I THINK.
ぼそ
WHISPER
ぼそ
WHISPER
DON'T MISS THE DAIKON RADISHES ...
ぼそ
WHISPER
今が旬！ 白菜 126円
大根 特価88円
SIGNS: DAIKON RADISH, SPECIAL! ¥88 / TODAY ONLY! CABBAGE ¥126
SPRING CHRYSANTHEMUM IS GOOD IN WINTER, SURPRISINGLY...
ぼそ
MUTTER
ぼそ
MUTTER
WOW, I DIDN'T REALIZE THAT.
NAGATO-SAN, YOU'RE TOO QUIET! THIS IS HOW YOU GET CUSTOMERS IN!
WEL-COME!
MIKURU! HOLD THE SIGN HIGHER!
WELCOME!

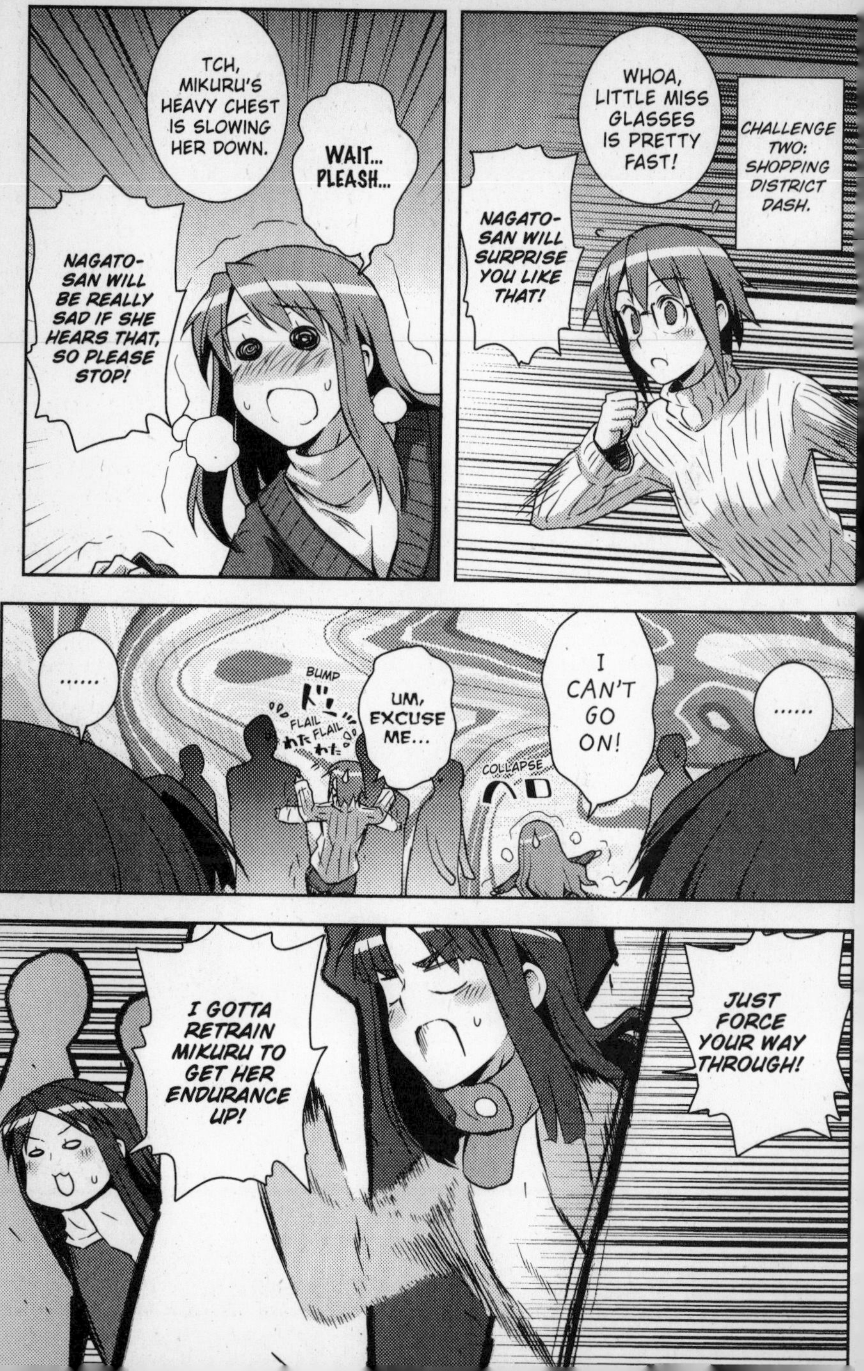
CHALLENGE TWO: SHOPPING DISTRICT DASH.
WHOA, LITTLE MISS GLASSES IS PRETTY FAST!
NAGATO-SAN WILL SURPRISE YOU LIKE THAT!
TCH, MIKURU'S HEAVY CHEST IS SLOWING HER DOWN.
WAIT... PLEASH...
NAGATO-SAN WILL BE REALLY SAD IF SHE HEARS THAT, SO PLEASE STOP!
......
I CAN'T GO ON!
COLLAPSE
UM, EXCUSE ME...
BUMP
FLAIL FLAIL
......
JUST FORCE YOUR WAY THROUGH!
I GOTTA RETRAIN MIKURU TO GET HER ENDURANCE UP!

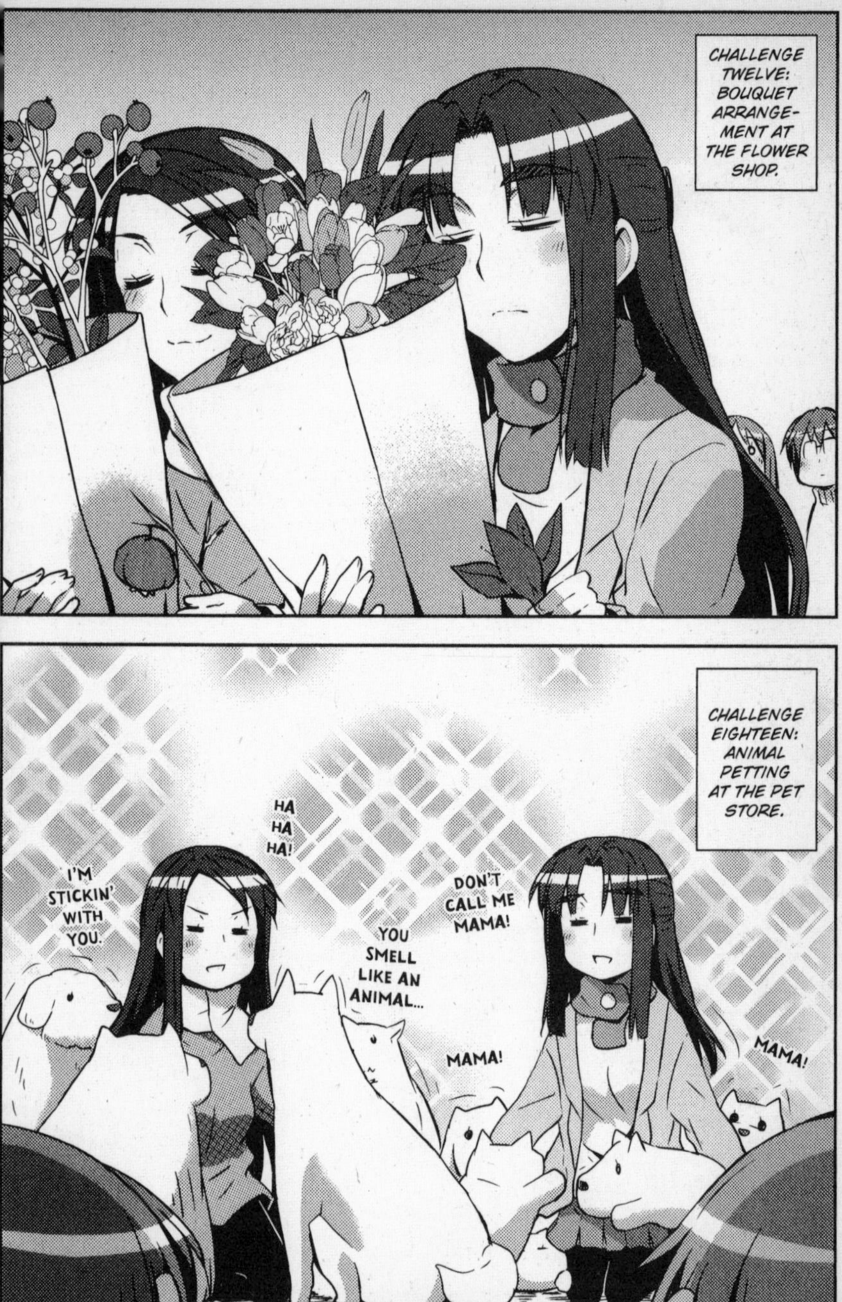
CHALLENGE TWELVE: BOUQUET ARRANGE-MENT AT THE FLOWER SHOP.
CHALLENGE EIGHTEEN: ANIMAL PETTING AT THE PET STORE.
MAMA!
DON'T CALL ME MAMA!
HA HA HA!
YOU SMELL LIKE AN ANIMAL...
MAMA!
I'M STICKIN' WITH YOU.

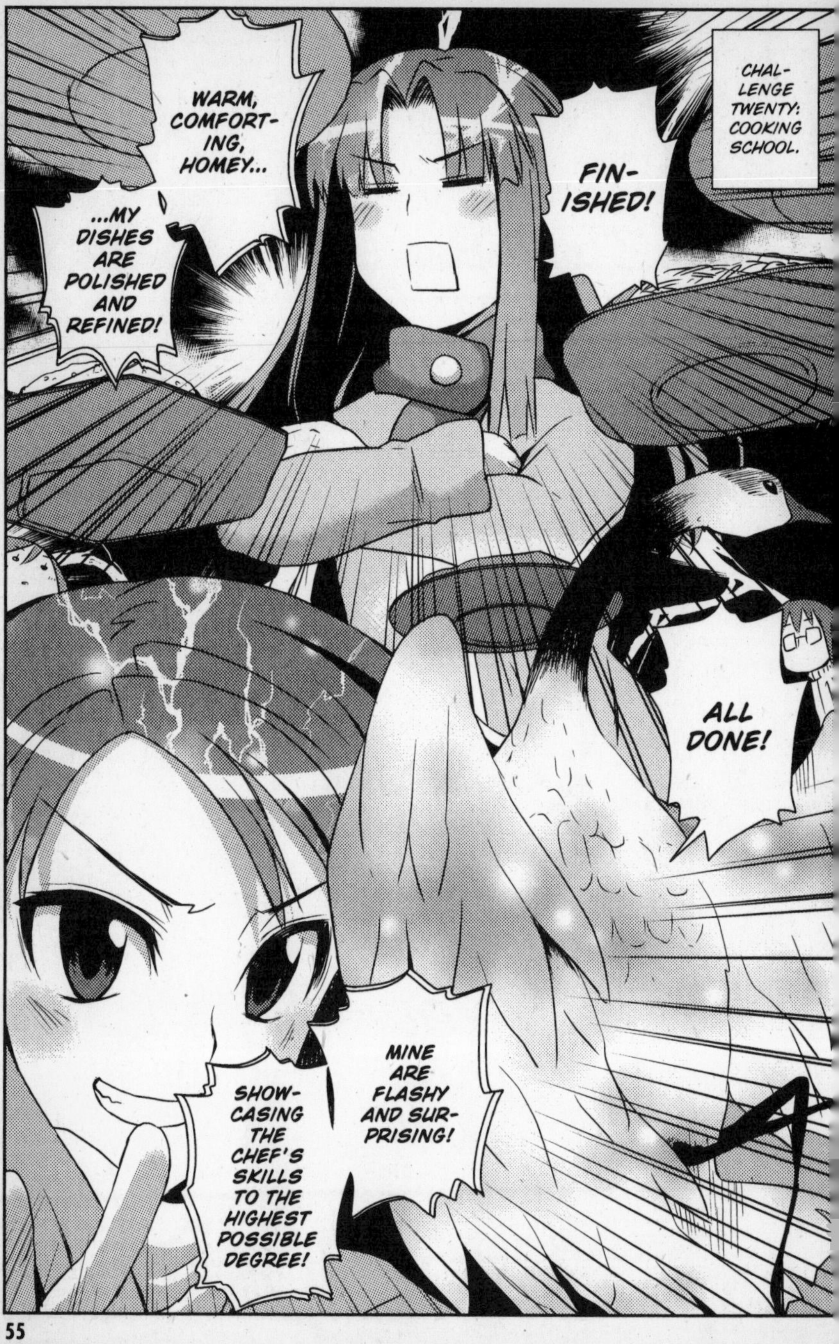
CHALLENGE TWENTY: COOKING SCHOOL.
FINISHED!
WARM, COMFORTING, HOMEY...
...MY DISHES ARE POLISHED AND REFINED!
ALL DONE!
MINE ARE FLASHY AND SURPRISING!
SHOWCASING THE CHEF'S SKILLS TO THE HIGHEST POSSIBLE DEGREE!

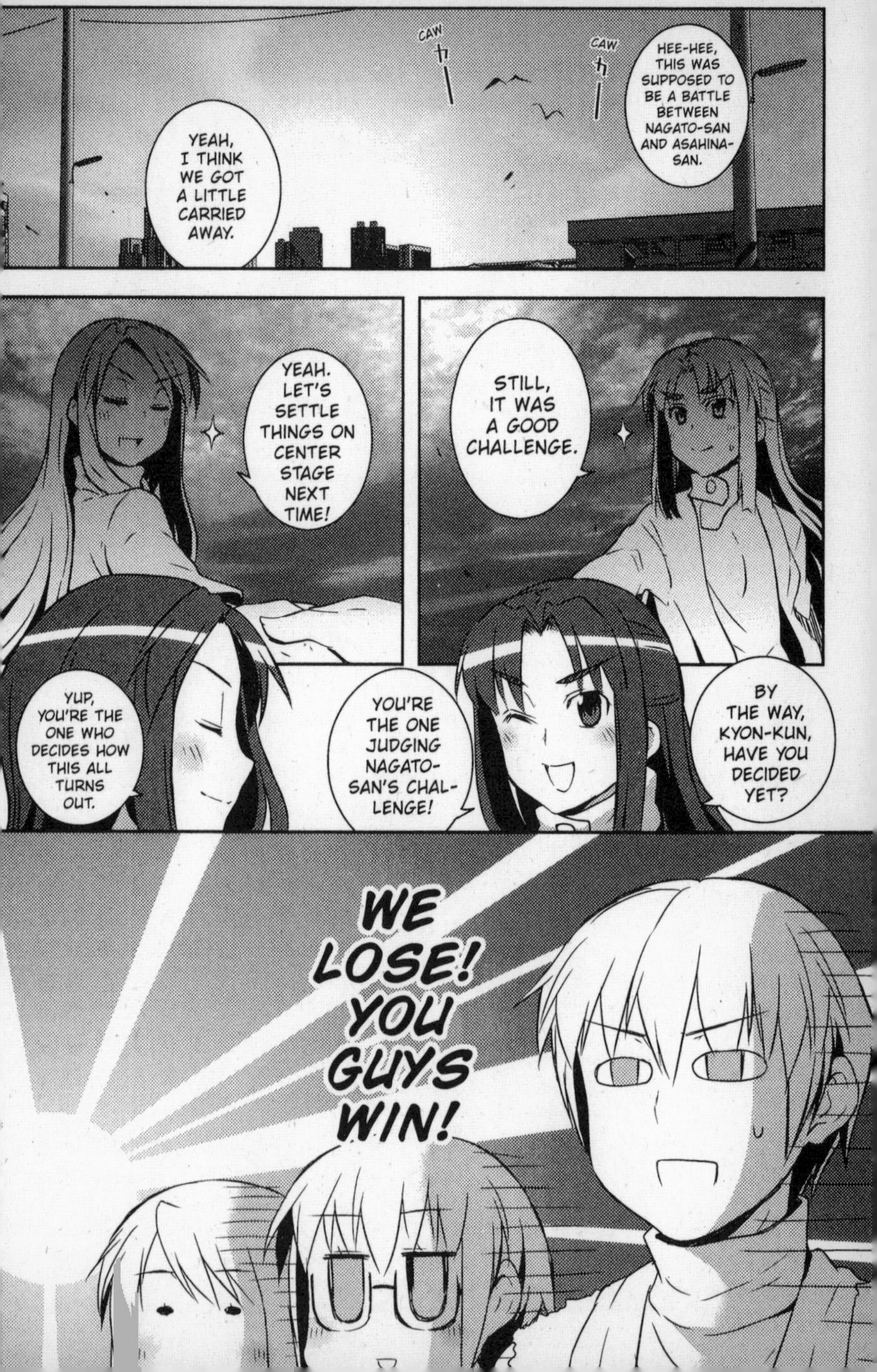
HEE-HEE, THIS WAS SUPPOSED TO BE A BATTLE BETWEEN NAGATO-SAN AND ASAHINA-SAN.
CAW
CAW
YEAH, I THINK WE GOT A LITTLE CARRIED AWAY.
STILL, IT WAS A GOOD CHALLENGE.
YEAH. LET'S SETTLE THINGS ON CENTER STAGE NEXT TIME!
BY THE WAY, KYON-KUN, HAVE YOU DECIDED YET?
YOU'RE THE ONE JUDGING NAGATO-SAN'S CHALLENGE!
YUP, YOU'RE THE ONE WHO DECIDES HOW THIS ALL TURNS OUT.
WE LOSE! YOU GUYS WIN!

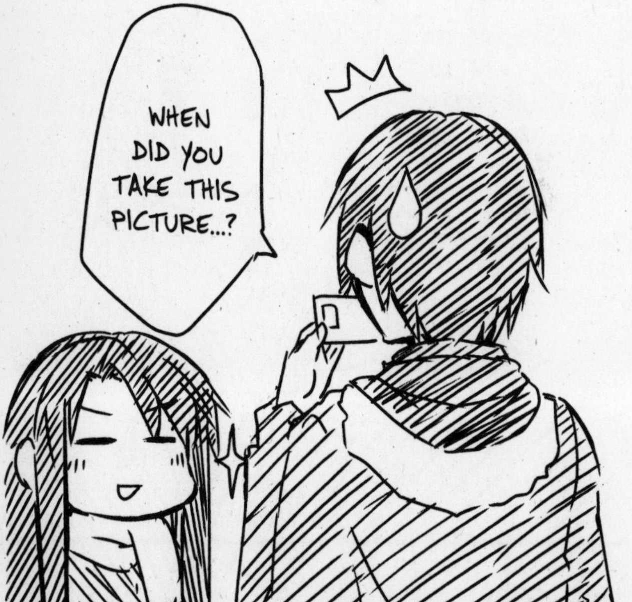
WHEN DID YOU TAKE THIS PICTURE...?

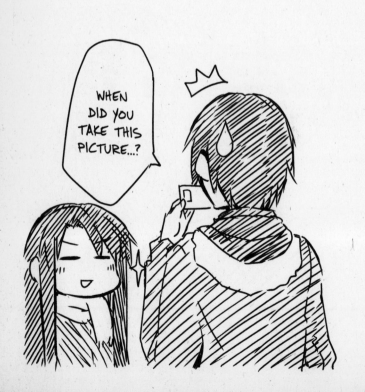

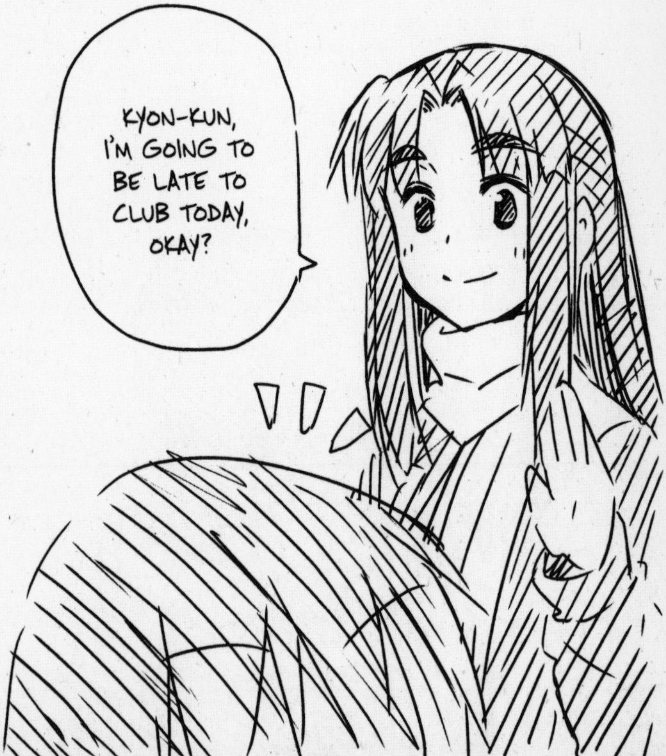
KYON-KUN, I'M GOING TO BE LATE TO CLUB TODAY, OKAY?

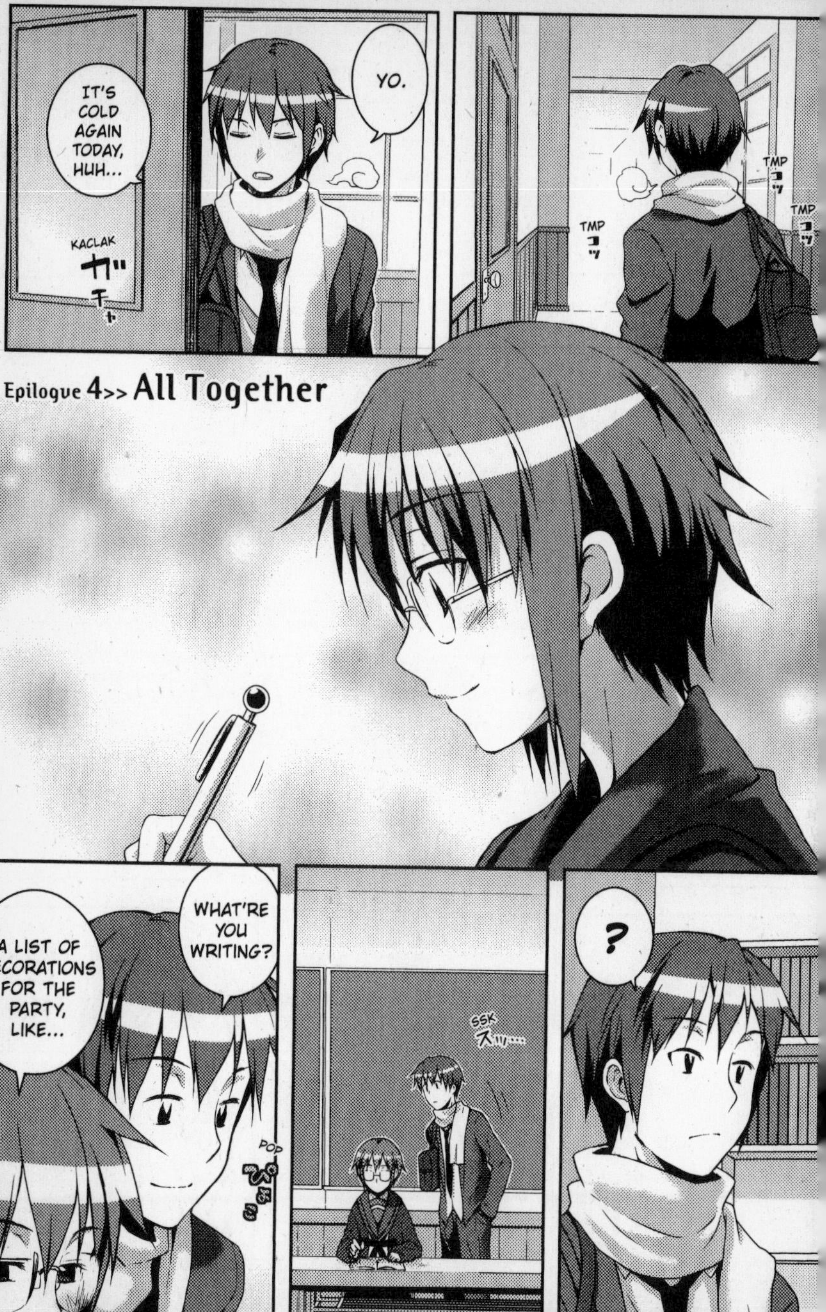
TMP
コッ
TMP
コッ
TMP
コッ
YO.
IT'S COLD AGAIN TODAY, HUH...
KACLAK
ガチャ
Epilogue 4>> All Together
?
SSK
スッ…
WHAT'RE YOU WRITING?
A LIST OF DECORATIONS FOR THE PARTY, LIKE...
POP
ぴょこ

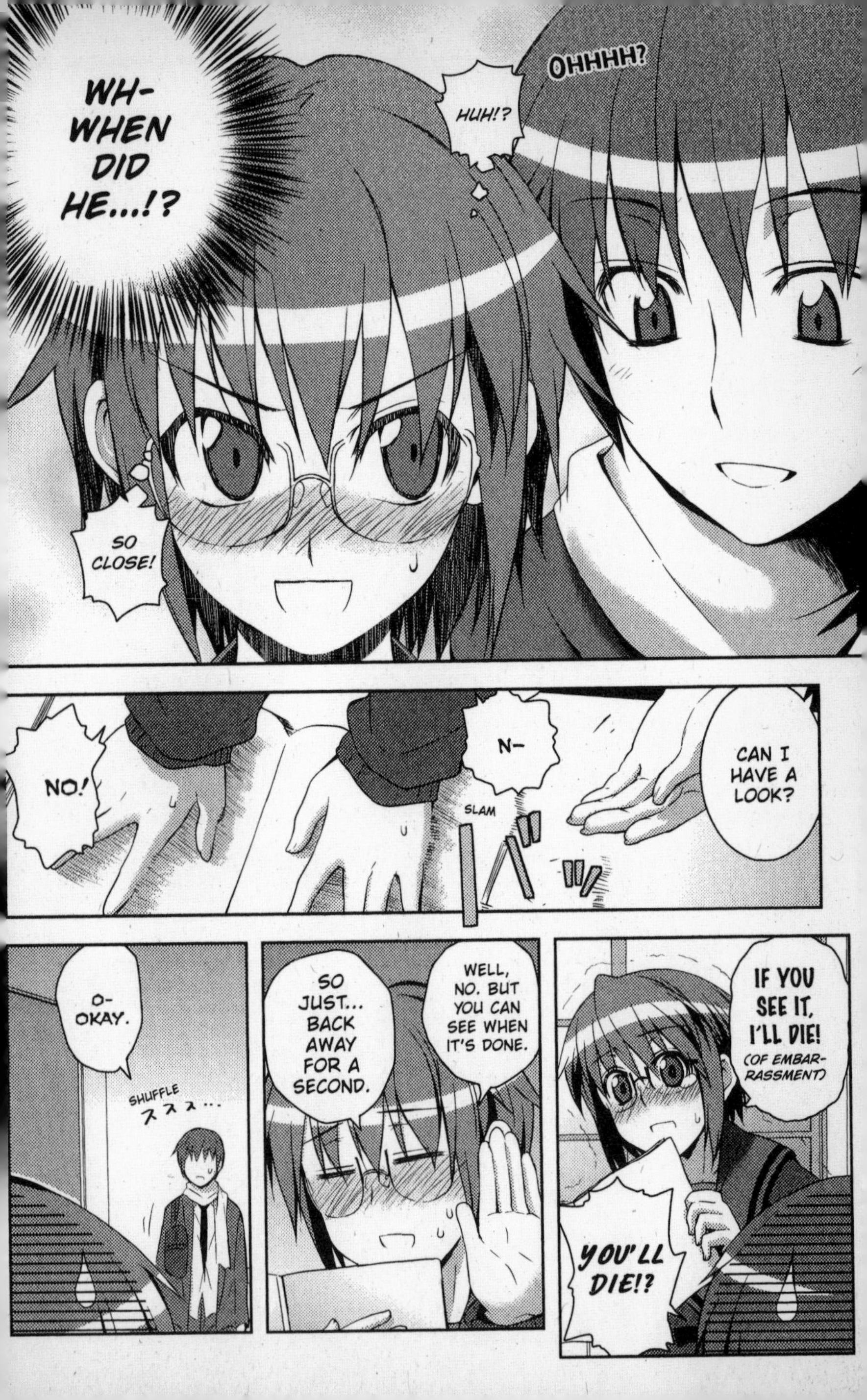
OHHHH?
HUH!?
WH- WHEN DID HE...!?
SO CLOSE!
CAN I HAVE A LOOK?
N-
SLAM
NO!
IF YOU SEE IT, I'LL DIE!
(OF EMBARRASSMENT)
YOU'LL DIE!?
WELL, NO. BUT YOU CAN SEE WHEN IT'S DONE.
SO JUST... BACK AWAY FOR A SECOND.
O-OKAY.
SHUFFLE
ススス…

As his cheek drew near, our faces

......

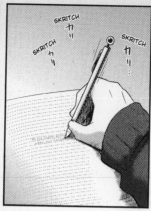

SKRITCH
カ
リ

SKRITCH
カ
リ

SKRITCH
カ
リ

......

......

RRRRIP

NAGA-
TO...

YOU'RE
PRETTY
INTENSE!

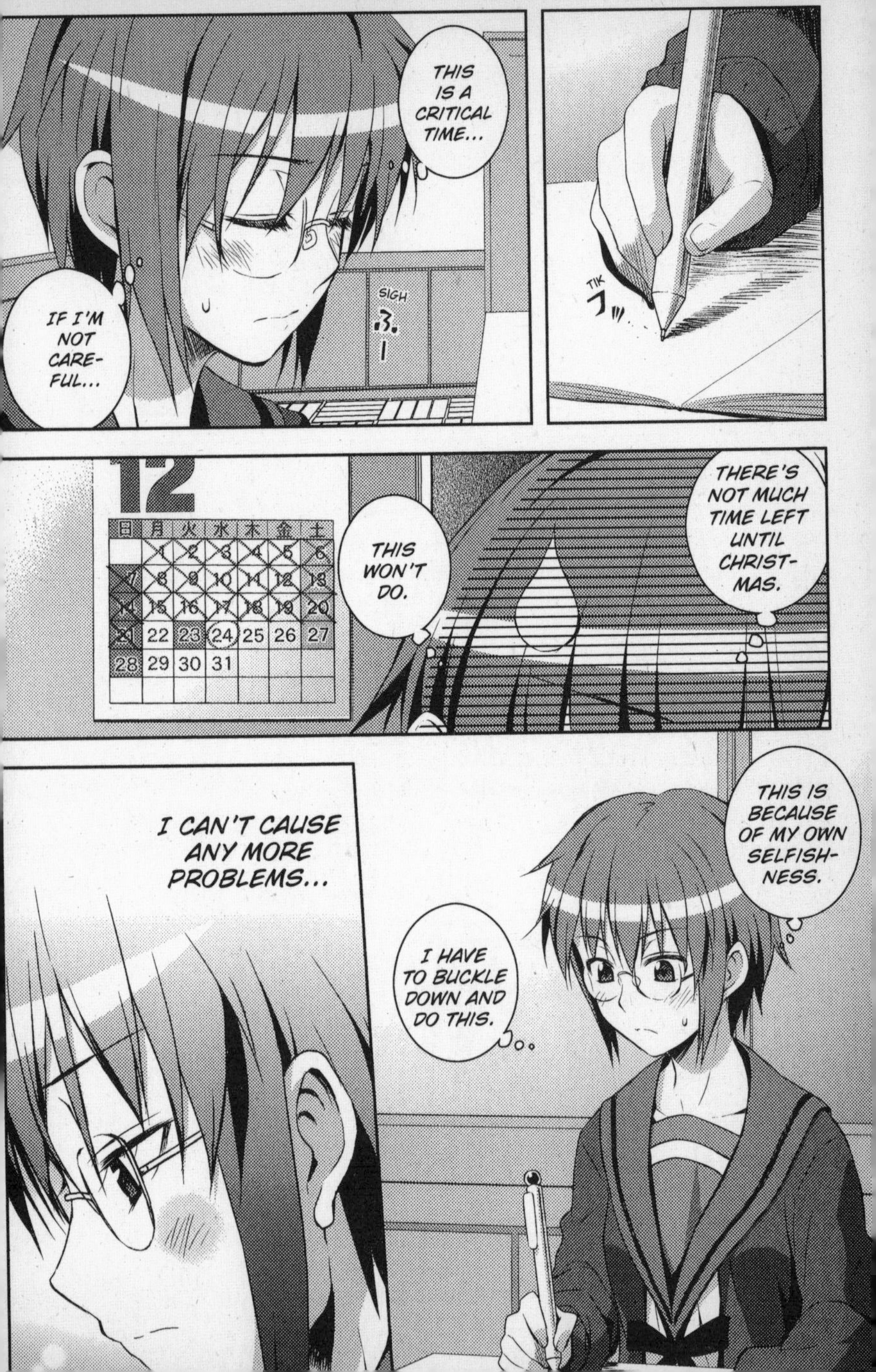
TIK
フッ
THIS IS A CRITICAL TIME...
SIGH
ふー
IF I'M NOT CAREFUL...
THERE'S NOT MUCH TIME LEFT UNTIL CHRISTMAS.
THIS WON'T DO.
12
日 月 火 水 木 金 土
1 2 3 4 5 6
7 8 9 10 11 12 13
14 15 16 17 18 19 20
21 22 23 24 25 26 27
28 29 30 31
THIS IS BECAUSE OF MY OWN SELFISHNESS.
I HAVE TO BUCKLE DOWN AND DO THIS.
I CAN'T CAUSE ANY MORE PROBLEMS...

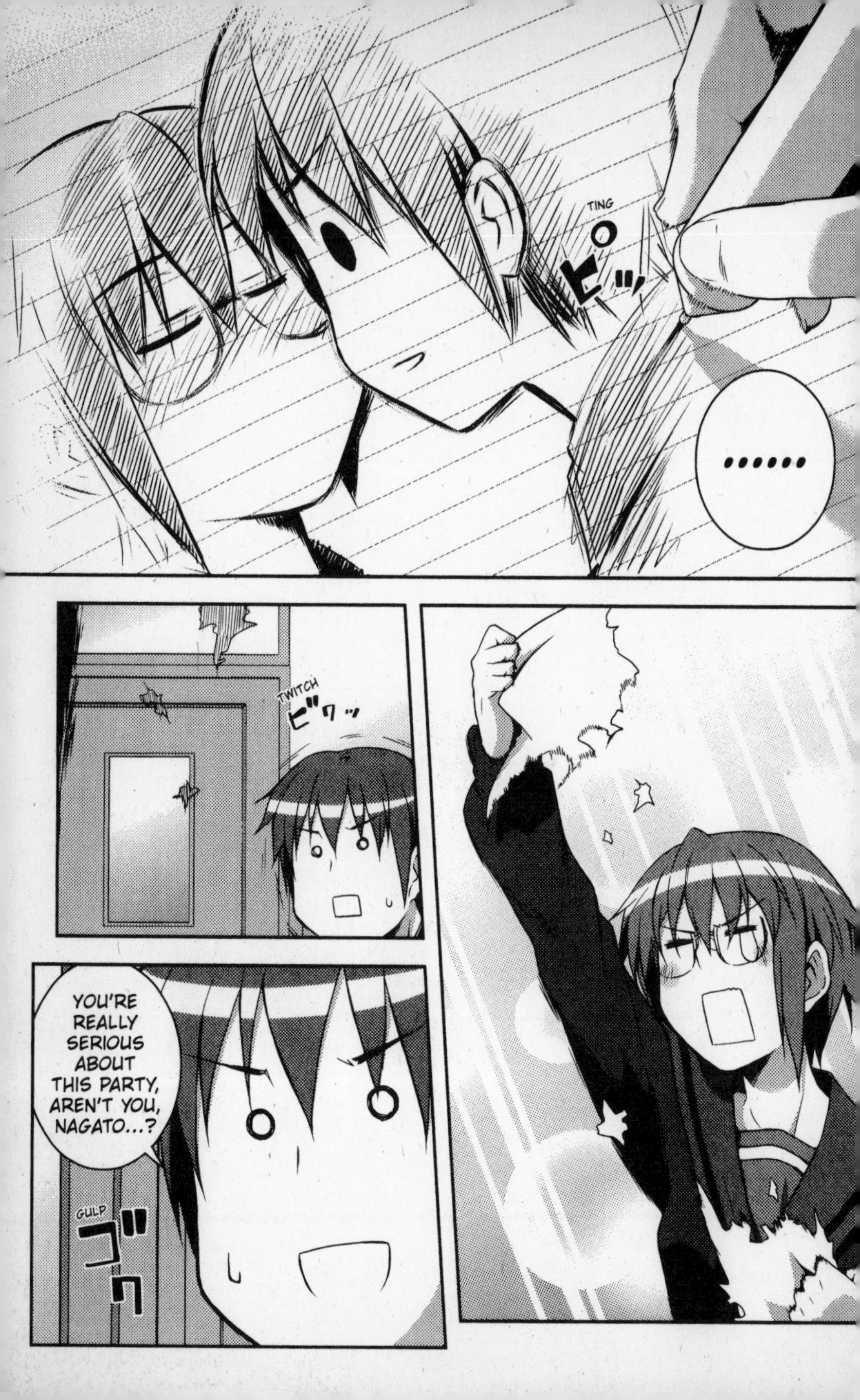
TING
......
TWITCH
YOU'RE REALLY SERIOUS ABOUT THIS PARTY, AREN'T YOU, NAGATO...?
GULP

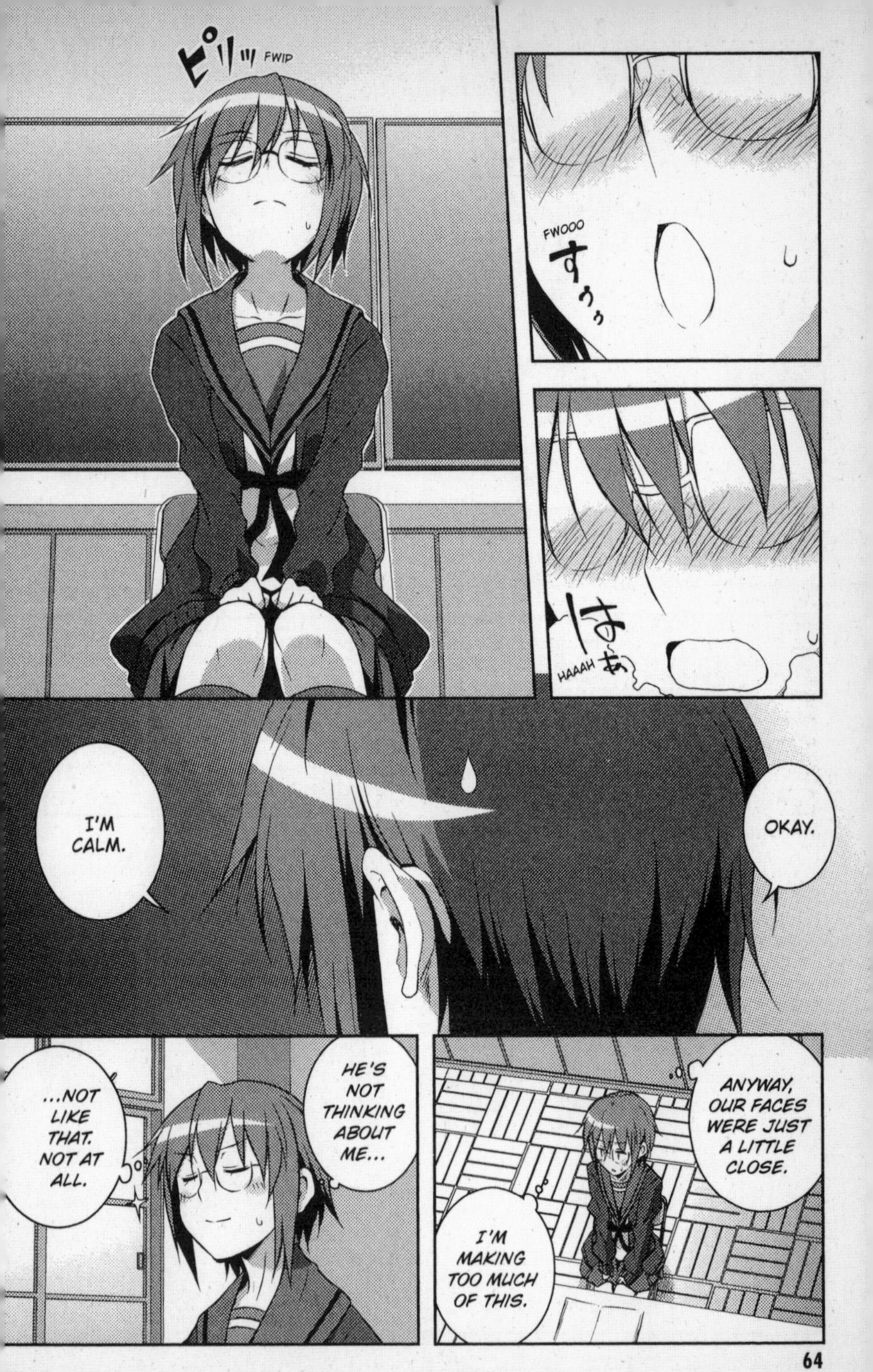
FWOOO
すぅぅ
はぁ
HAAAH
ピリッ
FWIP
OKAY.
I'M CALM.
ANYWAY, OUR FACES WERE JUST A LITTLE CLOSE.
I'M MAKING TOO MUCH OF THIS.
HE'S NOT THINKING ABOUT ME...
...NOT LIKE THAT. NOT AT ALL.

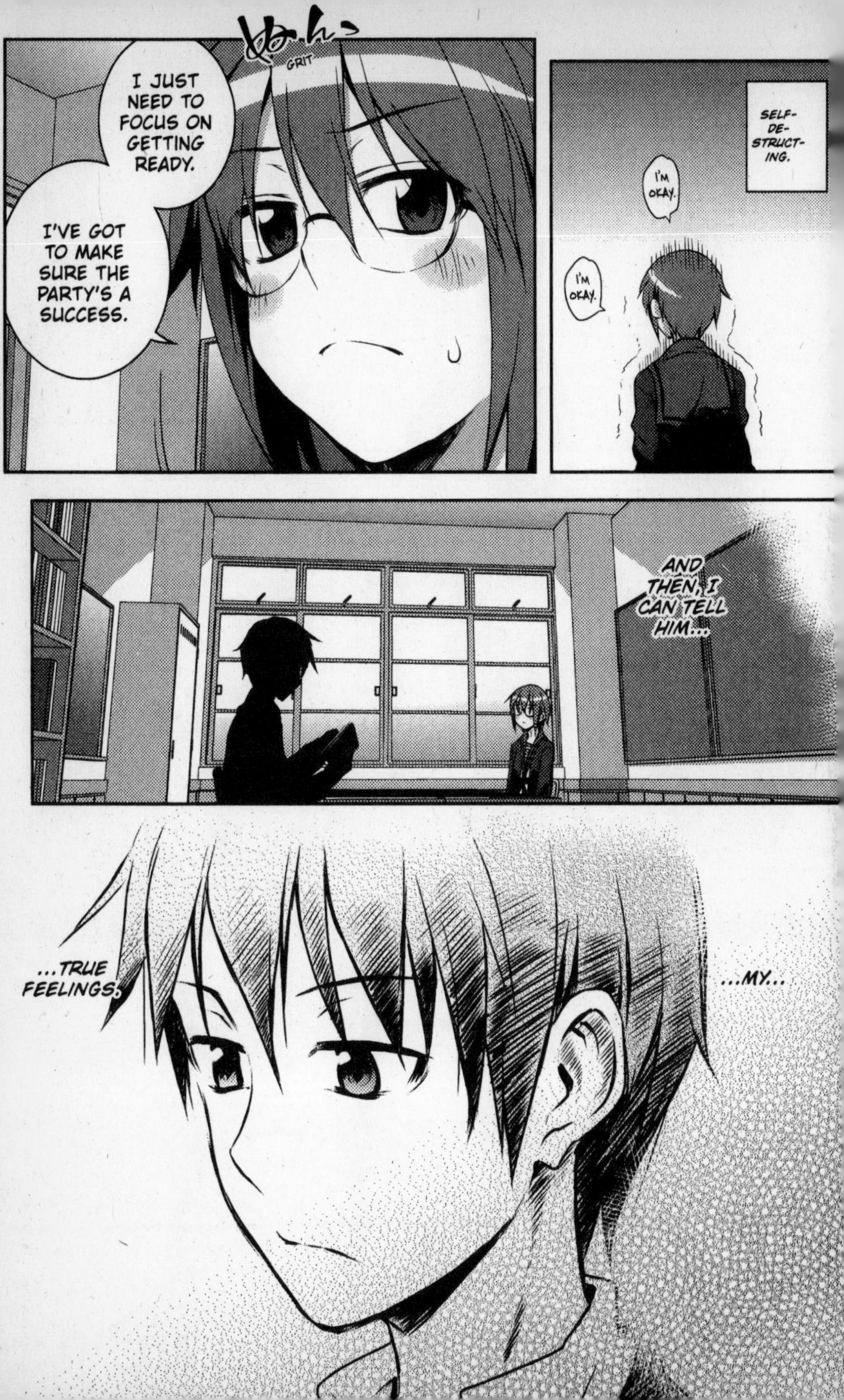
SELF-DESTRUCTING.
I'M OKAY.
I'M OKAY.
GRIT
I JUST NEED TO FOCUS ON GETTING READY.
I'VE GOT TO MAKE SURE THE PARTY'S A SUCCESS.
AND THEN, I CAN TELL HIM...
...MY...
...TRUE FEELINGS.

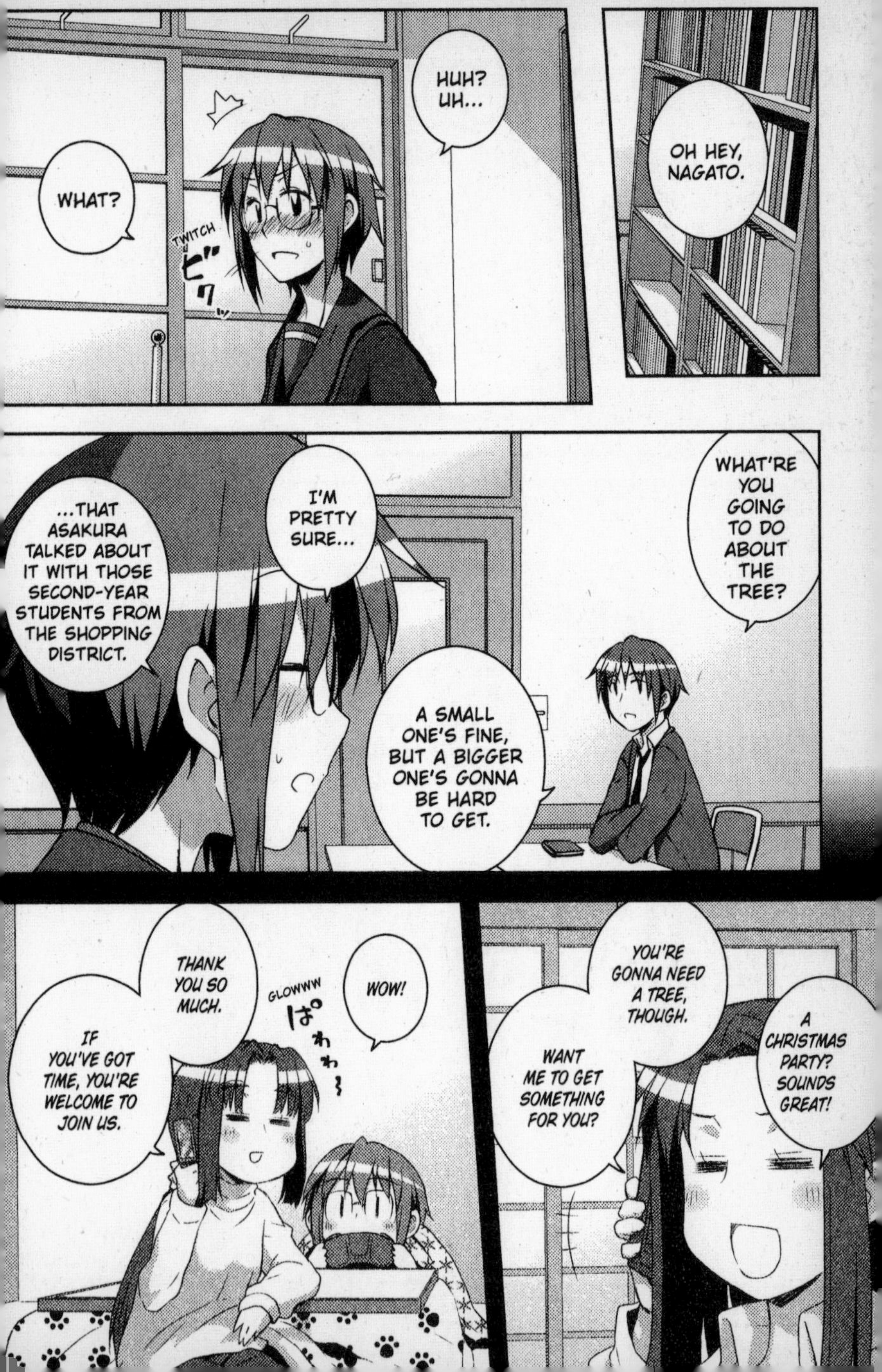
OH HEY, NAGATO.
HUH? UH...
WHAT?
TWITCH ビクッ
WHAT'RE YOU GOING TO DO ABOUT THE TREE?
I'M PRETTY SURE...
...THAT ASAKURA TALKED ABOUT IT WITH THOSE SECOND-YEAR STUDENTS FROM THE SHOPPING DISTRICT.
A SMALL ONE'S FINE, BUT A BIGGER ONE'S GONNA BE HARD TO GET.
A CHRISTMAS PARTY? SOUNDS GREAT!
YOU'RE GONNA NEED A TREE, THOUGH.
WANT ME TO GET SOMETHING FOR YOU?
WOW!
GLOWWW ぱわわ～
THANK YOU SO MUCH.
IF YOU'VE GOT TIME, YOU'RE WELCOME TO JOIN US.

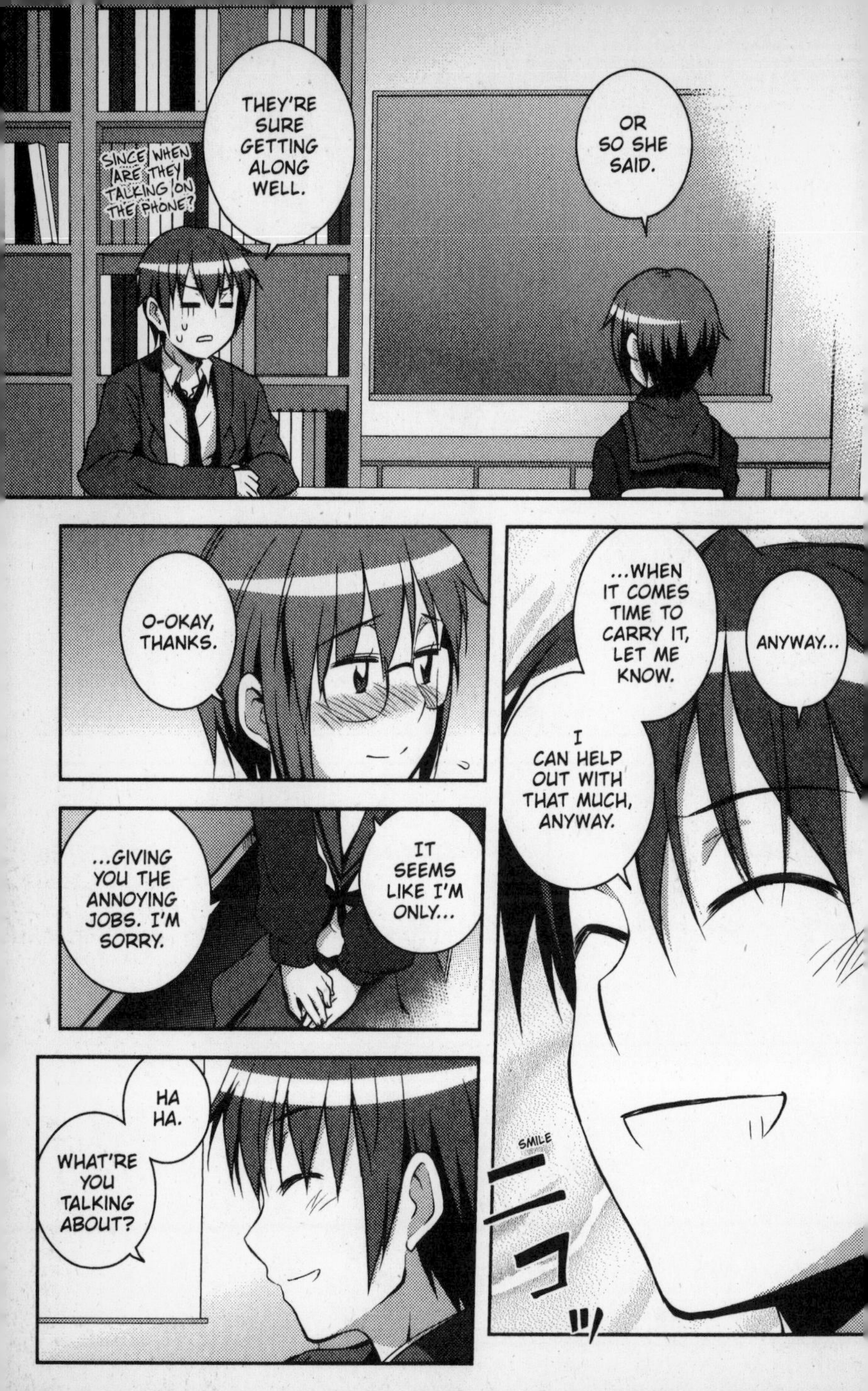
OR SO SHE SAID.
THEY'RE SURE GETTING ALONG WELL.
SINCE WHEN ARE THEY TALKING ON THE PHONE?
ANYWAY...
...WHEN IT COMES TIME TO CARRY IT, LET ME KNOW.
I CAN HELP OUT WITH THAT MUCH, ANYWAY.
SMILE
ニコッ
O-OKAY, THANKS.
IT SEEMS LIKE I'M ONLY...
...GIVING YOU THE ANNOYING JOBS. I'M SORRY.
HA HA.
WHAT'RE YOU TALKING ABOUT?

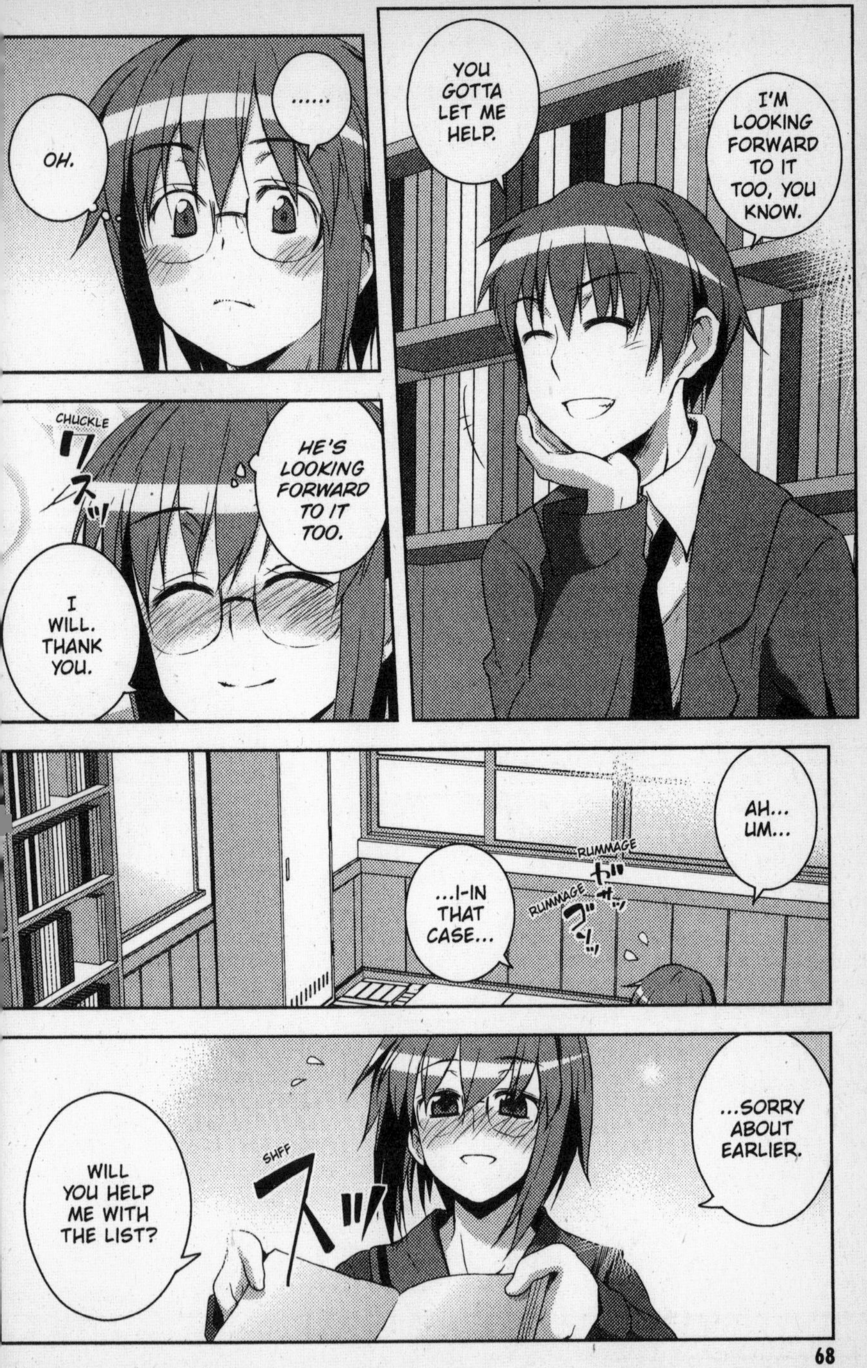
I'M LOOKING FORWARD TO IT TOO, YOU KNOW.
YOU GOTTA LET ME HELP.
......
OH.
CHUCKLE
HE'S LOOKING FORWARD TO IT TOO.
I WILL. THANK YOU.
AH... UM...
RUMMAGE
RUMMAGE
...I-IN THAT CASE...
...SORRY ABOUT EARLIER.
SHFF
WILL YOU HELP ME WITH THE LIST?

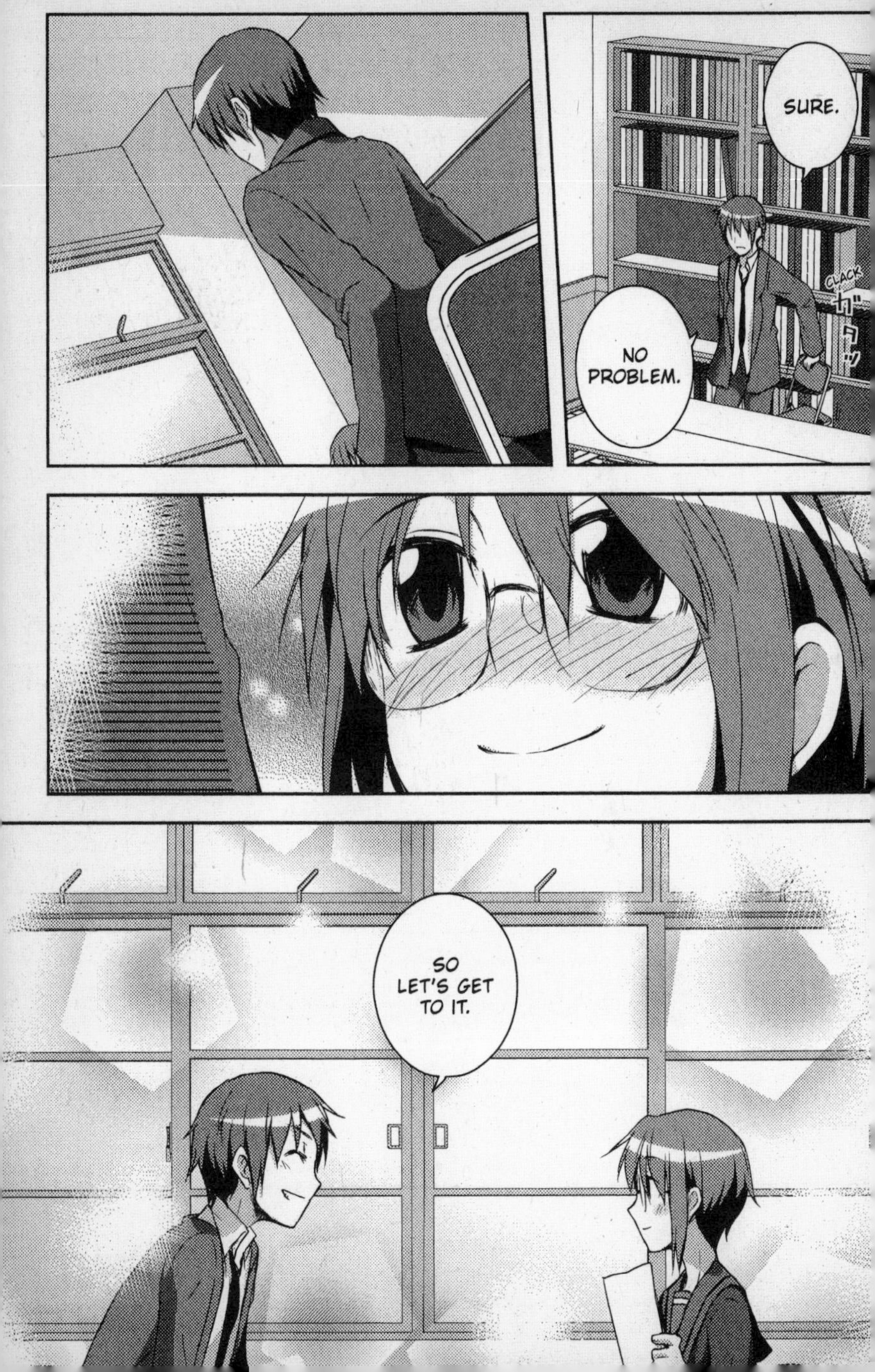
SURE.
NO PROBLEM.
CLACK
ガタッ
SO LET'S GET TO IT.

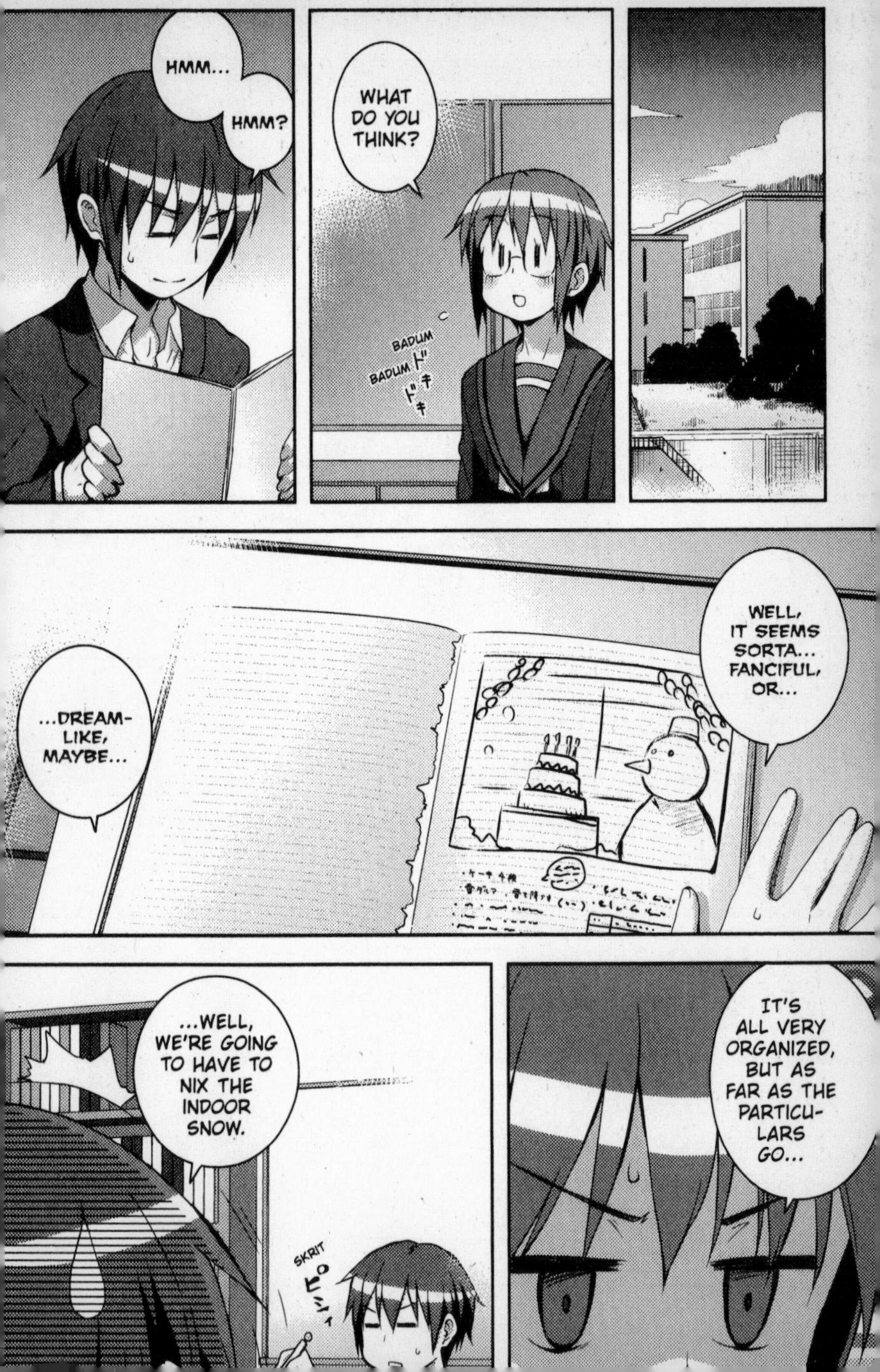
WHAT DO YOU THINK?
BADUM BADUM
ドキドキ
HMM...
HMM?
WELL, IT SEEMS SORTA... FANCIFUL, OR...
...DREAM-LIKE, MAYBE...
IT'S ALL VERY ORGANIZED, BUT AS FAR AS THE PARTICULARS GO...
...WELL, WE'RE GOING TO HAVE TO NIX THE INDOOR SNOW.
SKRIT

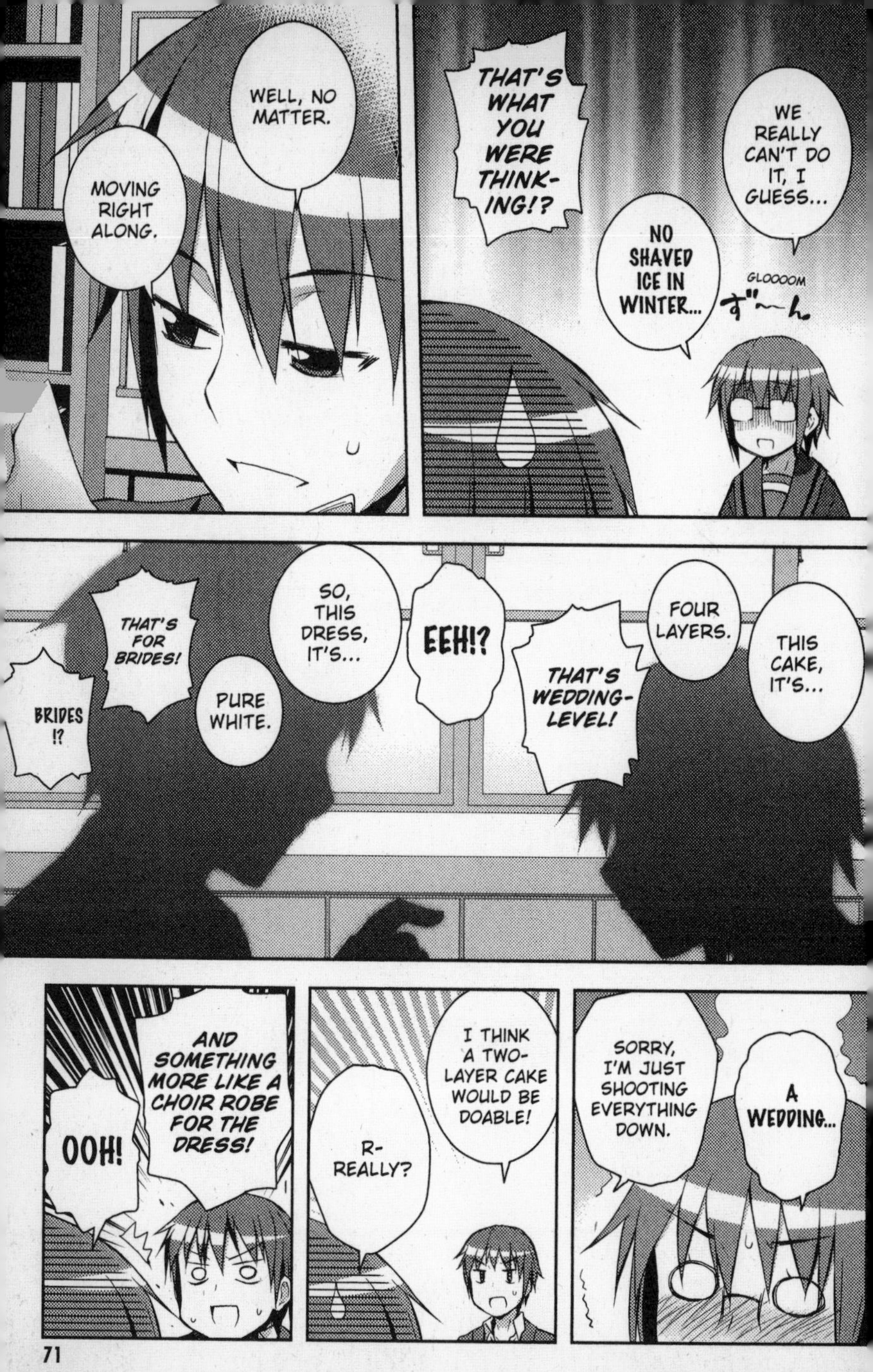
WE REALLY CAN'T DO IT, I GUESS...
NO SHAVED ICE IN WINTER...
GLOOOOM
ず〜ん
THAT'S WHAT YOU WERE THINKING!?
WELL, NO MATTER.
MOVING RIGHT ALONG.
THIS CAKE, IT'S...
FOUR LAYERS.
THAT'S WEDDING-LEVEL!
EEH!?
SO, THIS DRESS, IT'S...
PURE WHITE.
THAT'S FOR BRIDES!
BRIDES!?
A WEDDING...
SORRY, I'M JUST SHOOTING EVERYTHING DOWN.
I THINK A TWO-LAYER CAKE WOULD BE DOABLE!
R-REALLY?
AND SOMETHING MORE LIKE A CHOIR ROBE FOR THE DRESS!
OOH!

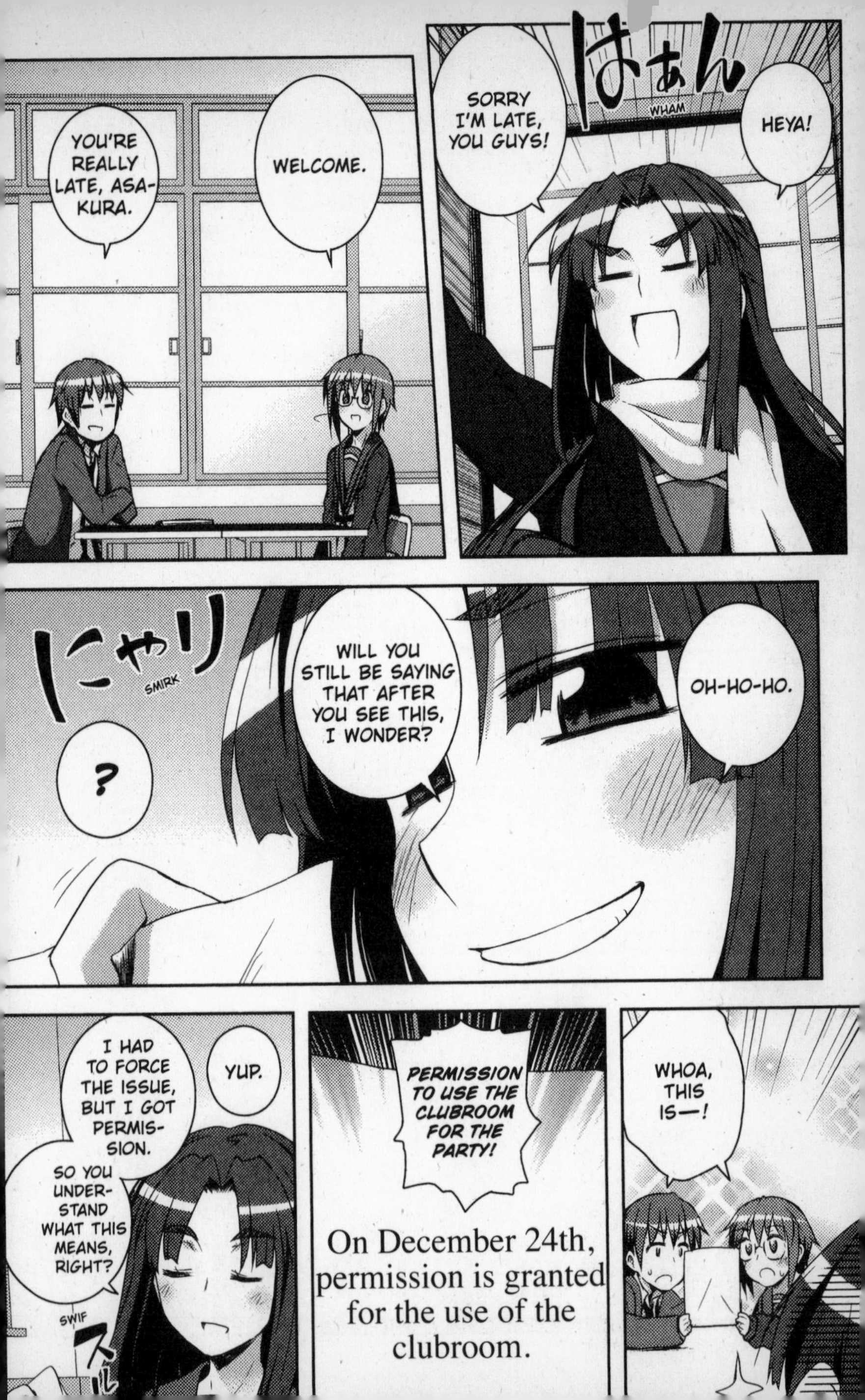
ばぁん
WHAM
HEYA!
SORRY I'M LATE, YOU GUYS!
WELCOME.
YOU'RE REALLY LATE, ASA-KURA.
OH-HO-HO.
WILL YOU STILL BE SAYING THAT AFTER YOU SEE THIS, I WONDER?
にやり
SMIRK
?
WHOA, THIS IS—!
PERMISSION TO USE THE CLUBROOM FOR THE PARTY!
On December 24th, permission is granted for the use of the clubroom.
YUP.
I HAD TO FORCE THE ISSUE, BUT I GOT PERMIS-SION.
SO YOU UNDER-STAND WHAT THIS MEANS, RIGHT?
スル
SWIF

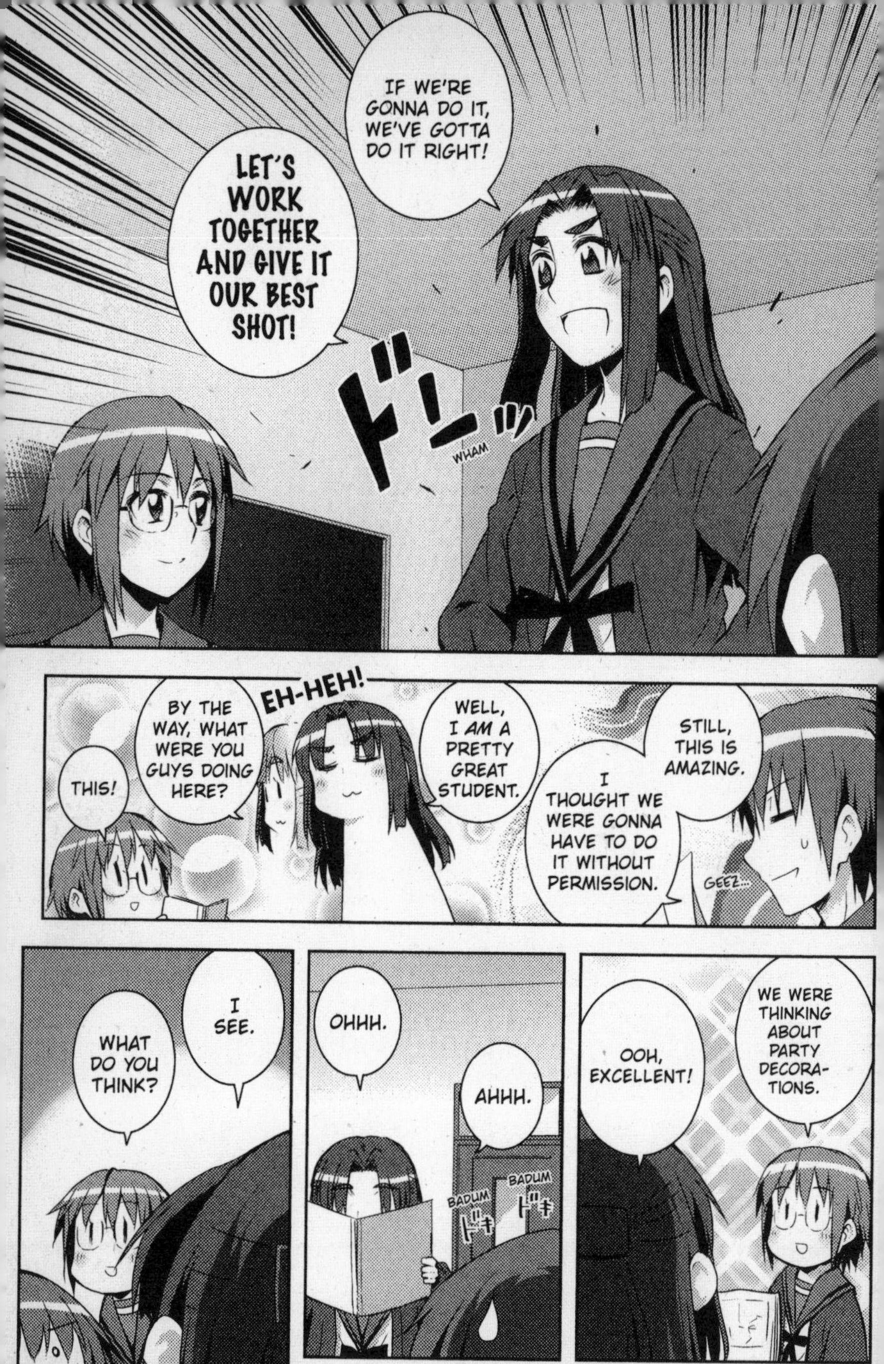
IF WE'RE GONNA DO IT, WE'VE GOTTA DO IT RIGHT!
LET'S WORK TOGETHER AND GIVE IT OUR BEST SHOT!
ドーンッ
WHAM
STILL, THIS IS AMAZING.
I THOUGHT WE WERE GONNA HAVE TO DO IT WITHOUT PERMISSION.
GEEZ...
WELL, I *AM* A PRETTY GREAT STUDENT.
EH-HEH!
BY THE WAY, WHAT WERE YOU GUYS DOING HERE?
THIS!
WE WERE THINKING ABOUT PARTY DECORATIONS.
OOH, EXCELLENT!
OHHH.
AHHH.
BADUM
ドキ
BADUM
ドキ
I SEE.
WHAT DO YOU THINK?

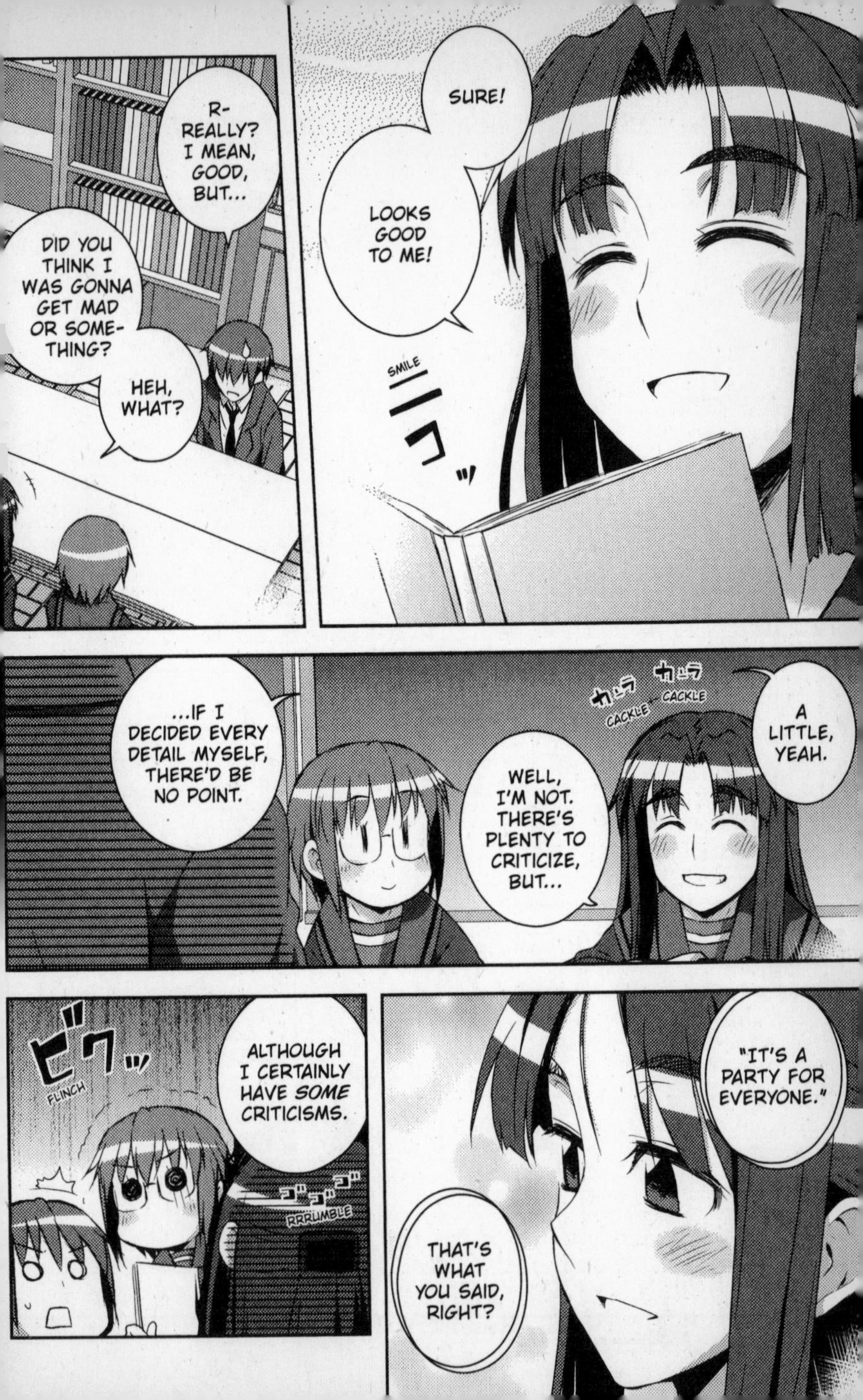
SURE!
LOOKS GOOD TO ME!
SMILE
R-REALLY? I MEAN, GOOD, BUT...
DID YOU THINK I WAS GONNA GET MAD OR SOME-THING?
HEH, WHAT?
A LITTLE, YEAH.
CACKLE CACKLE
WELL, I'M NOT. THERE'S PLENTY TO CRITICIZE, BUT...
...IF I DECIDED EVERY DETAIL MYSELF, THERE'D BE NO POINT.
"IT'S A PARTY FOR EVERYONE."
THAT'S WHAT YOU SAID, RIGHT?
ALTHOUGH I CERTAINLY HAVE *SOME* CRITICISMS.
FLINCH
RRRUMBLE

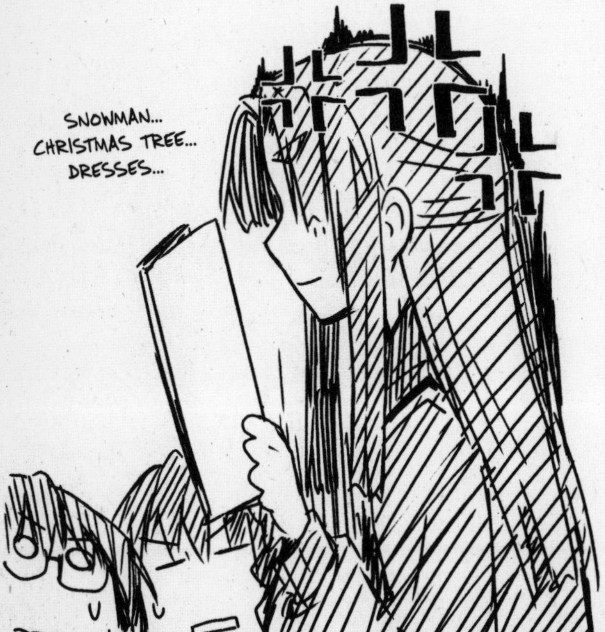
SNOWMAN...
CHRISTMAS TREE...
DRESSES...

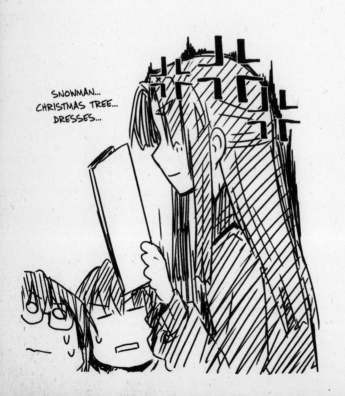

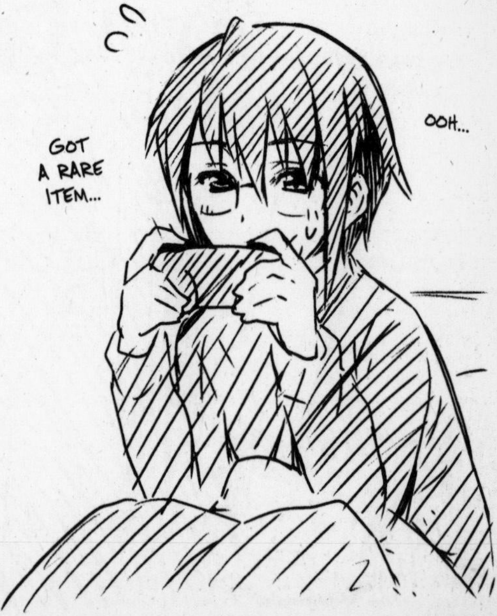
OOH...
GOT A RARE ITEM...

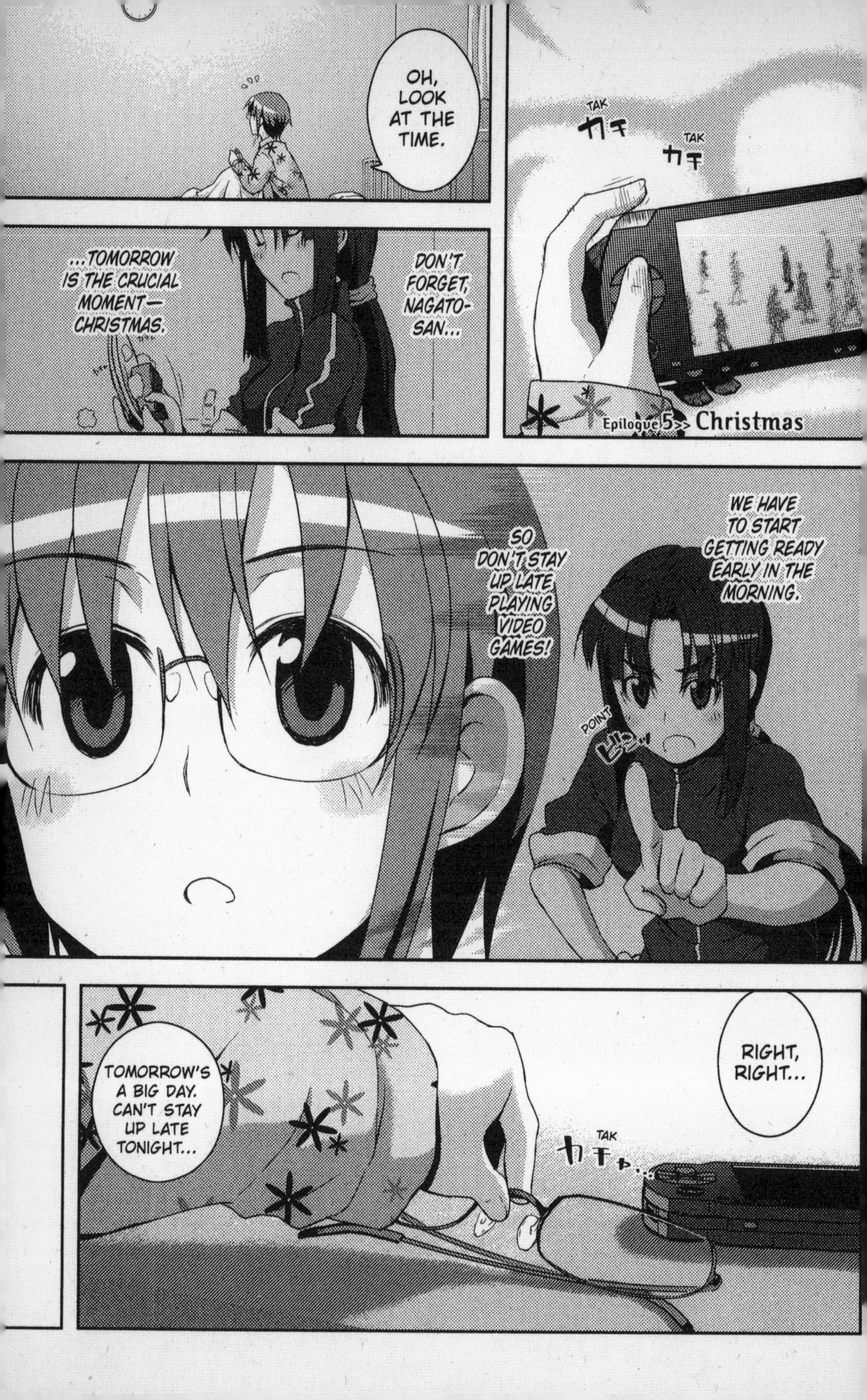
TAK
TAK
Epilogue 5>> Christmas
OH, LOOK AT THE TIME.
DON'T FORGET, NAGATO-SAN...
...TOMORROW IS THE CRUCIAL MOMENT—CHRISTMAS.
WE HAVE TO START GETTING READY EARLY IN THE MORNING.
SO DON'T STAY UP LATE PLAYING VIDEO GAMES!
POINT
RIGHT, RIGHT...
TAK
TOMORROW'S A BIG DAY. CAN'T STAY UP LATE TONIGHT...

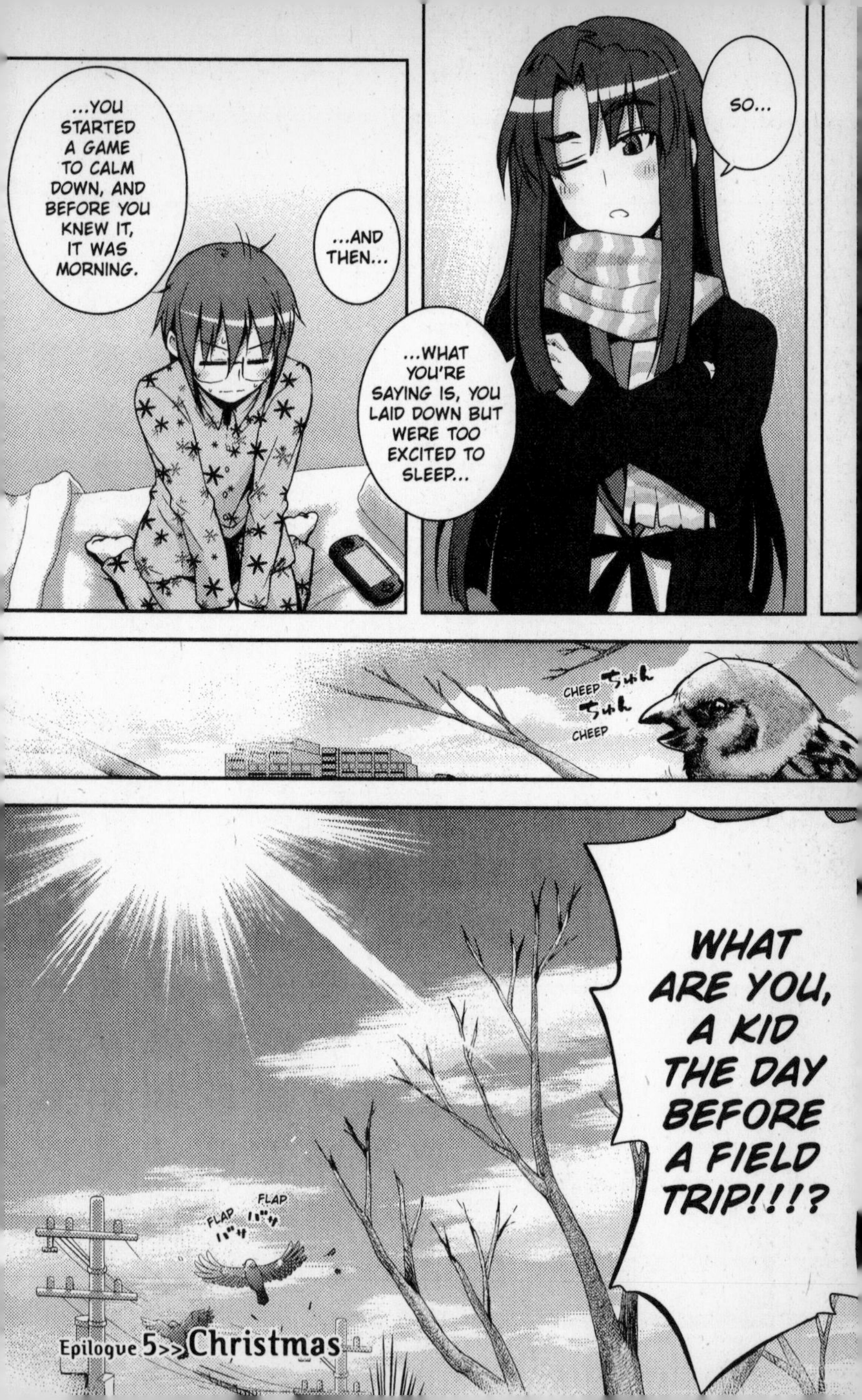
SO...
...WHAT YOU'RE SAYING IS, YOU LAID DOWN BUT WERE TOO EXCITED TO SLEEP...
...AND THEN...
...YOU STARTED A GAME TO CALM DOWN, AND BEFORE YOU KNEW IT, IT WAS MORNING.
CHEEP ちゅん
ちゅん CHEEP
WHAT ARE YOU, A KID THE DAY BEFORE A FIELD TRIP!!!?
FLAP バサ
FLAP バサ

Epilogue 5>> Christmas

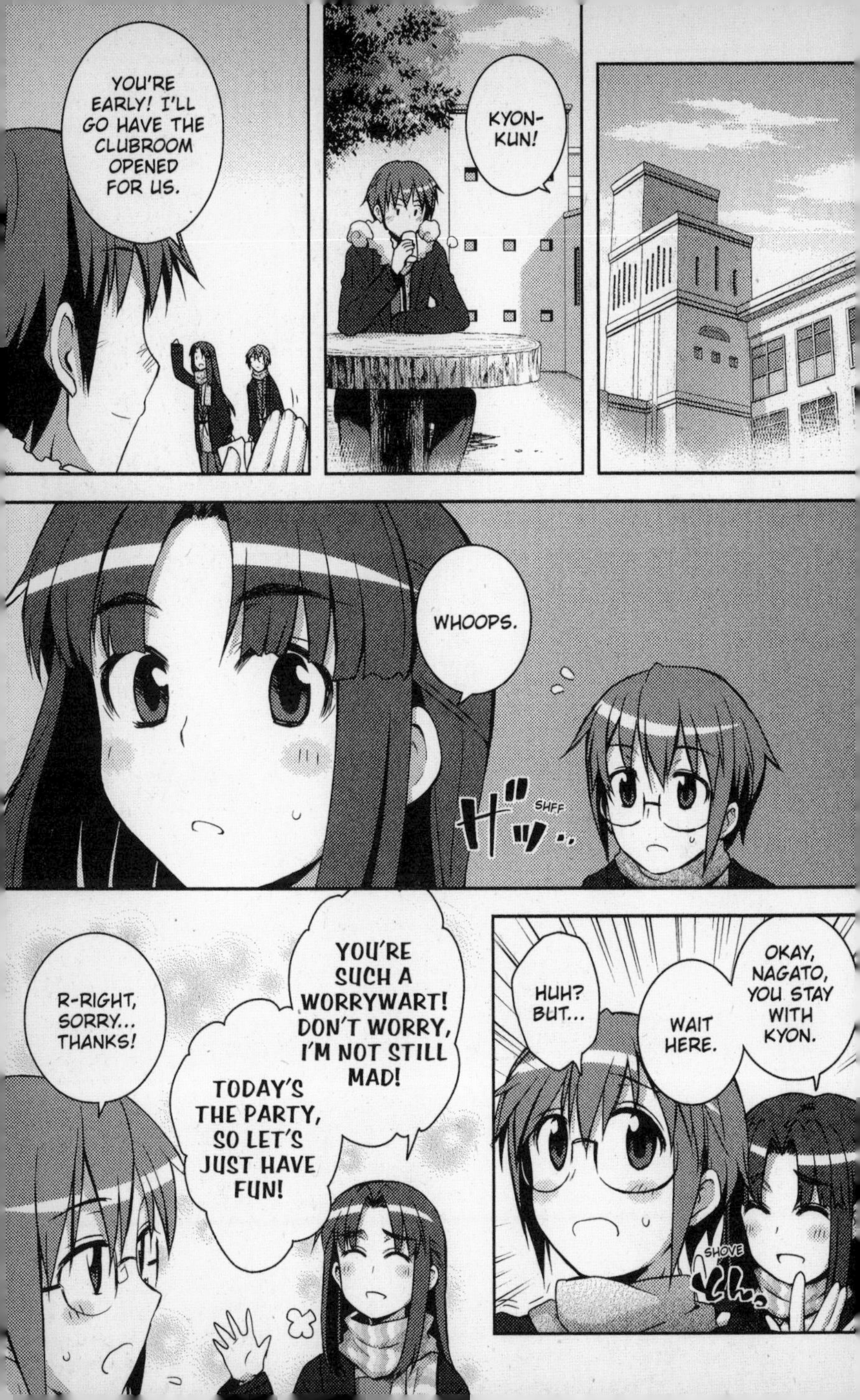
KYON-KUN!
YOU'RE EARLY! I'LL GO HAVE THE CLUBROOM OPENED FOR US.
WHOOPS.
SHFF
OKAY, NAGATO, YOU STAY WITH KYON.
WAIT HERE.
HUH? BUT...
SHOVE
YOU'RE SUCH A WORRYWART! DON'T WORRY, I'M NOT STILL MAD!
TODAY'S THE PARTY, SO LET'S JUST HAVE FUN!
R-RIGHT, SORRY... THANKS!

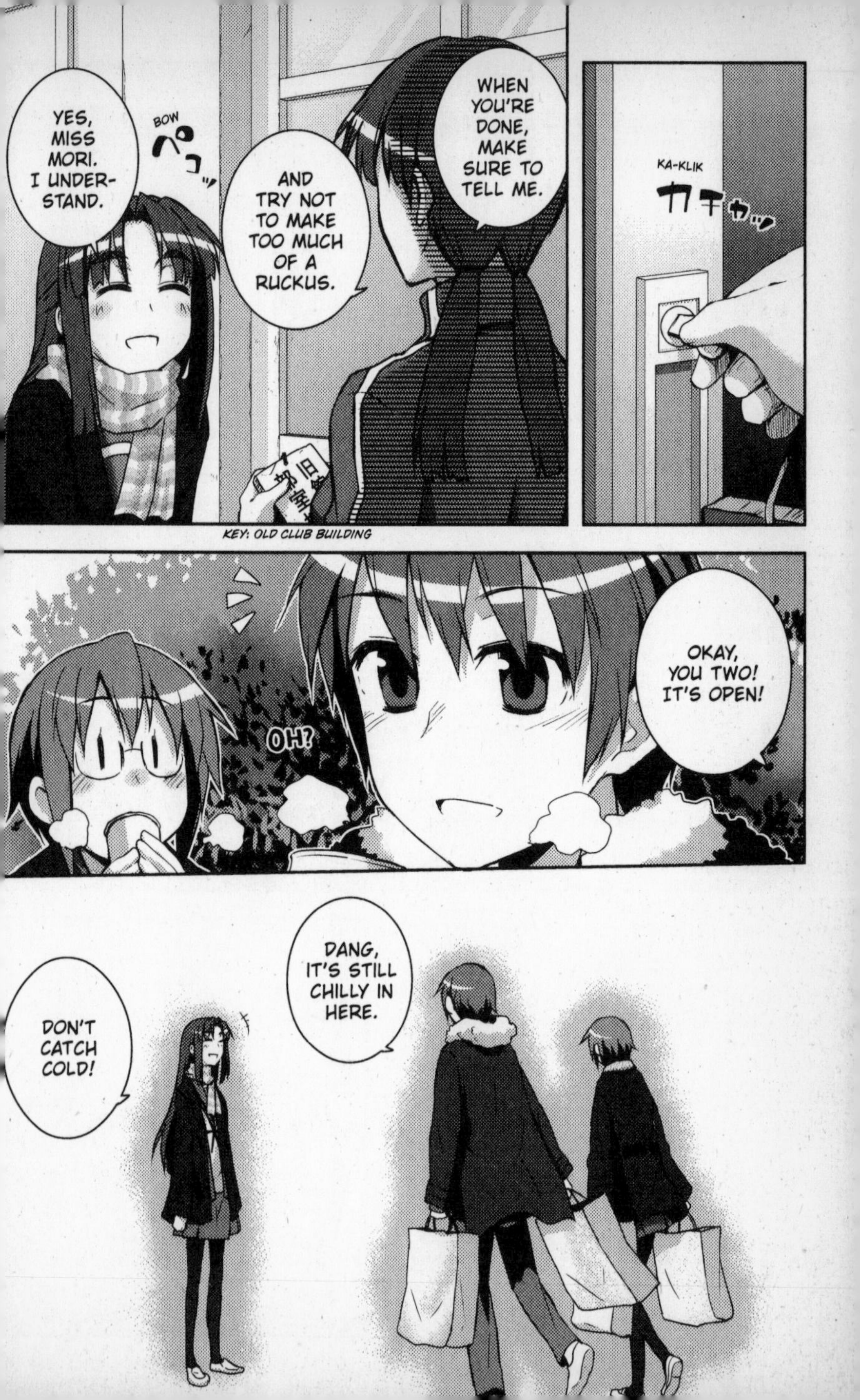
KA-KLIK
カチャッ
WHEN YOU'RE DONE, MAKE SURE TO TELL ME.
AND TRY NOT TO MAKE TOO MUCH OF A RUCKUS.
BOW
ペコッ
YES, MISS MORI. I UNDER-STAND.
KEY: OLD CLUB BUILDING
OKAY, YOU TWO! IT'S OPEN!
OH?
DANG, IT'S STILL CHILLY IN HERE.
DON'T CATCH COLD!

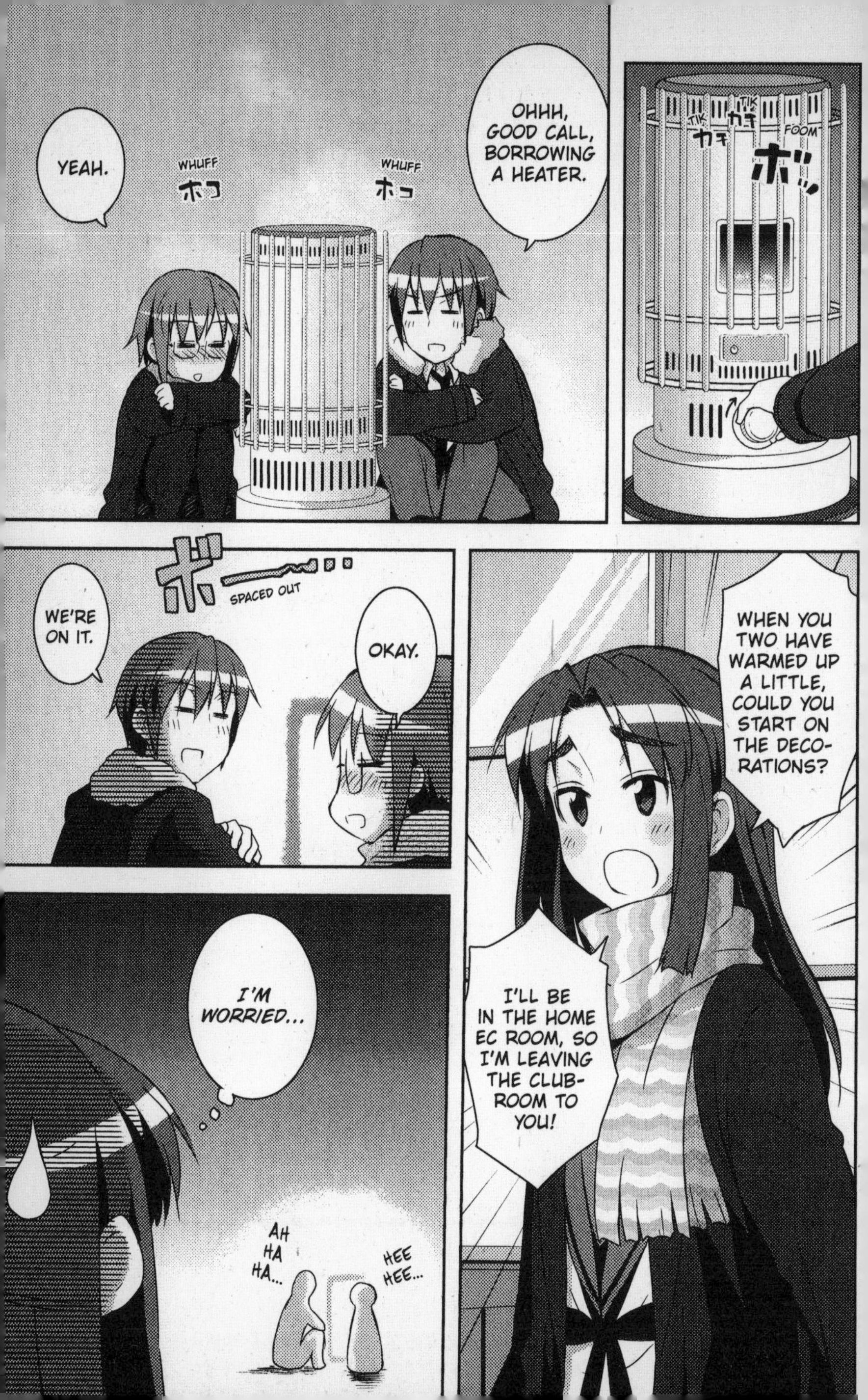
TIK TIK
カチ カチ
FOOM
ボッ
OHHH, GOOD CALL, BORROWING A HEATER.
WHUFF
ホッ
WHUFF
ホッ
YEAH.
WHEN YOU TWO HAVE WARMED UP A LITTLE, COULD YOU START ON THE DECO-RATIONS?
I'LL BE IN THE HOME EC ROOM, SO I'M LEAVING THE CLUB-ROOM TO YOU!
OKAY.
WE'RE ON IT.
ボー
SPACED OUT
I'M WORRIED...
HEE HEE...
AH HA HA...

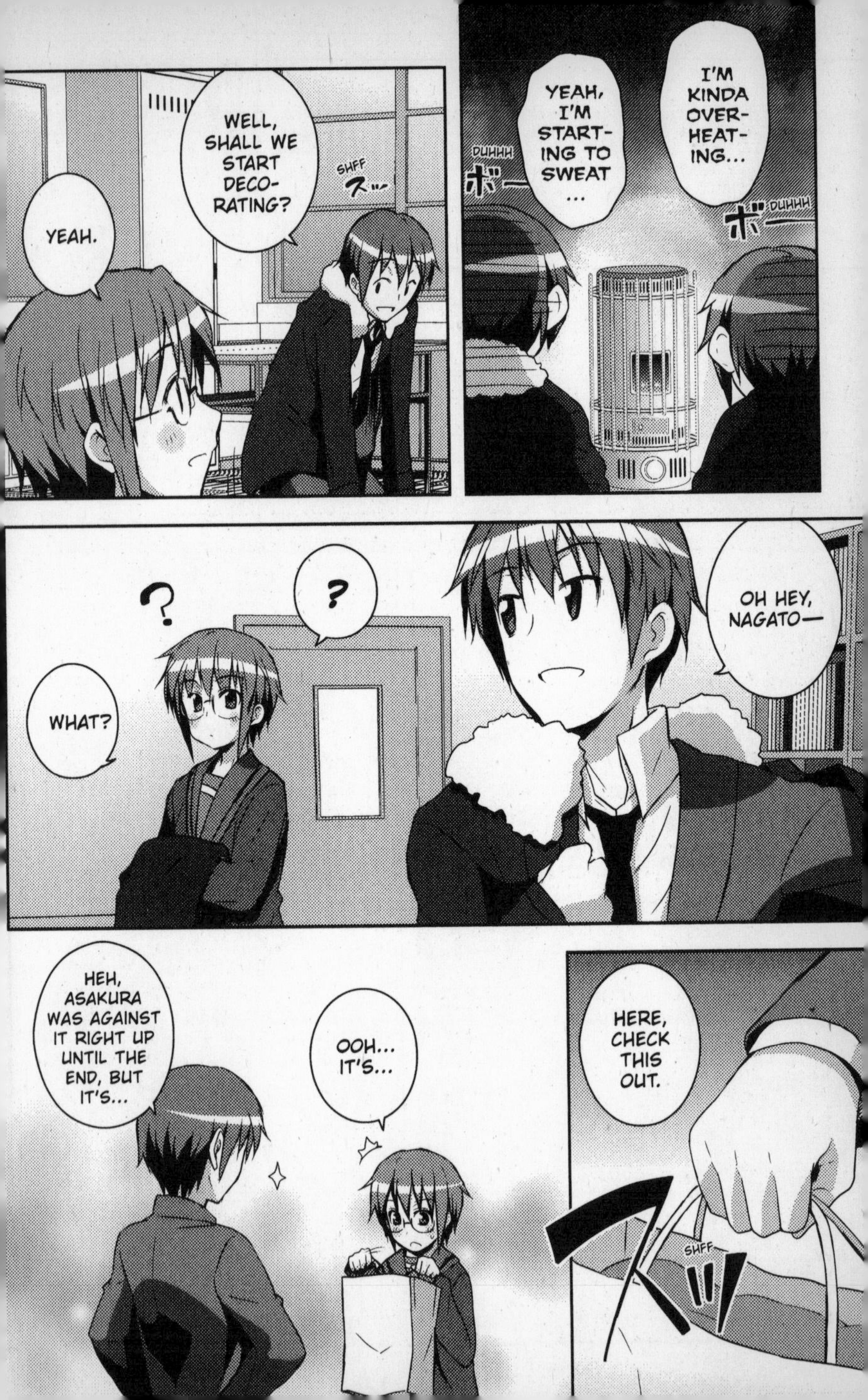
I'M KINDA OVER-HEAT-ING...
YEAH, I'M START-ING TO SWEAT...
DUHHH ボー
DUHHH ボー
WELL, SHALL WE START DECO-RATING?
SHFF ス
YEAH.
OH HEY, NAGATO—
?
?
WHAT?
HERE, CHECK THIS OUT.
SHFF ス
OOH... IT'S...
HEH, ASAKURA WAS AGAINST IT RIGHT UP UNTIL THE END, BUT IT'S...

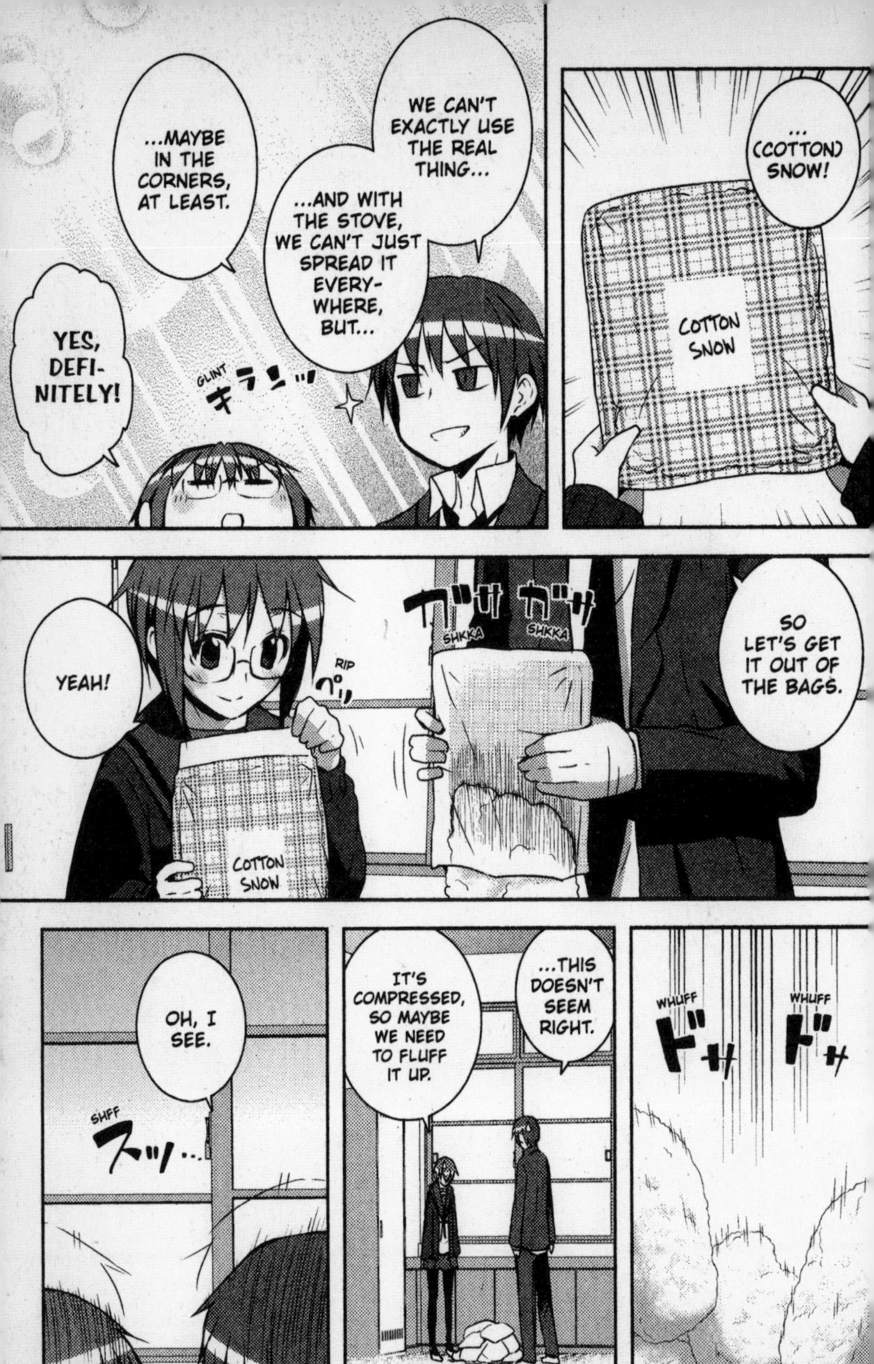
...
(COTTON)
SNOW!
COTTON SNOW
WE CAN'T EXACTLY USE THE REAL THING...
...AND WITH THE STOVE, WE CAN'T JUST SPREAD IT EVERY-WHERE, BUT...
...MAYBE IN THE CORNERS, AT LEAST.
GLINT
YES, DEFI-NITELY!
SO LET'S GET IT OUT OF THE BAGS.
SHKKA
SHKKA
RIP
YEAH!
COTTON SNOW
WHUFF
WHUFF
...THIS DOESN'T SEEM RIGHT.
IT'S COMPRESSED, SO MAYBE WE NEED TO FLUFF IT UP.
OH, I SEE.
SHFF

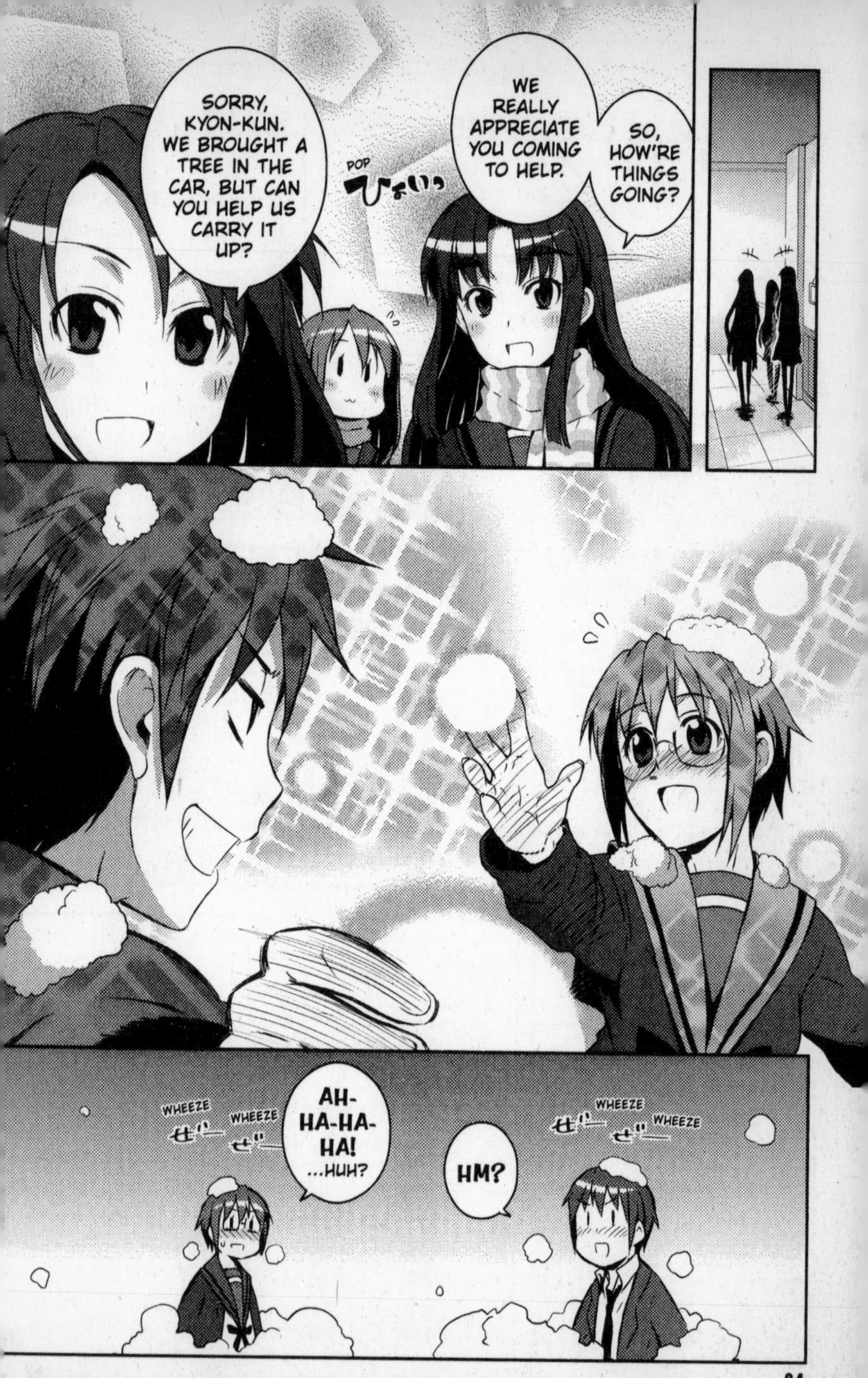
SO, HOW'RE THINGS GOING?
WE REALLY APPRECIATE YOU COMING TO HELP.
POP
SORRY, KYON-KUN. WE BROUGHT A TREE IN THE CAR, BUT CAN YOU HELP US CARRY IT UP?
WHEEZE
WHEEZE
HM?
AH-HA-HA-HA! ...HUH?
WHEEZE
WHEEZE

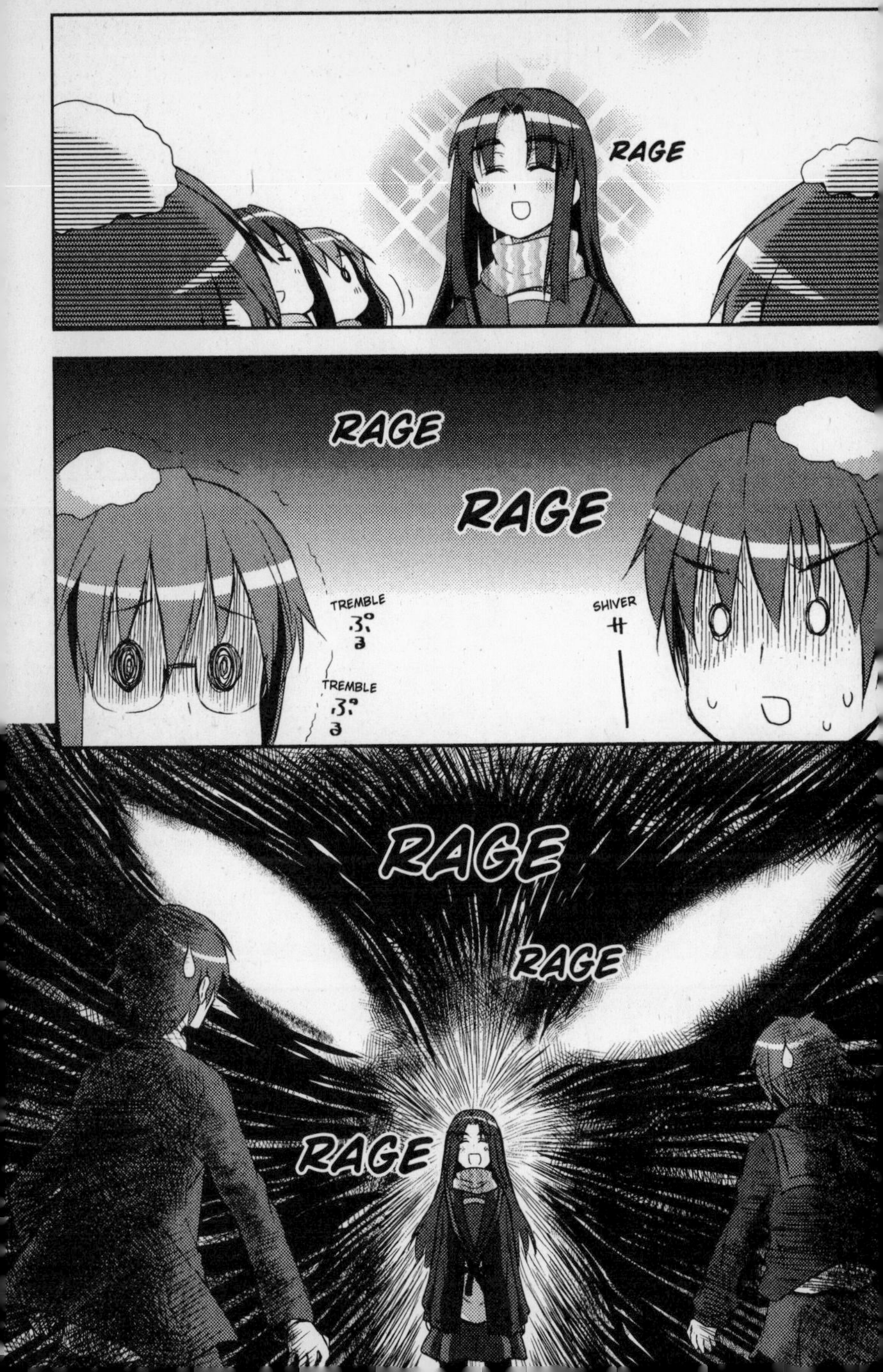
RAGE
RAGE
RAGE
SHIVER
TREMBLE
ぷる
TREMBLE
ぷる
RAGE
RAGE
RAGE

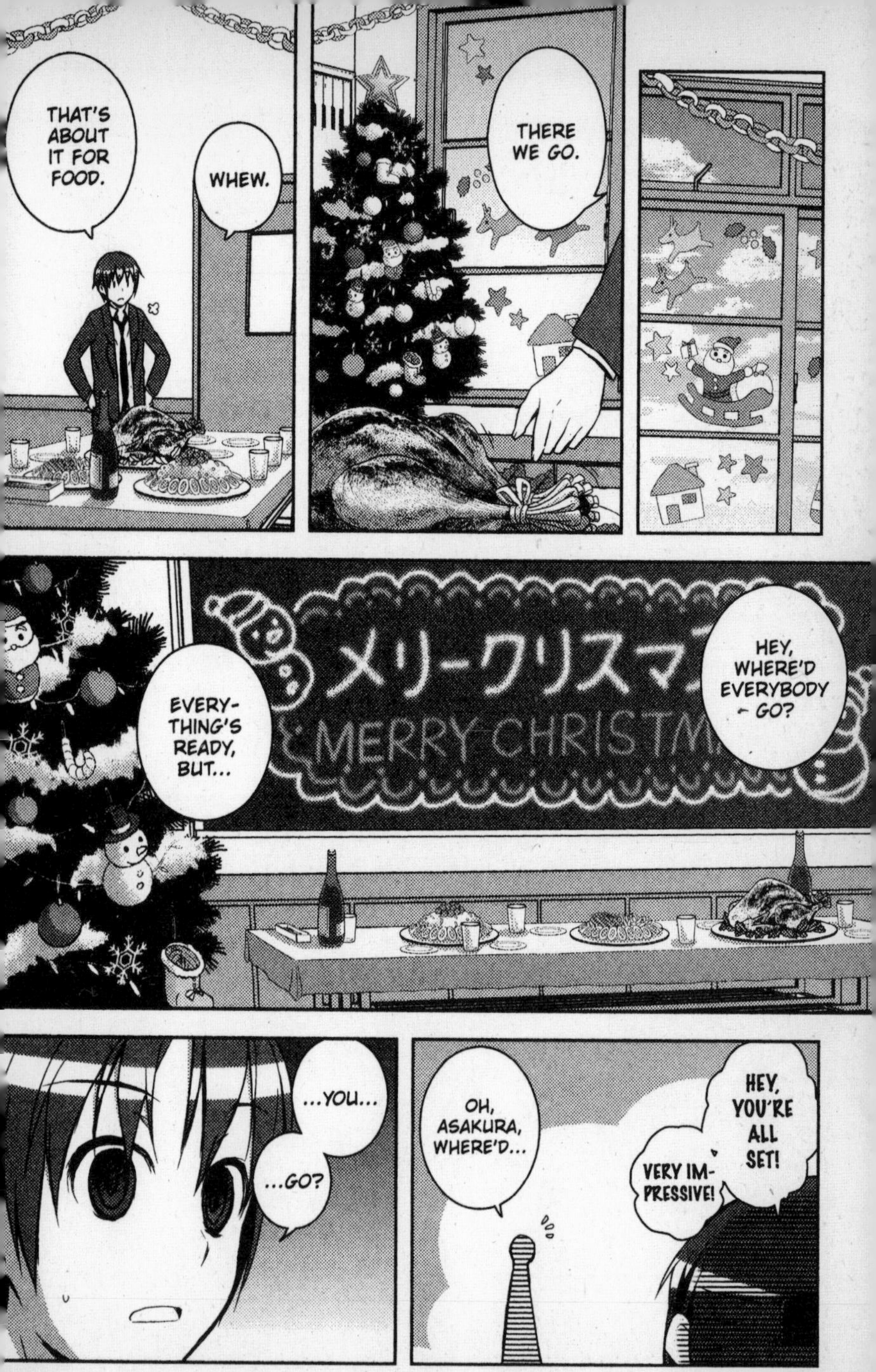
THERE WE GO.
WHEW.
THAT'S ABOUT IT FOR FOOD.
HEY, WHERE'D EVERYBODY GO?
メリークリスマ
MERRY CHRISTM
EVERY-THING'S READY, BUT...
HEY, YOU'RE ALL SET!
VERY IM-PRESSIVE!
OH, ASAKURA, WHERE'D...
...YOU...
...GO?

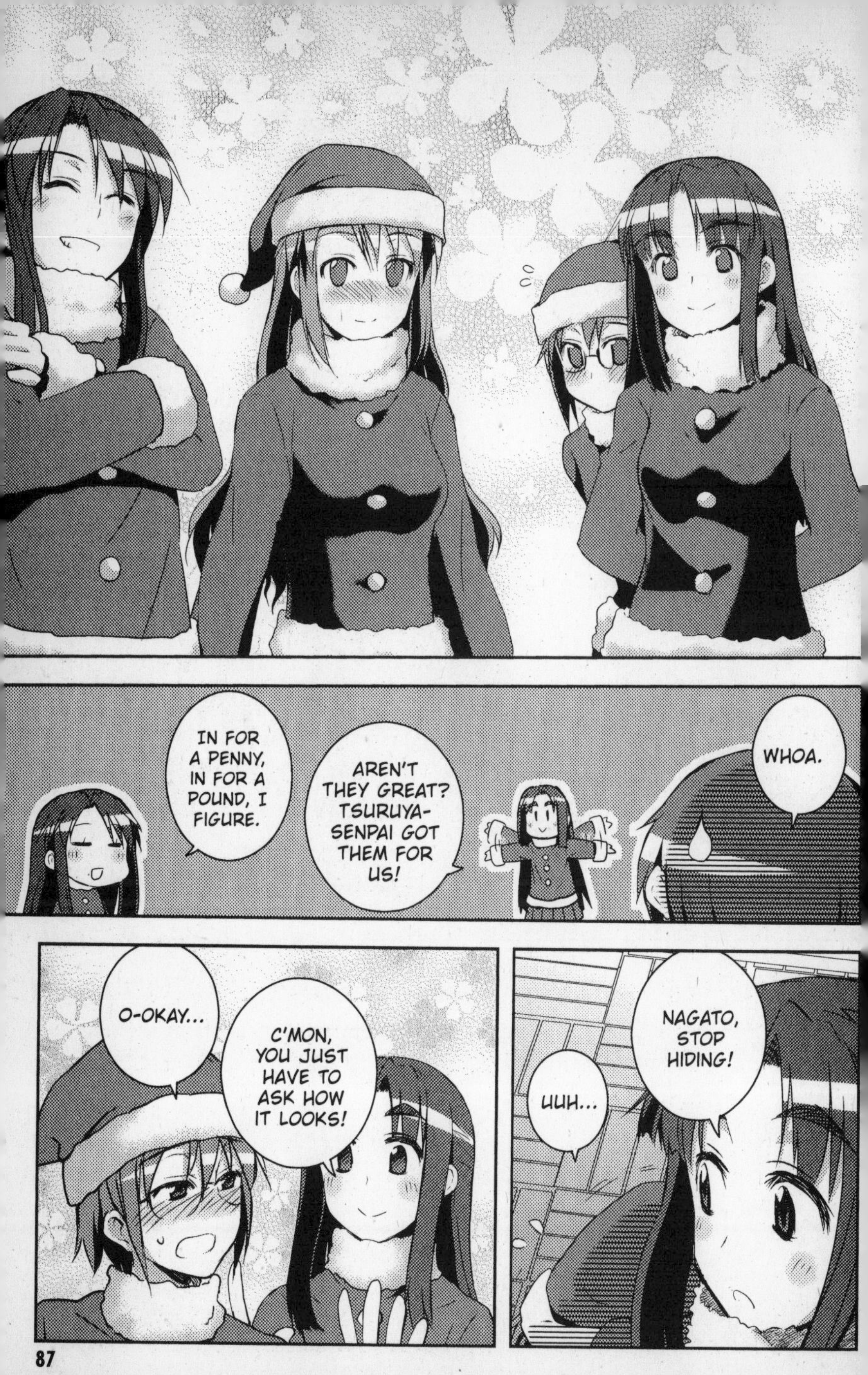
WHOA.
AREN'T THEY GREAT? TSURUYA-SENPAI GOT THEM FOR US!
IN FOR A PENNY, IN FOR A POUND, I FIGURE.
NAGATO, STOP HIDING!
UUH...
C'MON, YOU JUST HAVE TO ASK HOW IT LOOKS!
O-OKAY...

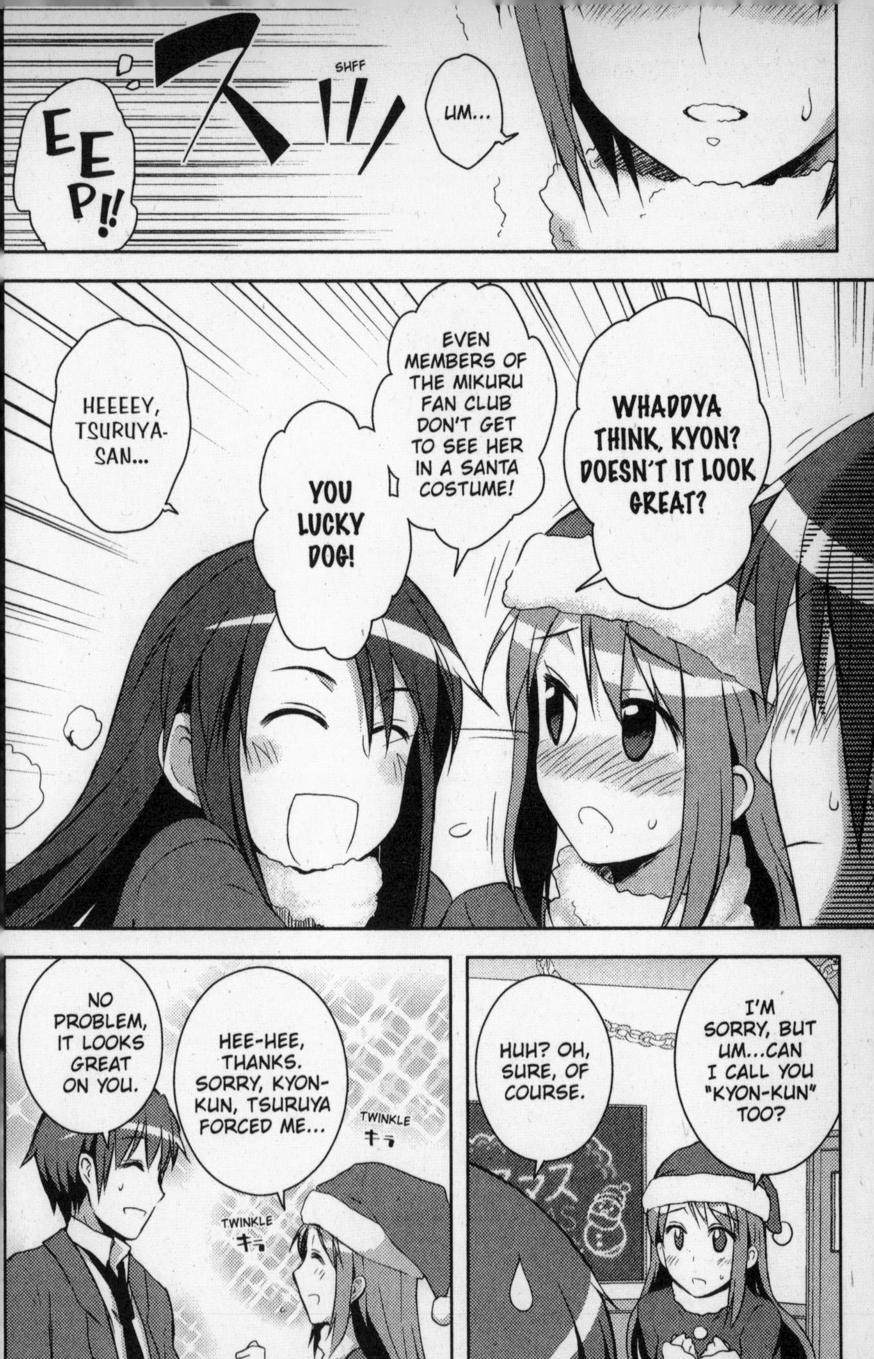
UM...
SHFF
EEP!!
WHADDYA THINK, KYON? DOESN'T IT LOOK GREAT?
EVEN MEMBERS OF THE MIKURU FAN CLUB DON'T GET TO SEE HER IN A SANTA COSTUME!
YOU LUCKY DOG!
HEEEEY, TSURUYA-SAN...
I'M SORRY, BUT UM...CAN I CALL YOU "KYON-KUN" TOO?
HUH? OH, SURE, OF COURSE.
HEE-HEE, THANKS. SORRY, KYON-KUN, TSURUYA FORCED ME...
TWINKLE
キラ
TWINKLE
キラ
NO PROBLEM, IT LOOKS GREAT ON YOU.

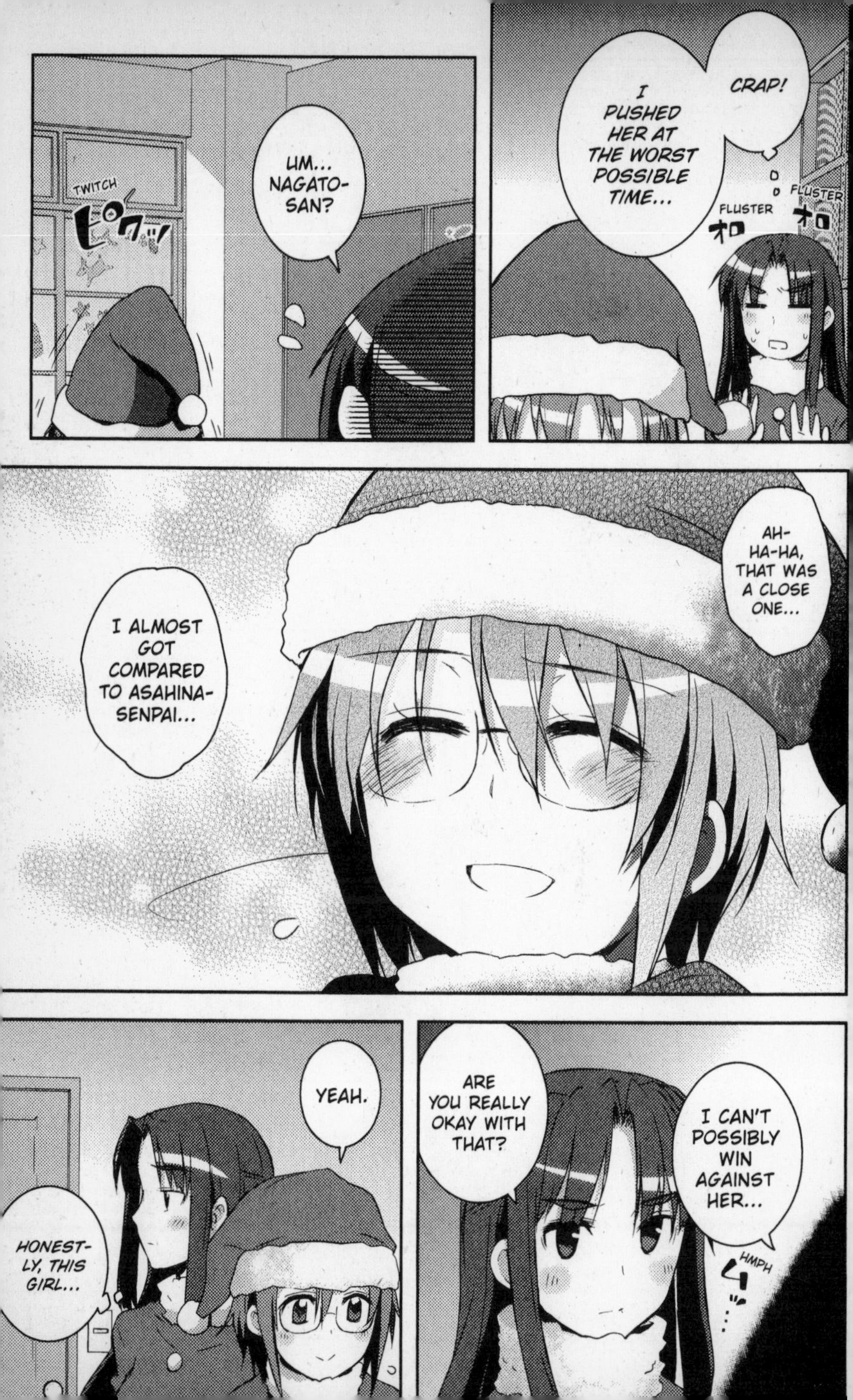
CRAP!
I PUSHED HER AT THE WORST POSSIBLE TIME...
FLUSTER オロ
FLUSTER オロ
UM... NAGATO-SAN?
TWITCH ピクッ
AH-HA-HA, THAT WAS A CLOSE ONE...
I ALMOST GOT COMPARED TO ASAHINA-SENPAI...
I CAN'T POSSIBLY WIN AGAINST HER...
HMPH
ARE YOU REALLY OKAY WITH THAT?
YEAH.
HONEST-LY, THIS GIRL...

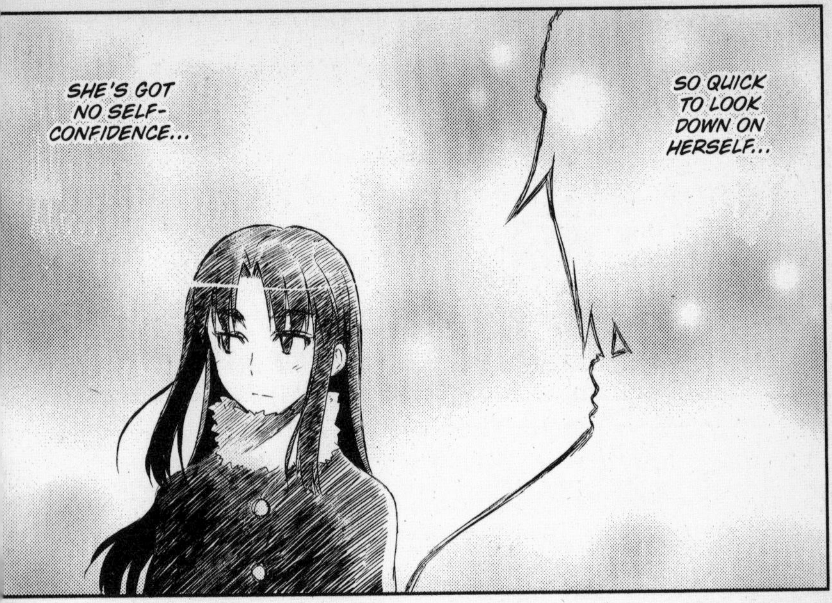
SO QUICK TO LOOK DOWN ON HERSELF...
SHE'S GOT NO SELF-CONFIDENCE...

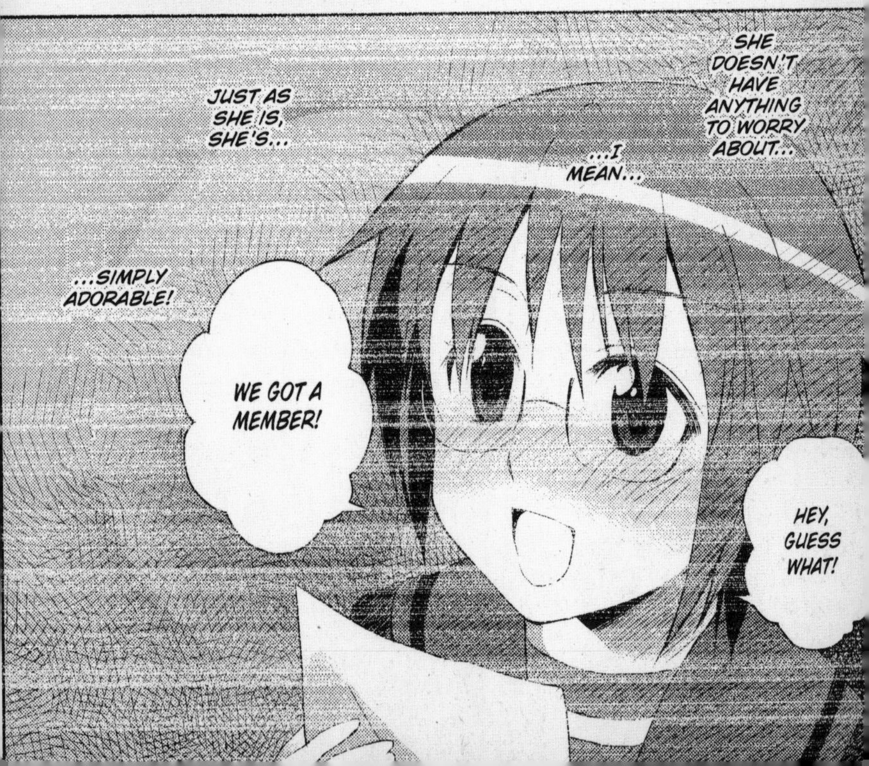
SHE DOESN'T HAVE ANYTHING TO WORRY ABOUT...
...I MEAN...
JUST AS SHE IS, SHE'S...
...SIMPLY ADORABLE!
HEY, GUESS WHAT!
WE GOT A MEMBER!

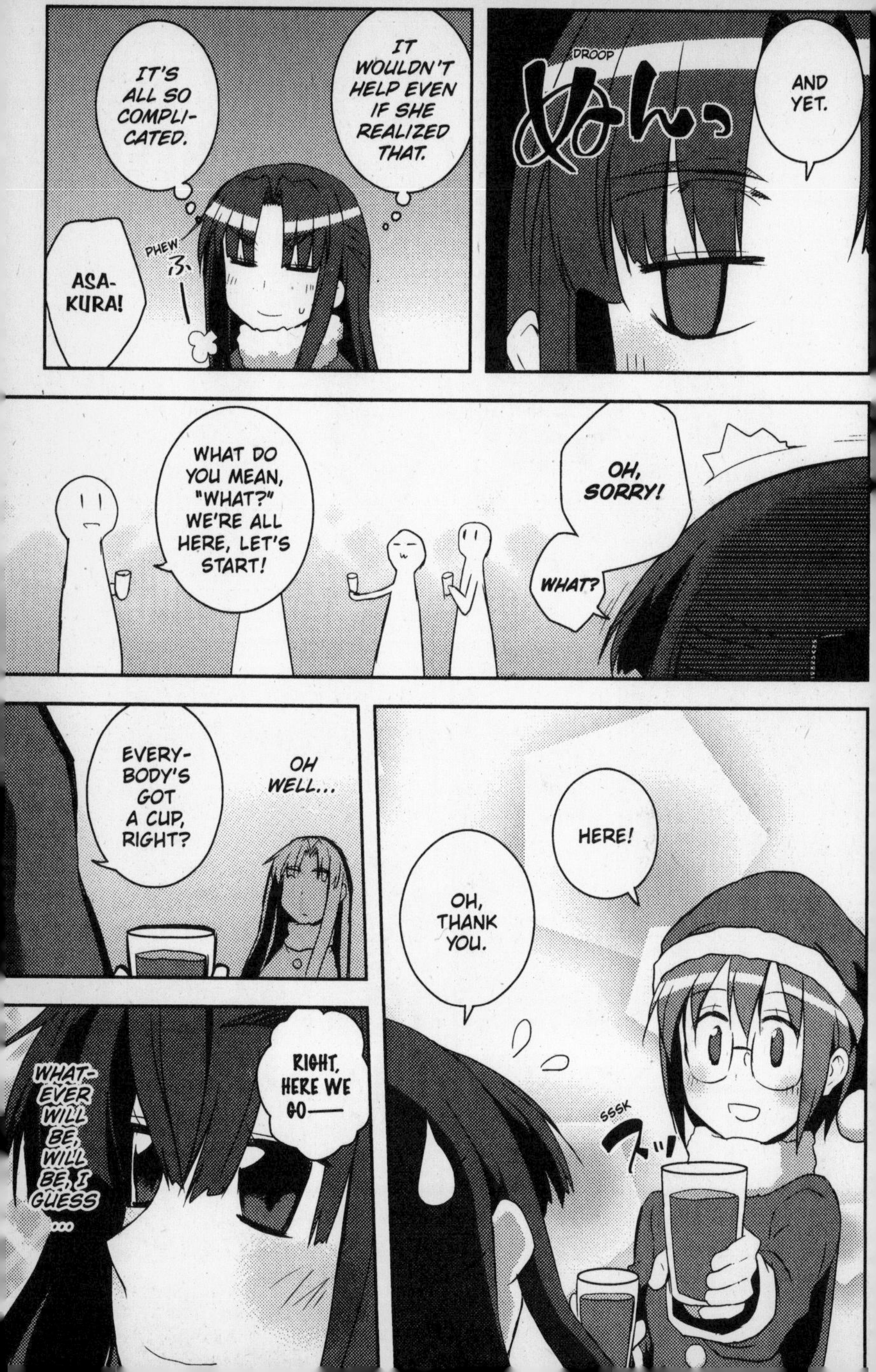
DROOP
ぬんっ
AND YET.
IT WOULDN'T HELP EVEN IF SHE REALIZED THAT.
IT'S ALL SO COMPLICATED.
PHEW
ふ
ASA-KURA!
OH, SORRY!
WHAT?
WHAT DO YOU MEAN, "WHAT?" WE'RE ALL HERE, LET'S START!
HERE!
OH, THANK YOU.
SSSK
スッ
EVERY-BODY'S GOT A CUP, RIGHT?
OH WELL...
RIGHT, HERE WE GO—
WHAT-EVER WILL BE, WILL BE, I GUESS...

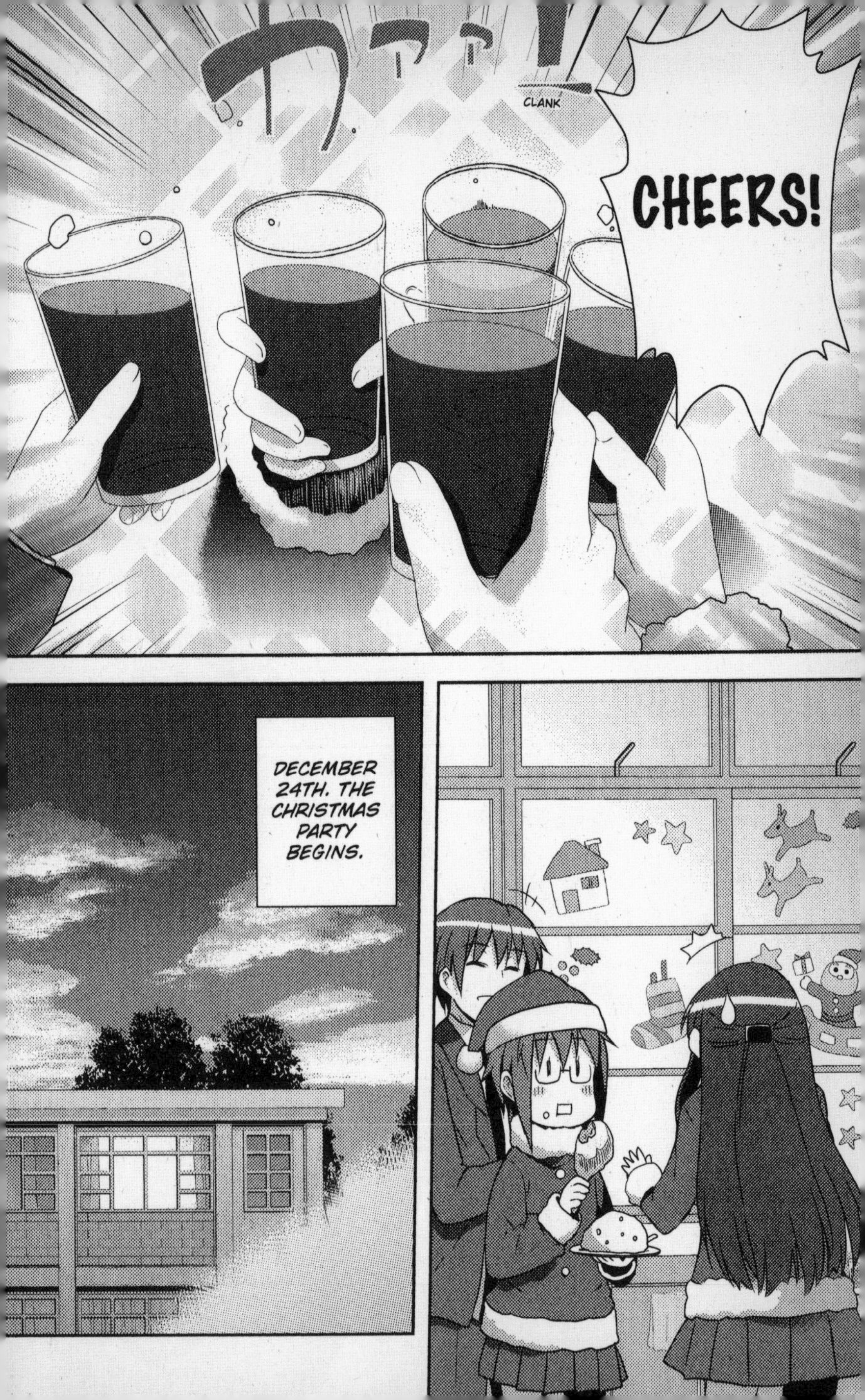
CLANK
CHEERS!
DECEMBER 24TH. THE CHRISTMAS PARTY BEGINS.

TURKEY! TURKEY!

AND NOW
THE CHRISTMAS
PARTY CONTINUES!

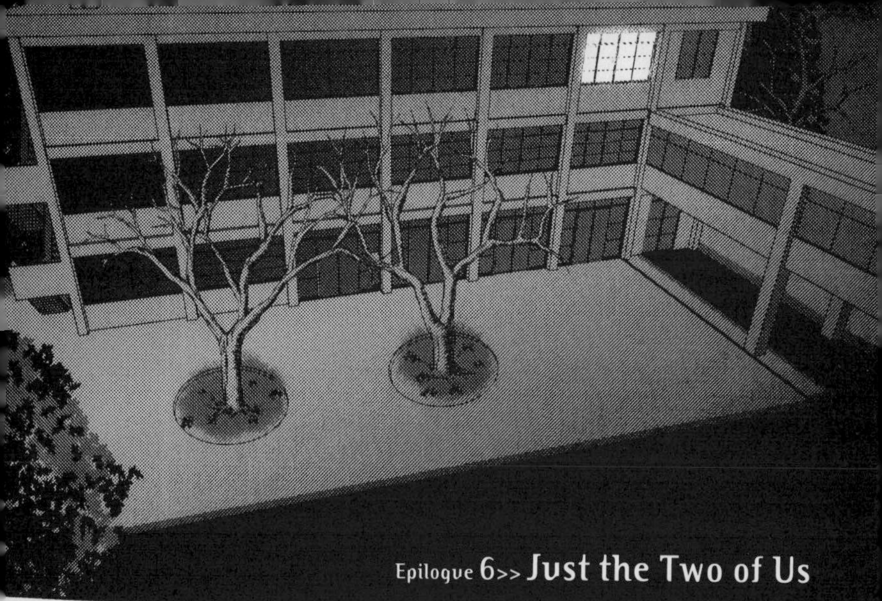

Epilogue 6>> Just the Two of Us

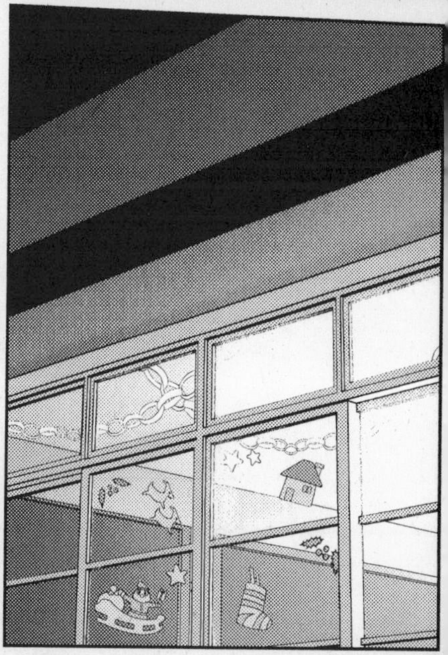

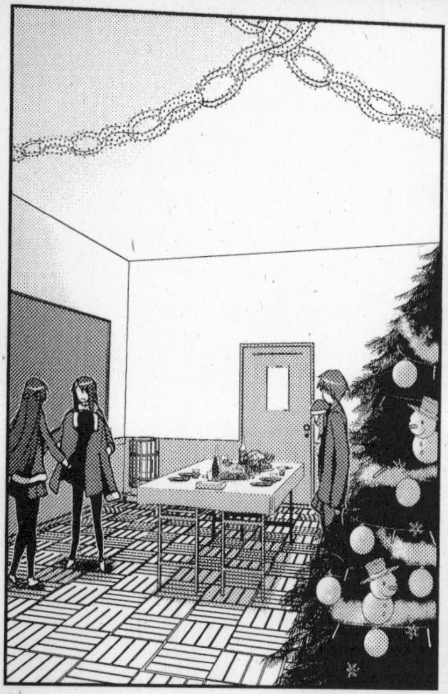

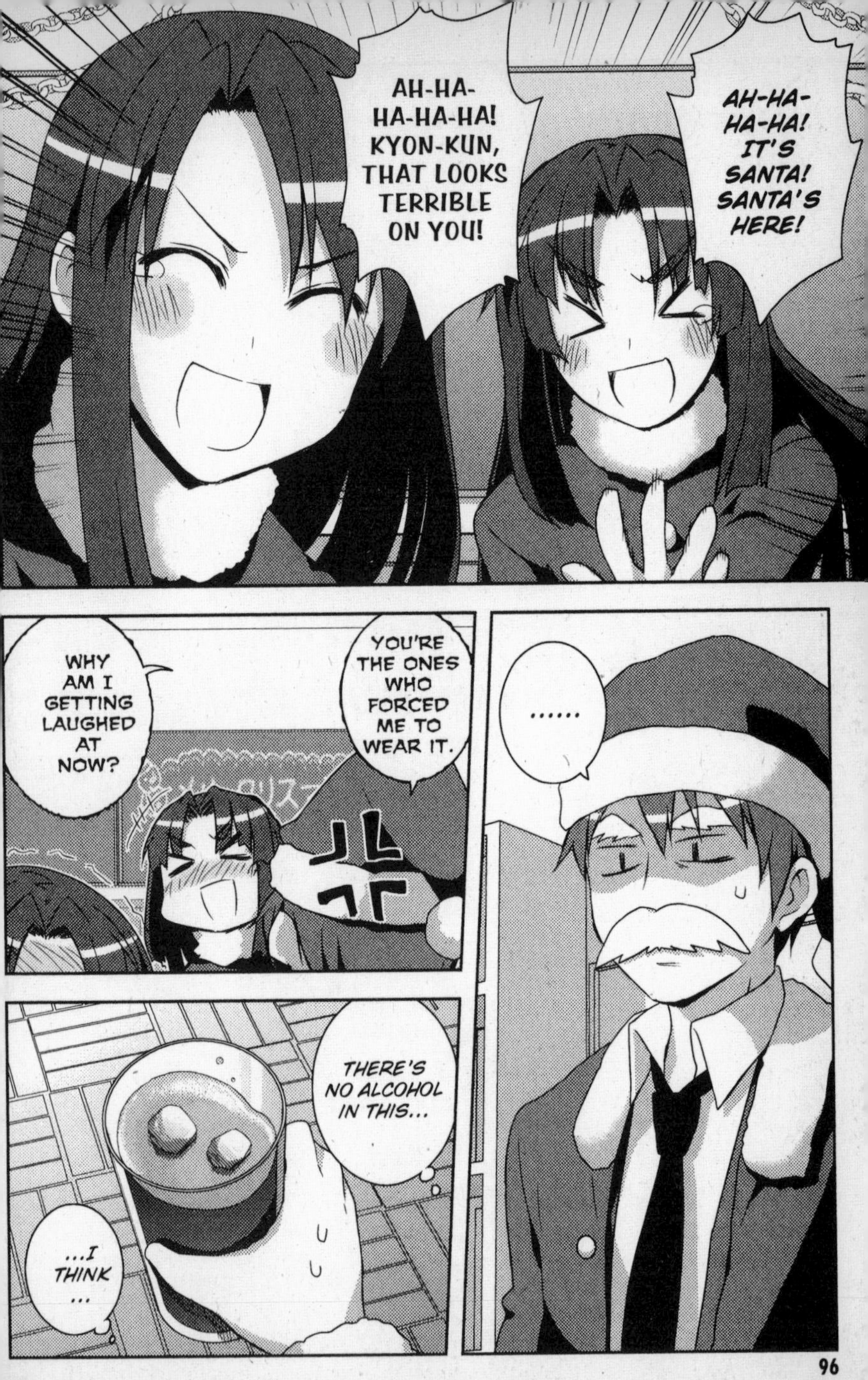
AH-HA-HA-HA! IT'S SANTA! SANTA'S HERE!
AH-HA-HA-HA-HA! KYON-KUN, THAT LOOKS TERRIBLE ON YOU!
......
YOU'RE THE ONES WHO FORCED ME TO WEAR IT.
WHY AM I GETTING LAUGHED AT NOW?
THERE'S NO ALCOHOL IN THIS...
...I THINK...

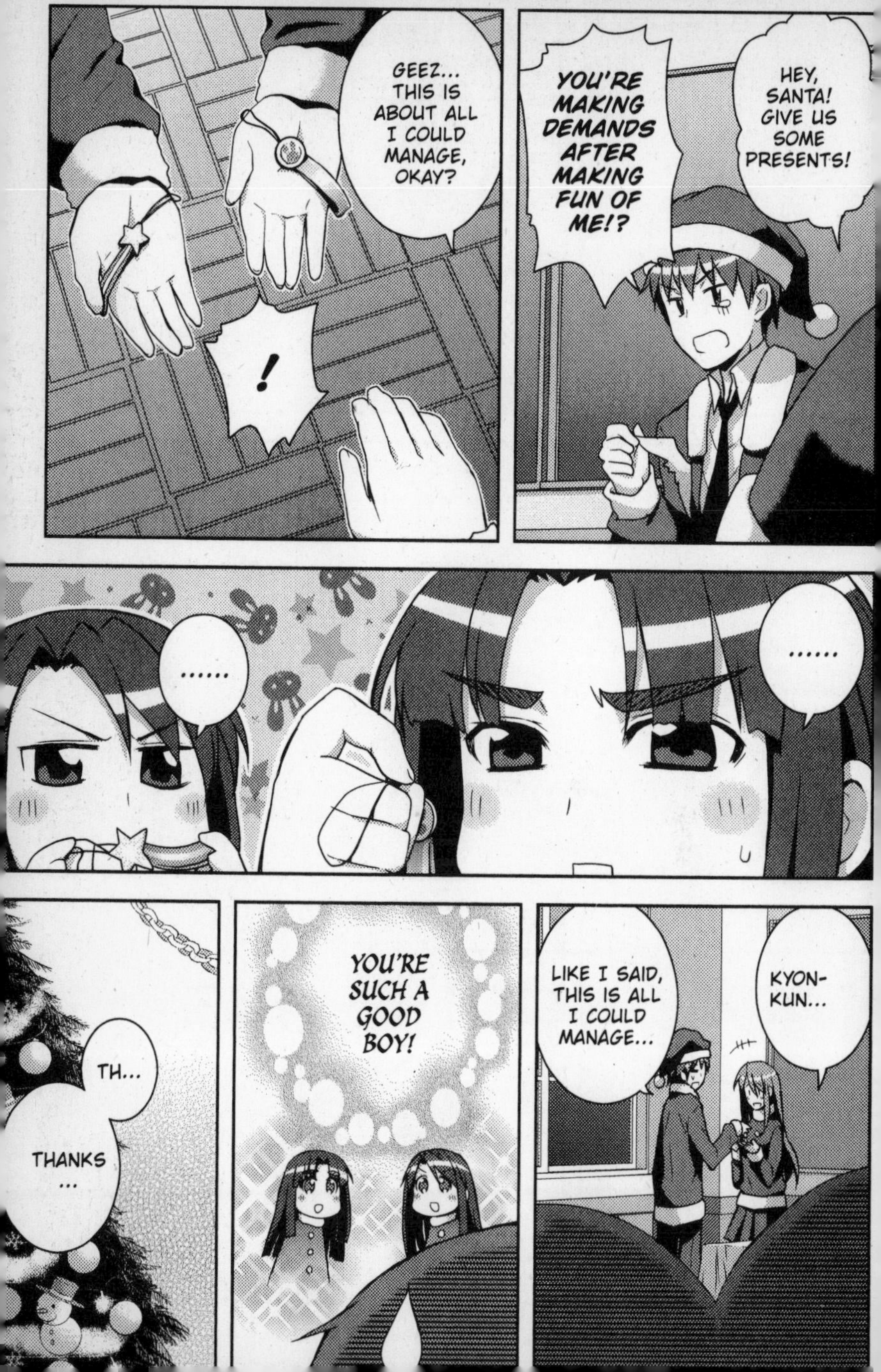
HEY, SANTA! GIVE US SOME PRESENTS!
YOU'RE MAKING DEMANDS AFTER MAKING FUN OF ME!?
GEEZ... THIS IS ABOUT ALL I COULD MANAGE, OKAY?
!
......
......
KYON-KUN...
LIKE I SAID, THIS IS ALL I COULD MANAGE...
YOU'RE SUCH A GOOD BOY!
TH...
THANKS ...

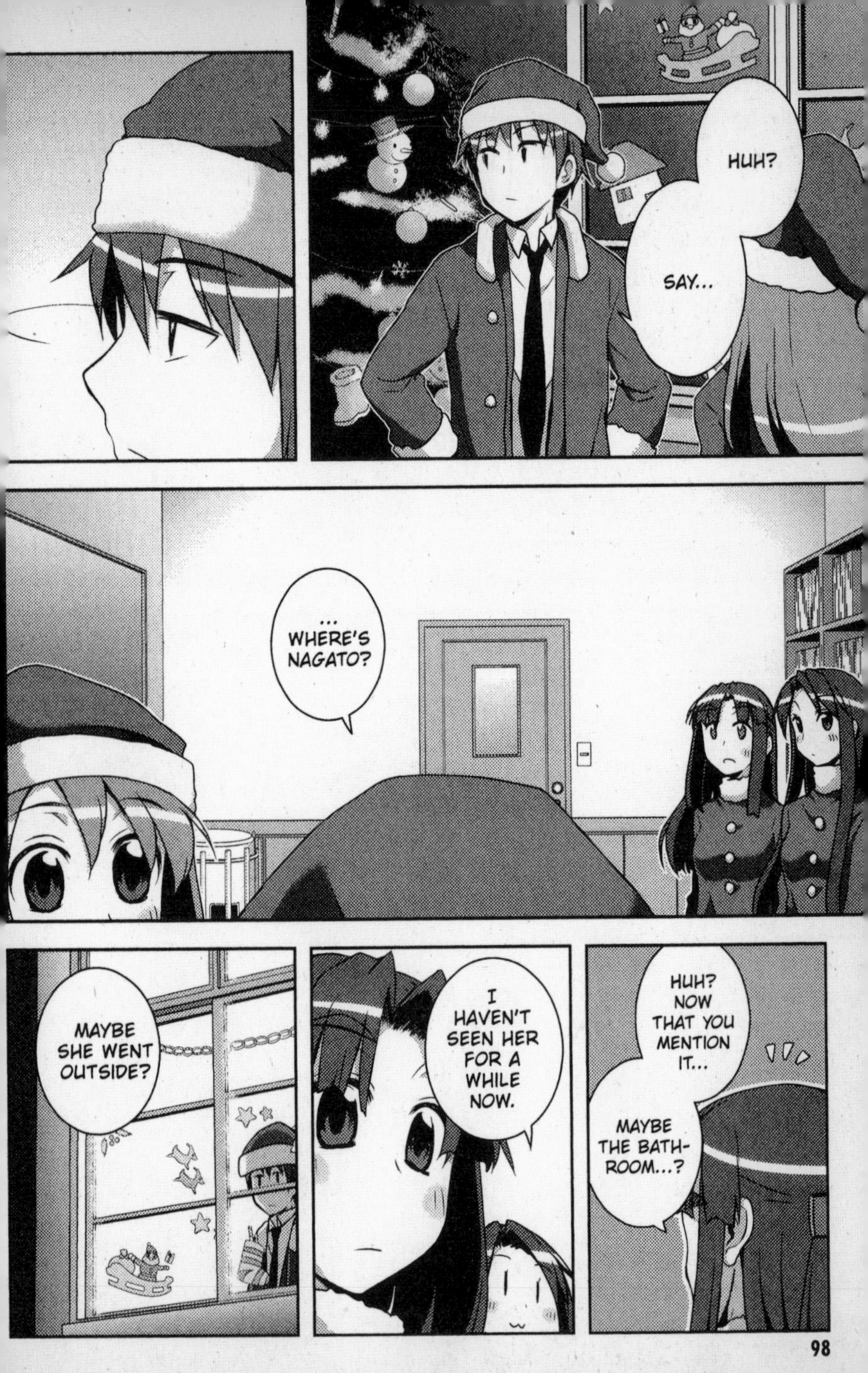
HUH?
SAY...
... WHERE'S NAGATO?
HUH? NOW THAT YOU MENTION IT...
MAYBE THE BATH-ROOM...?
I HAVEN'T SEEN HER FOR A WHILE NOW.
MAYBE SHE WENT OUTSIDE?

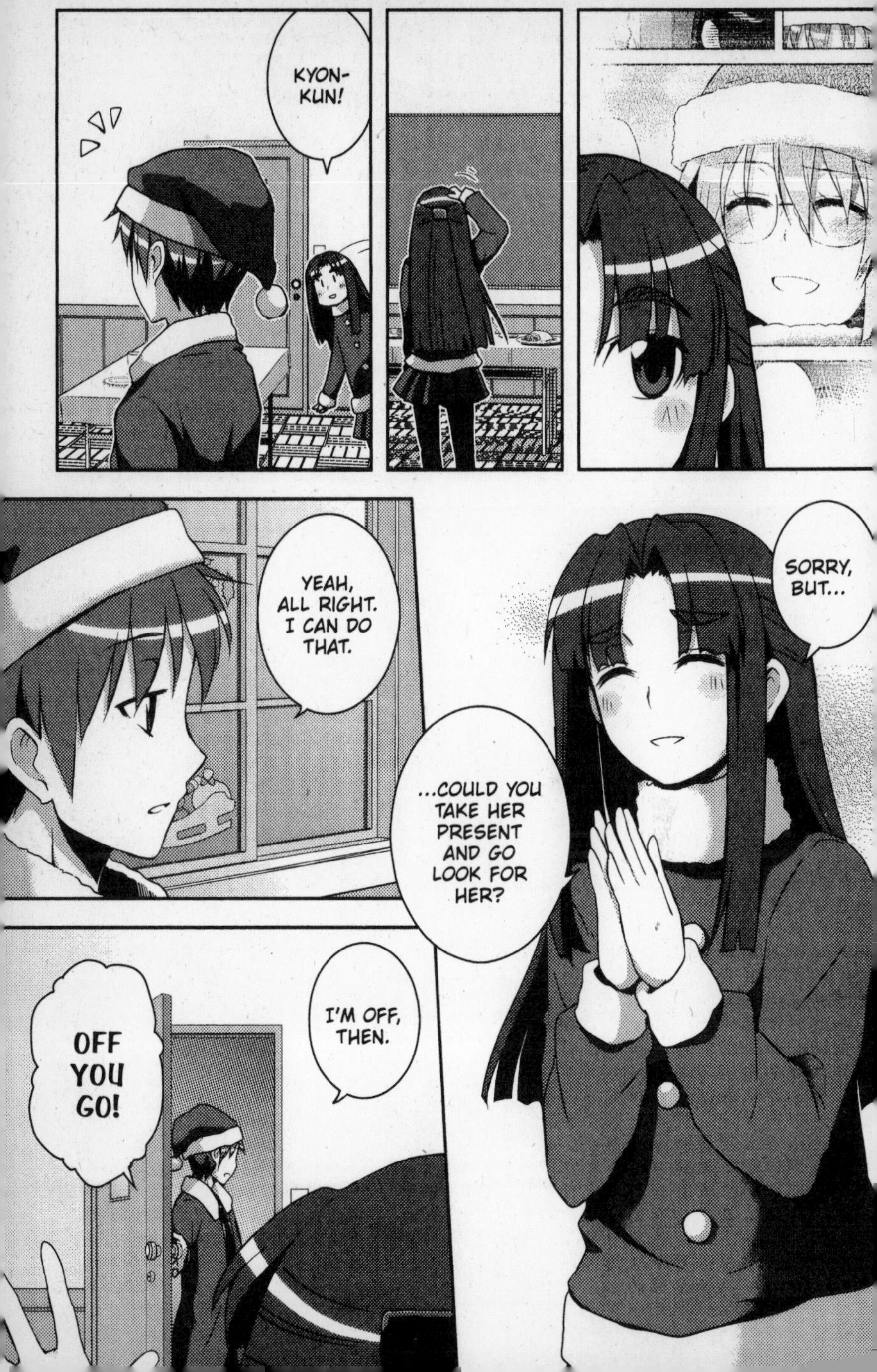
KYON-KUN!
SORRY, BUT...
...COULD YOU TAKE HER PRESENT AND GO LOOK FOR HER?
YEAH, ALL RIGHT. I CAN DO THAT.
I'M OFF, THEN.
OFF YOU GO!

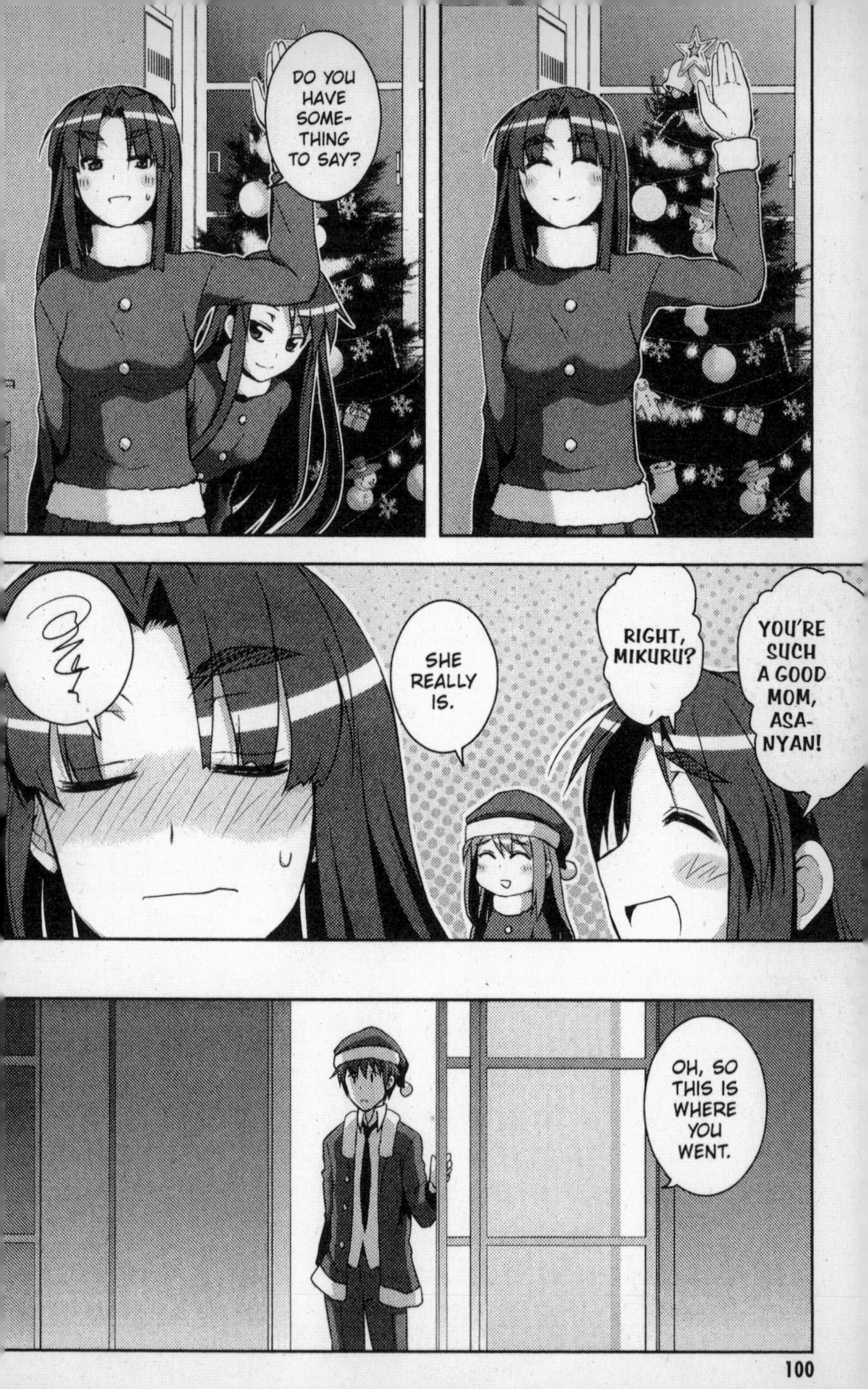
DO YOU HAVE SOME-THING TO SAY?
YOU'RE SUCH A GOOD MOM, ASA-NYAN!
RIGHT, MIKURU?
SHE REALLY IS.
OH, SO THIS IS WHERE YOU WENT.

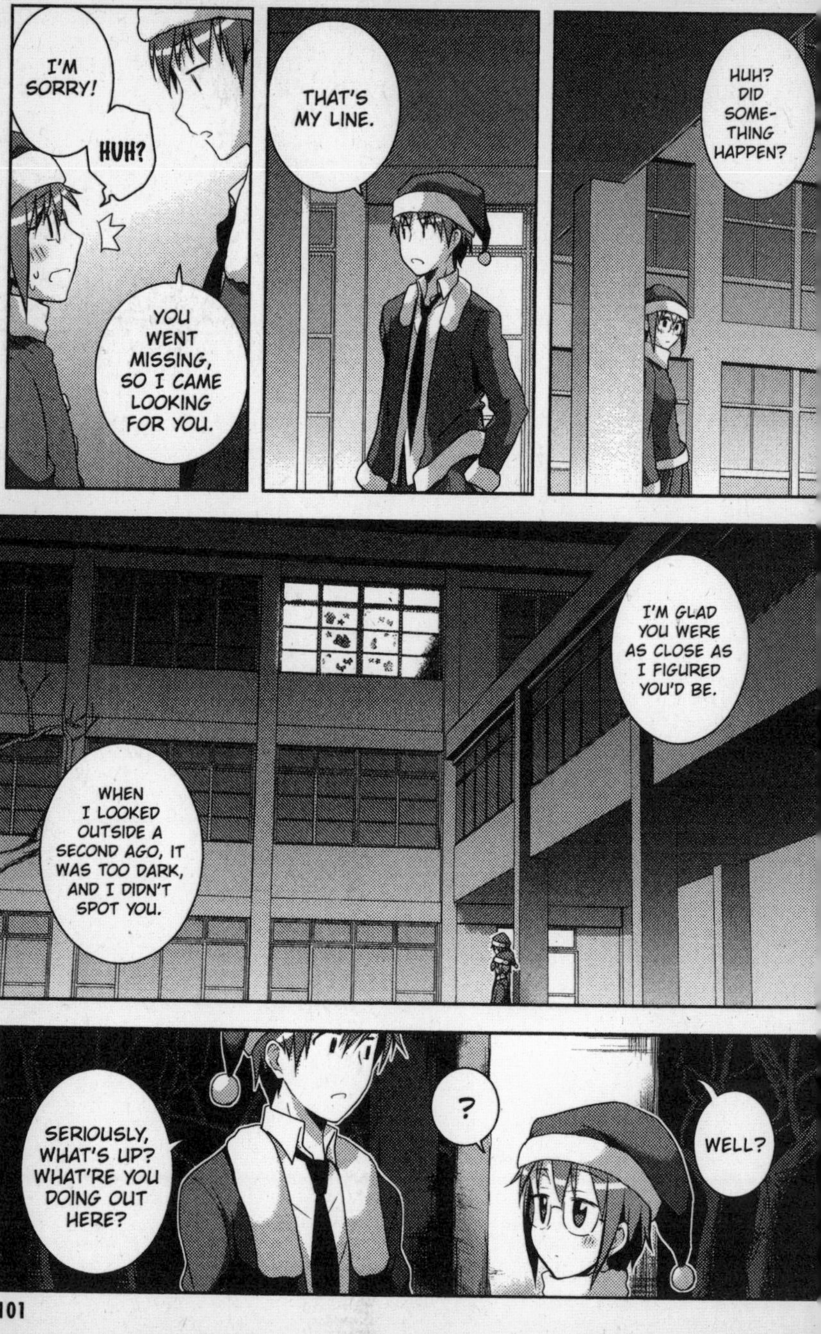
HUH? DID SOME-THING HAPPEN?
THAT'S MY LINE.
I'M SORRY!
HUH?
YOU WENT MISSING, SO I CAME LOOKING FOR YOU.
I'M GLAD YOU WERE AS CLOSE AS I FIGURED YOU'D BE.
WHEN I LOOKED OUTSIDE A SECOND AGO, IT WAS TOO DARK, AND I DIDN'T SPOT YOU.
WELL?
?
SERIOUSLY, WHAT'S UP? WHAT'RE YOU DOING OUT HERE?

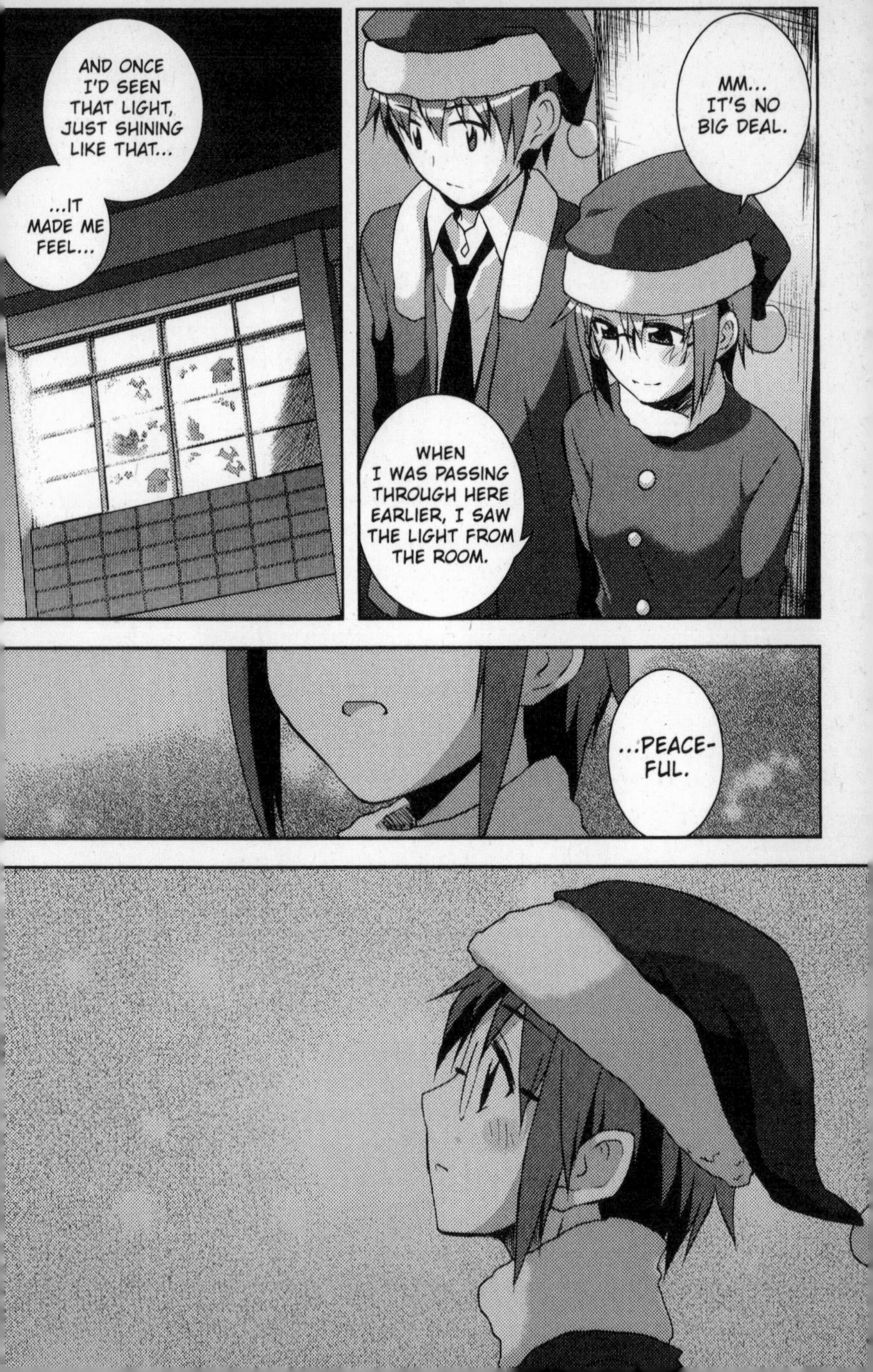
MM... IT'S NO BIG DEAL.
WHEN I WAS PASSING THROUGH HERE EARLIER, I SAW THE LIGHT FROM THE ROOM.
AND ONCE I'D SEEN THAT LIGHT, JUST SHINING LIKE THAT...
...IT MADE ME FEEL...
...PEACE-FUL.

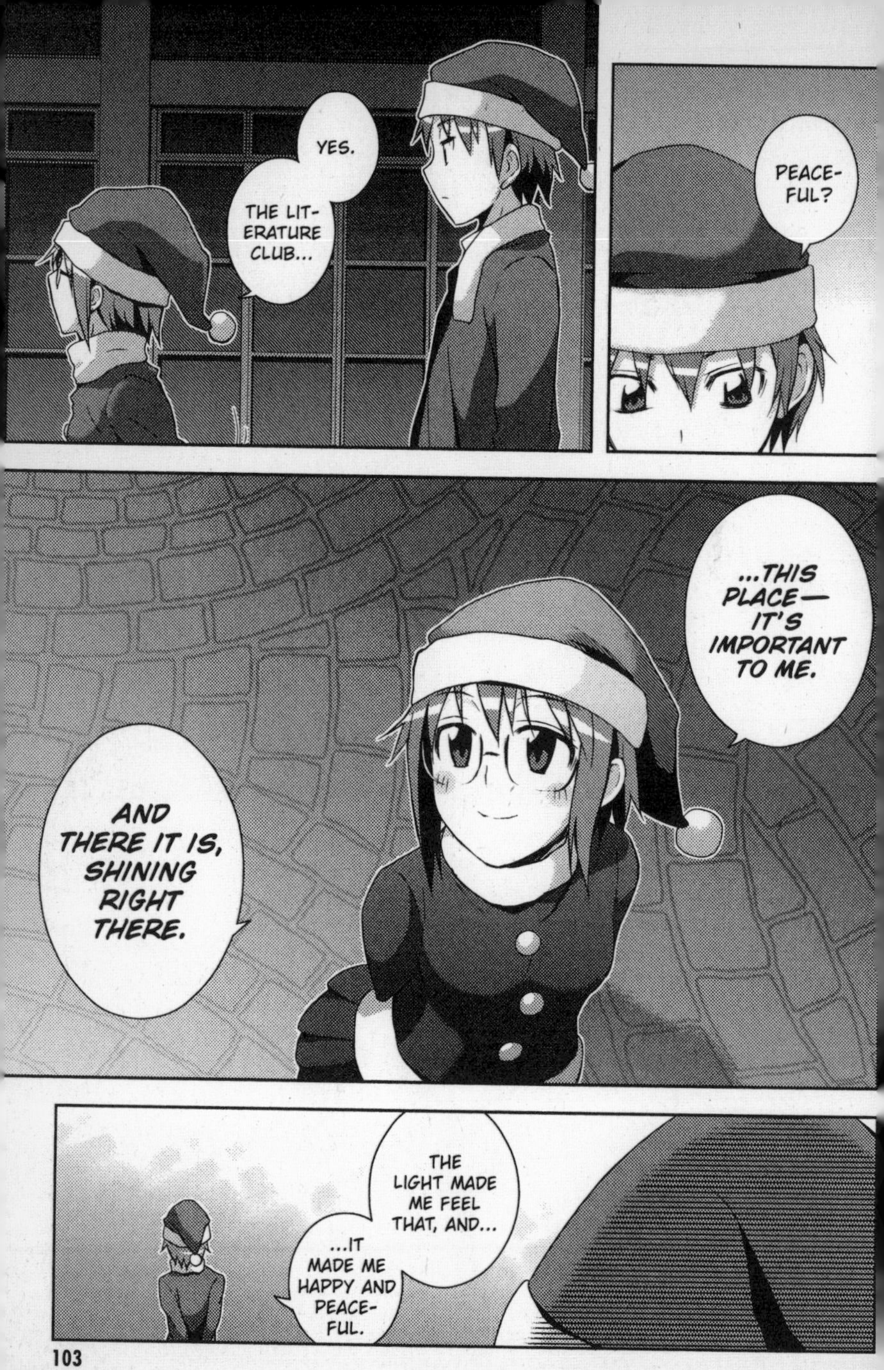
PEACE-FUL?
YES.
THE LIT-ERATURE CLUB...
...THIS PLACE—IT'S IMPORTANT TO ME.
AND THERE IT IS, SHINING RIGHT THERE.
THE LIGHT MADE ME FEEL THAT, AND...
...IT MADE ME HAPPY AND PEACE-FUL.

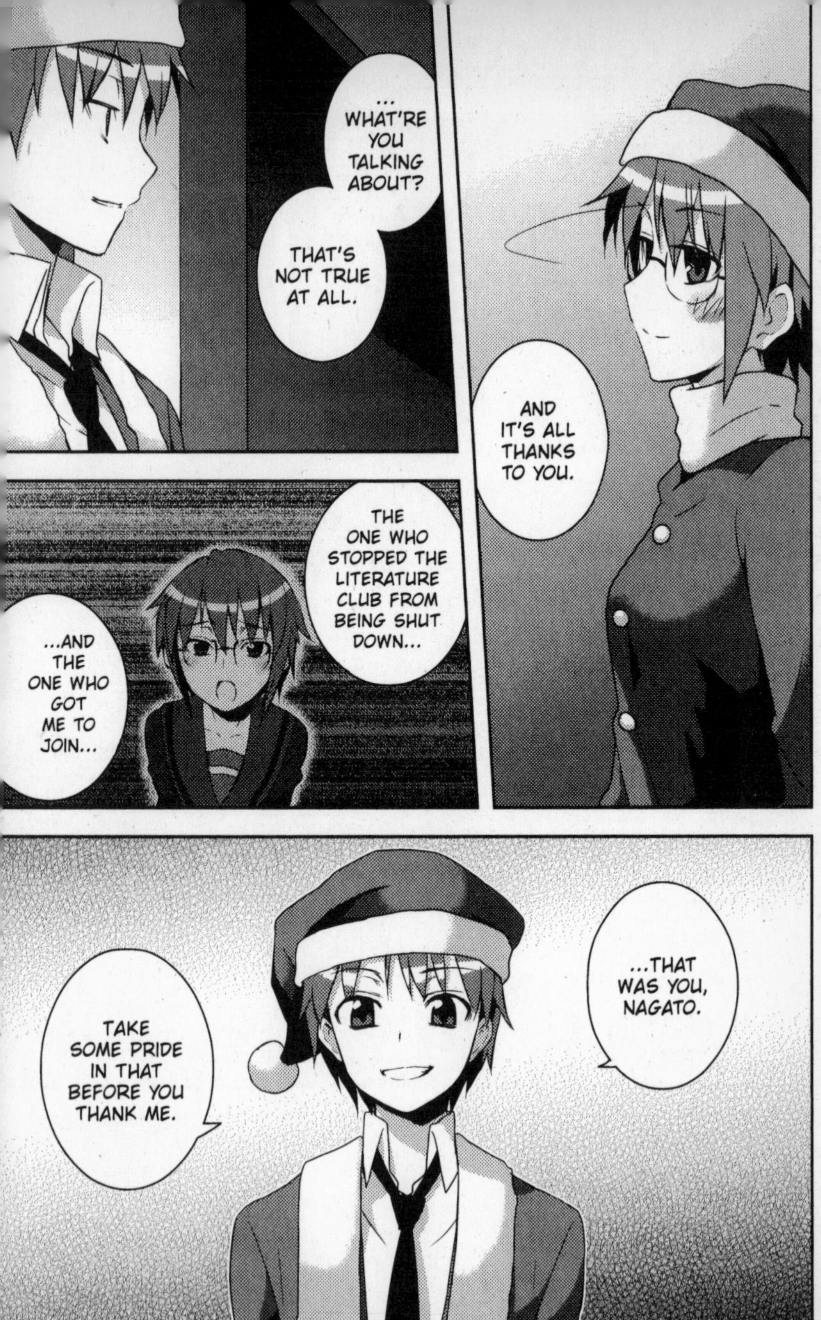
AND IT'S ALL THANKS TO YOU.
... WHAT'RE YOU TALKING ABOUT?
THAT'S NOT TRUE AT ALL.
THE ONE WHO STOPPED THE LITERATURE CLUB FROM BEING SHUT DOWN...
...AND THE ONE WHO GOT ME TO JOIN...
...THAT WAS YOU, NAGATO.
TAKE SOME PRIDE IN THAT BEFORE YOU THANK ME.

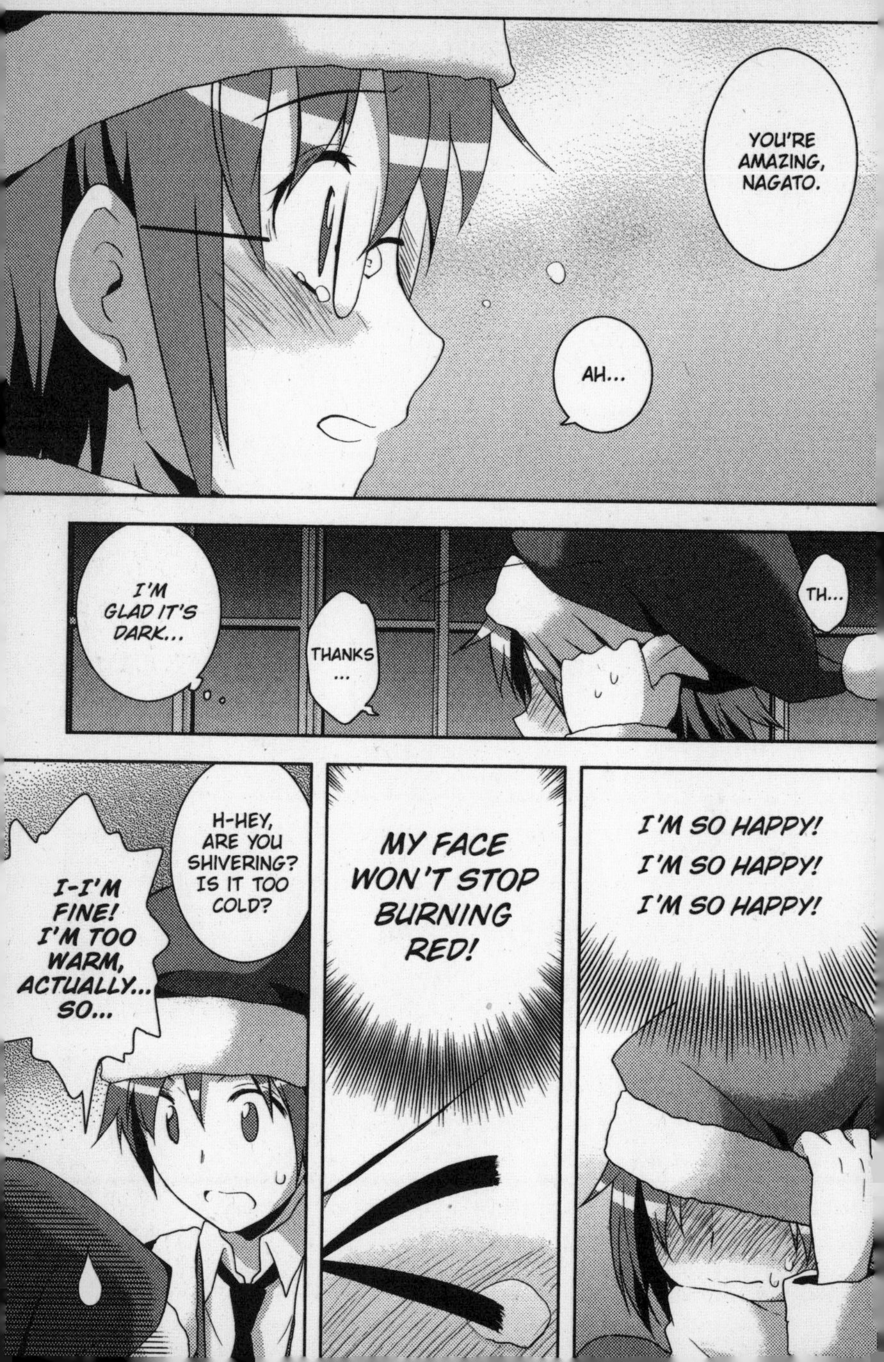
YOU'RE AMAZING, NAGATO.
AH...
TH...
THANKS...
I'M GLAD IT'S DARK...
I'M SO HAPPY! I'M SO HAPPY! I'M SO HAPPY!
MY FACE WON'T STOP BURNING RED!
H-HEY, ARE YOU SHIVERING? IS IT TOO COLD?
I-I'M FINE! I'M TOO WARM, ACTUALLY... SO...

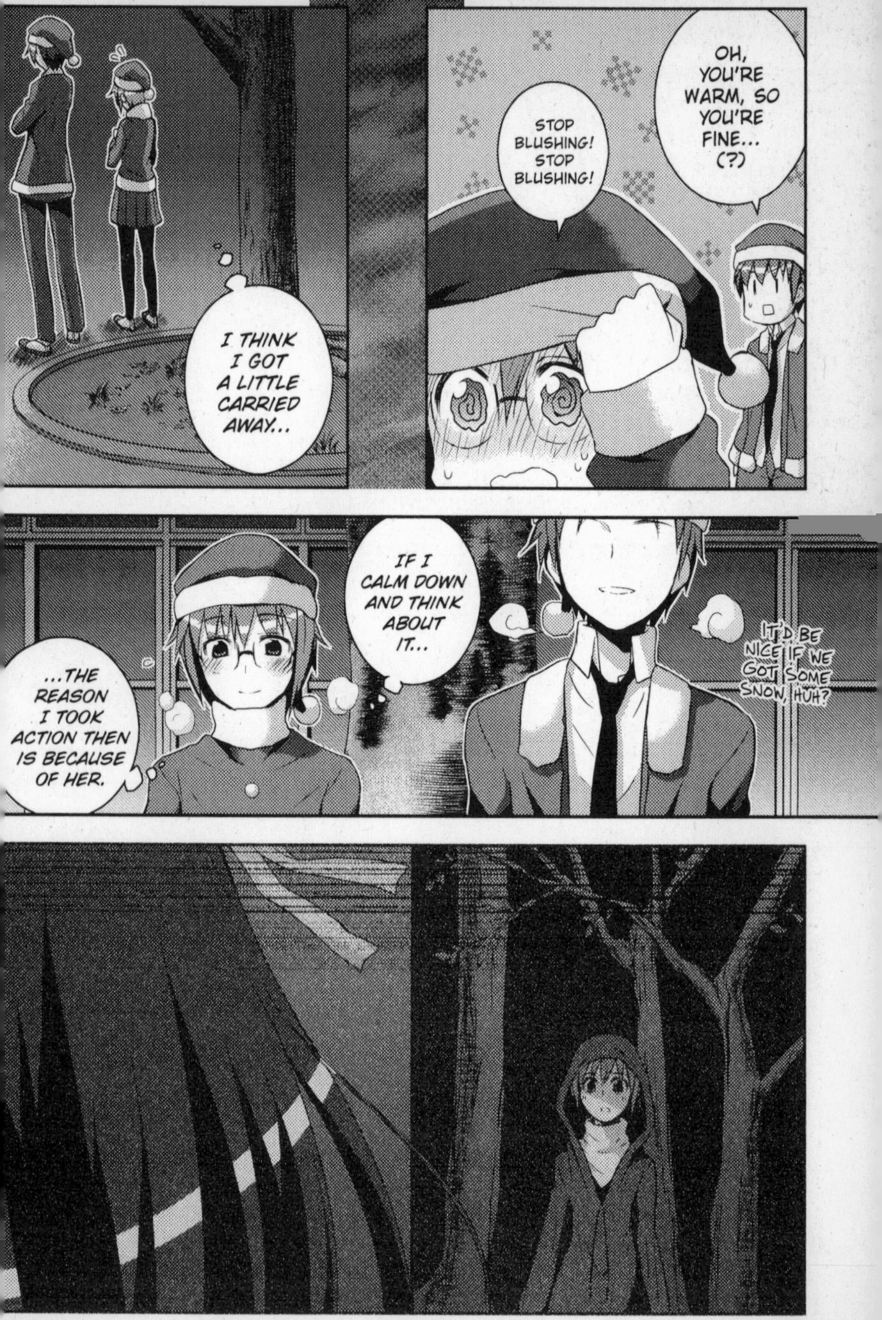
OH, YOU'RE WARM, SO YOU'RE FINE... (?)
STOP BLUSHING! STOP BLUSHING!
I THINK I GOT A LITTLE CARRIED AWAY...
IT'D BE NICE IF WE GOT SOME SNOW, HUH?
IF I CALM DOWN AND THINK ABOUT IT...
...THE REASON I TOOK ACTION THEN IS BECAUSE OF HER.

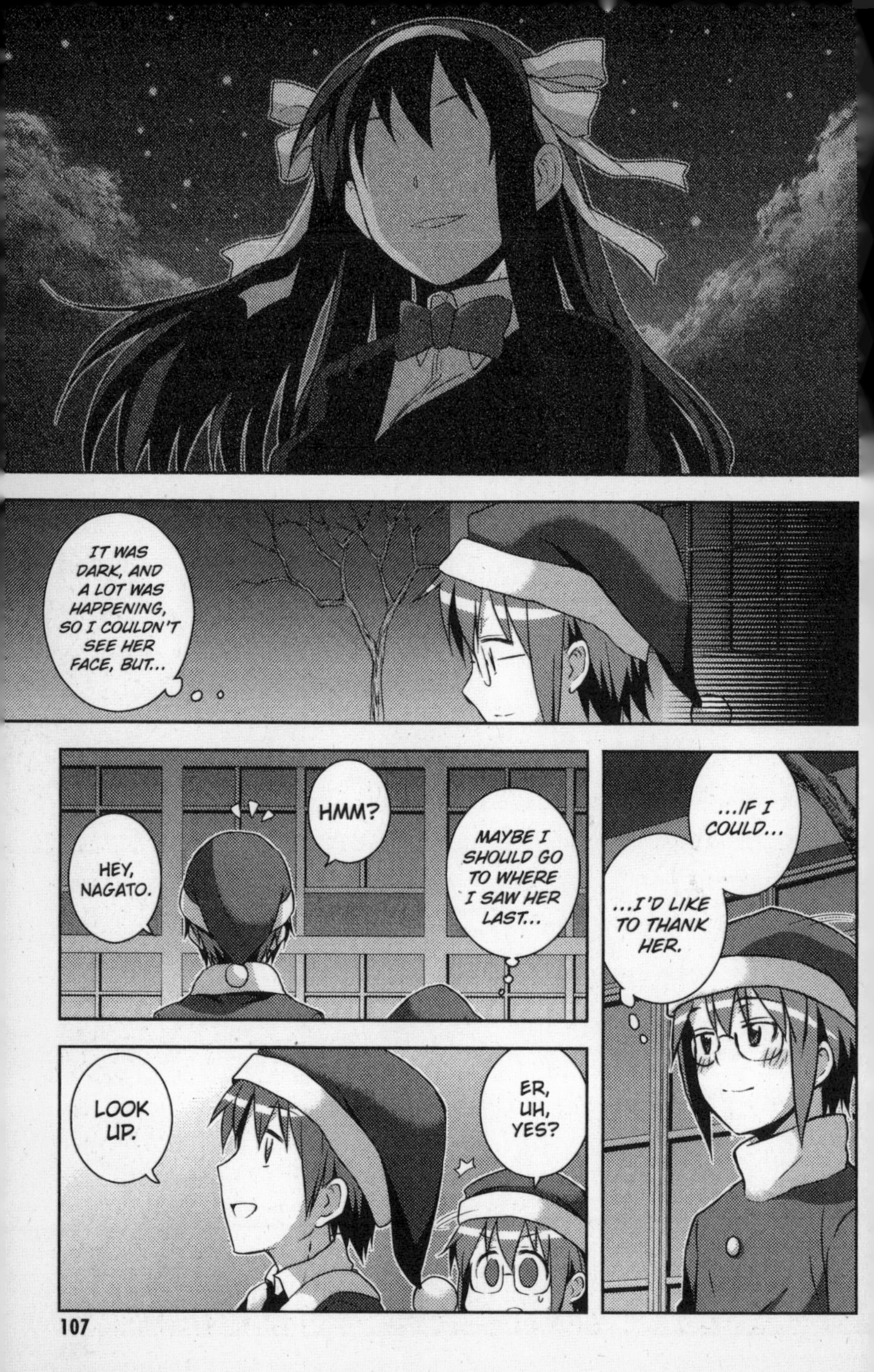
IT WAS DARK, AND A LOT WAS HAPPENING, SO I COULDN'T SEE HER FACE, BUT...
...IF I COULD...
...I'D LIKE TO THANK HER.
MAYBE I SHOULD GO TO WHERE I SAW HER LAST...
HMM?
HEY, NAGATO.
ER, UH, YES?
LOOK UP.

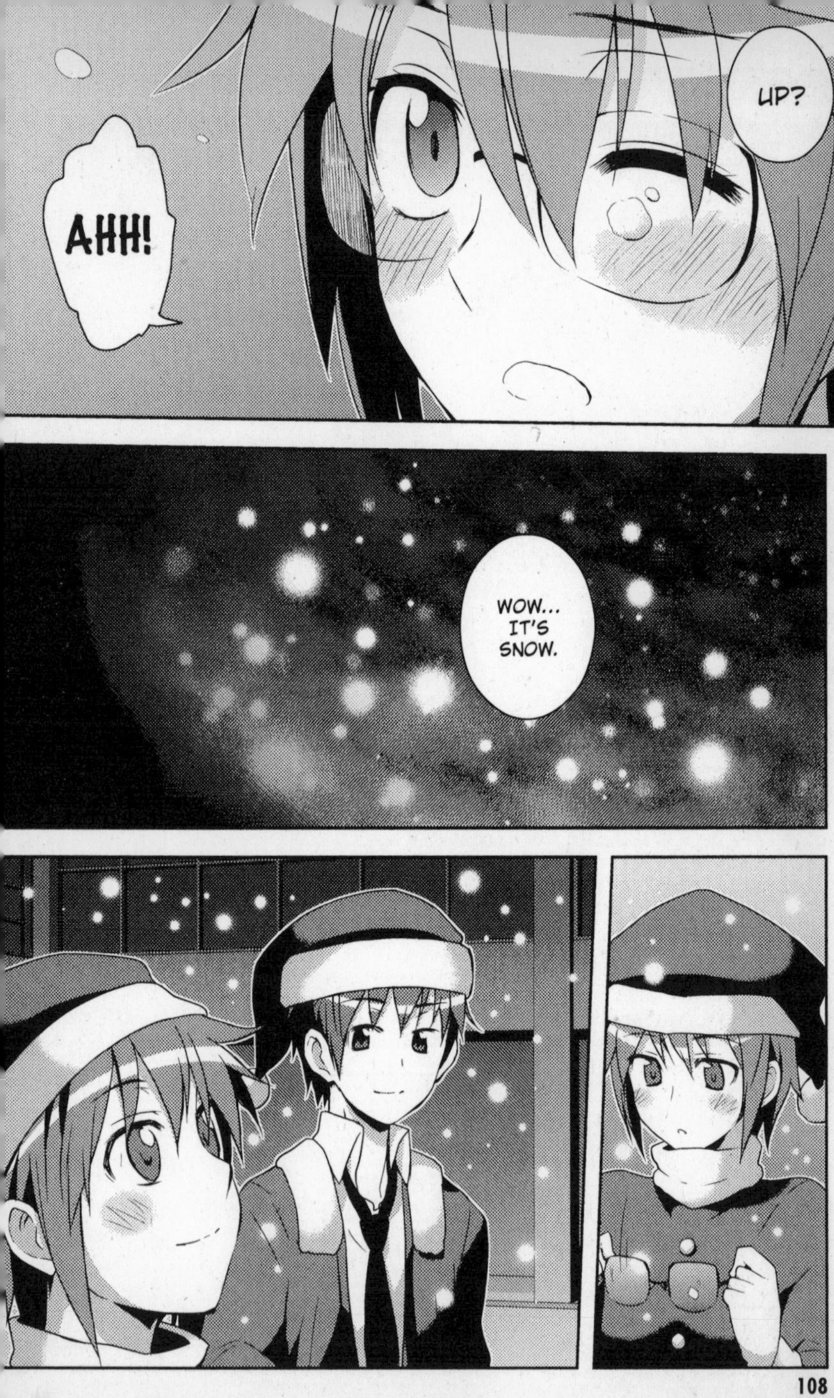
UP?
AHH!
WOW... IT'S SNOW.

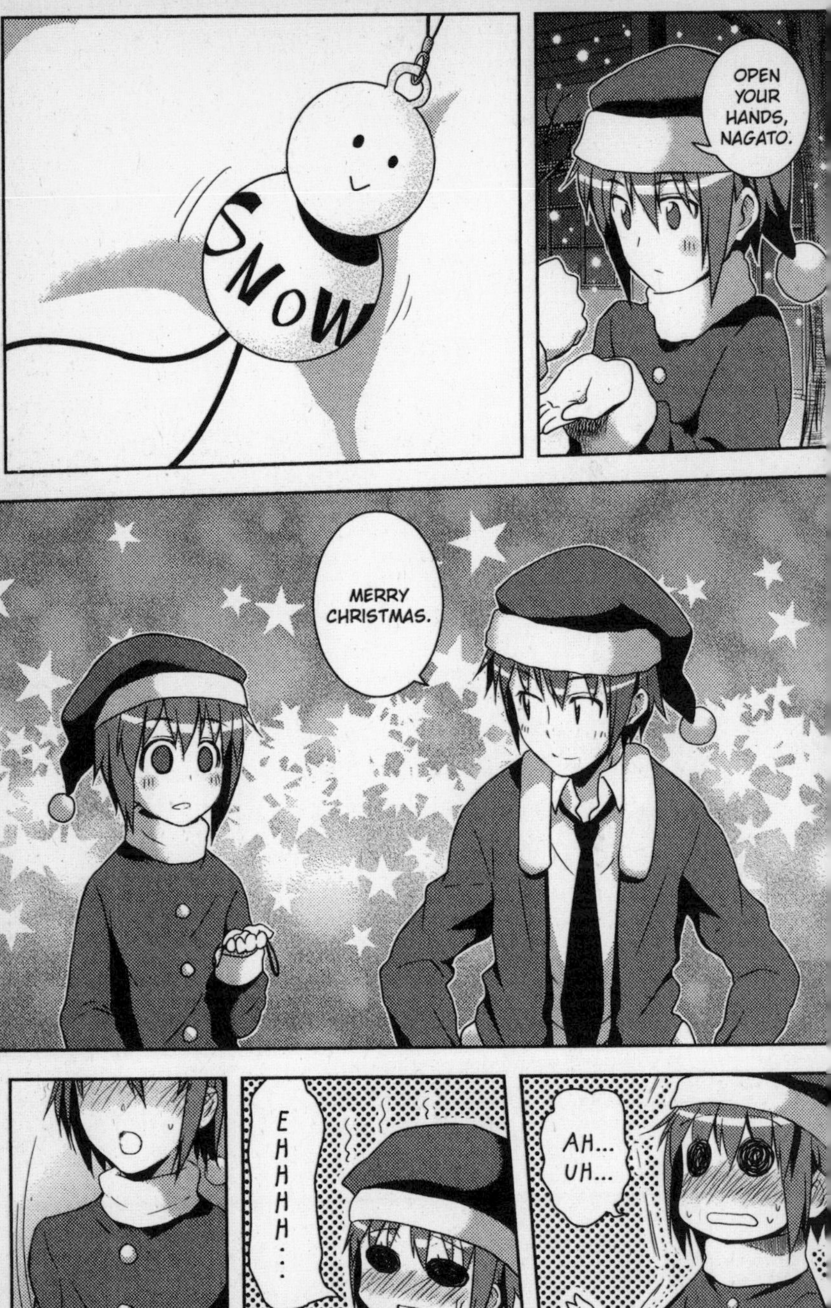
OPEN YOUR HANDS, NAGATO.
SNOW
MERRY CHRISTMAS.
AH... UH...
EHHHHH...

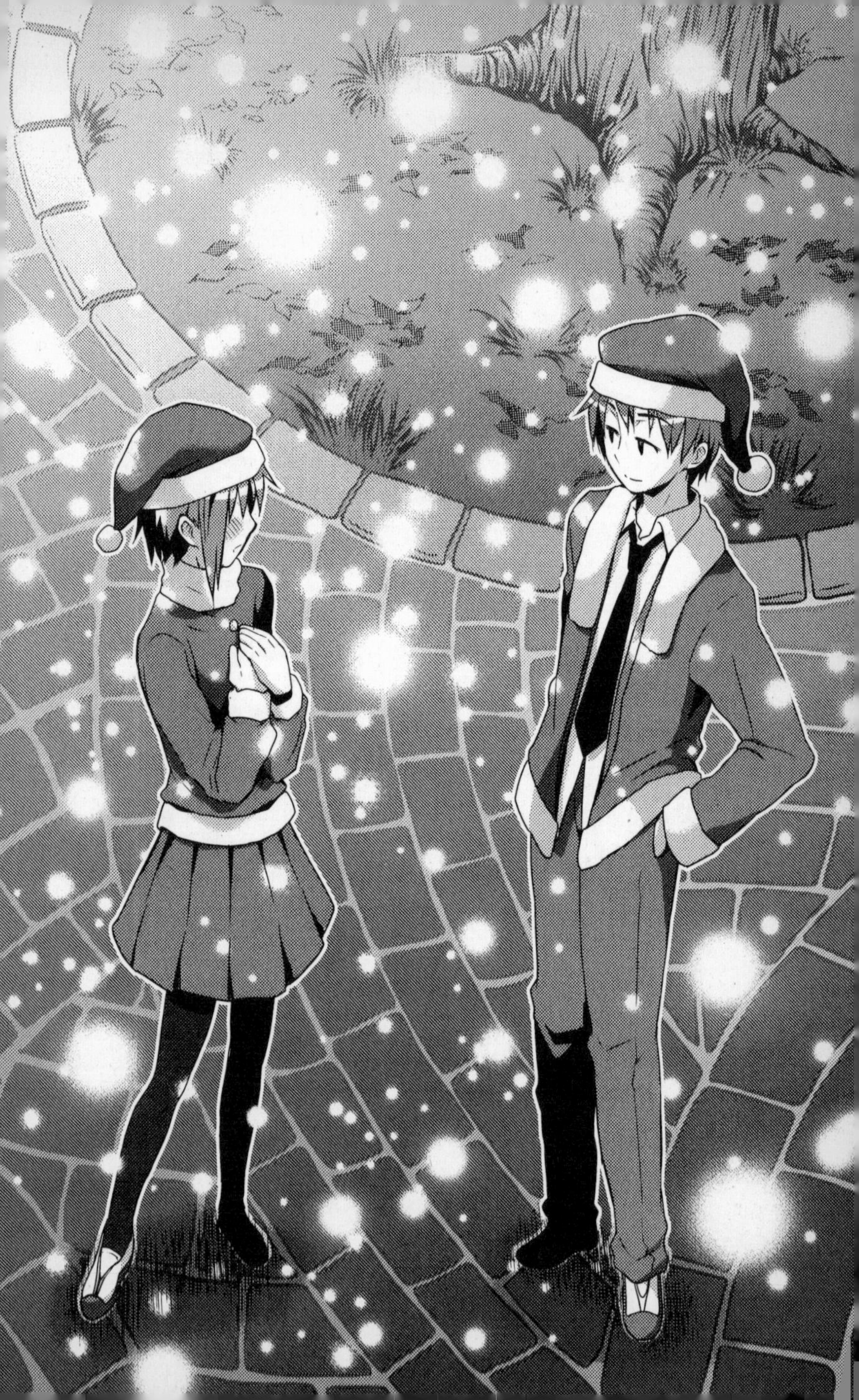

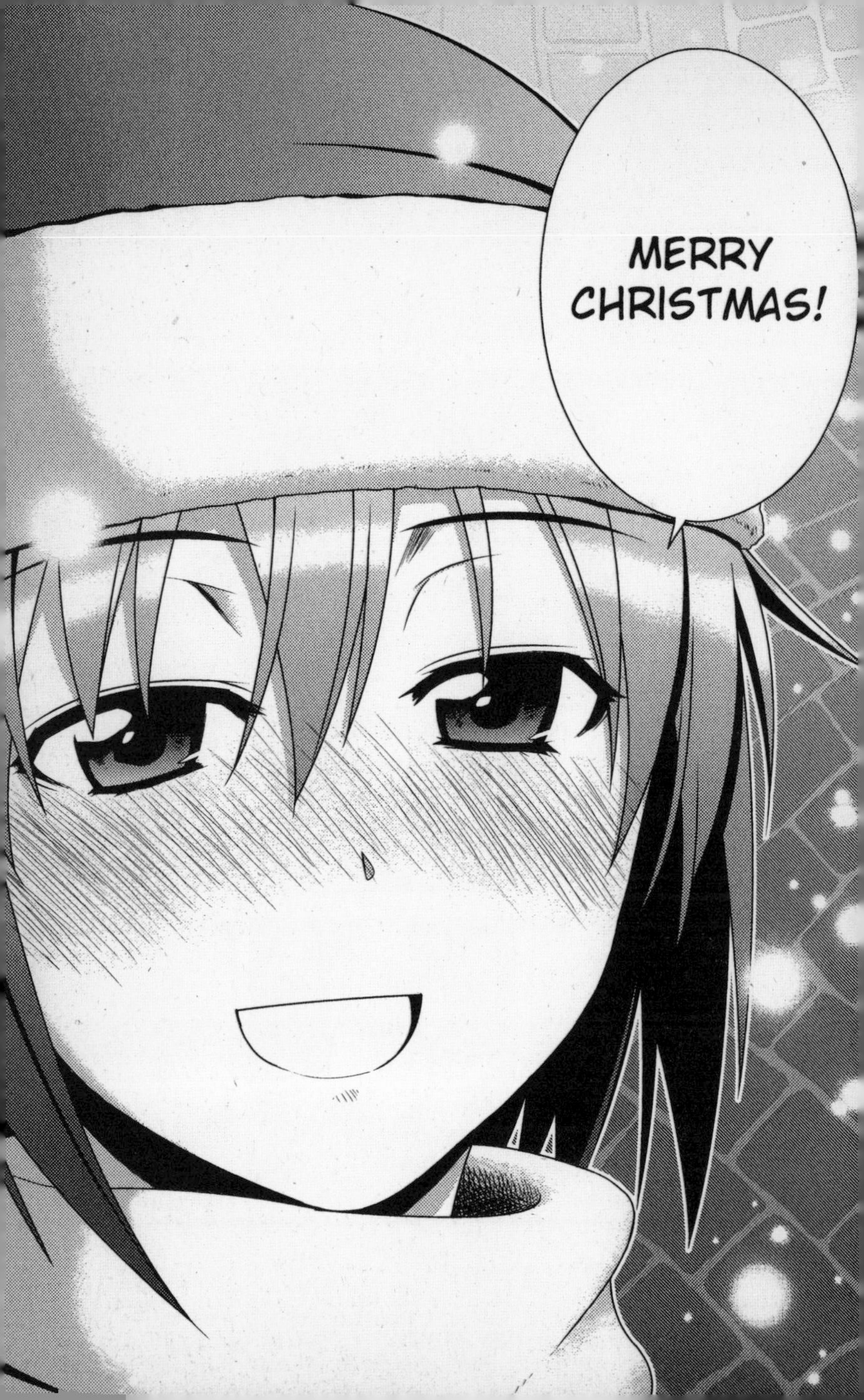
MERRY CHRISTMAS!

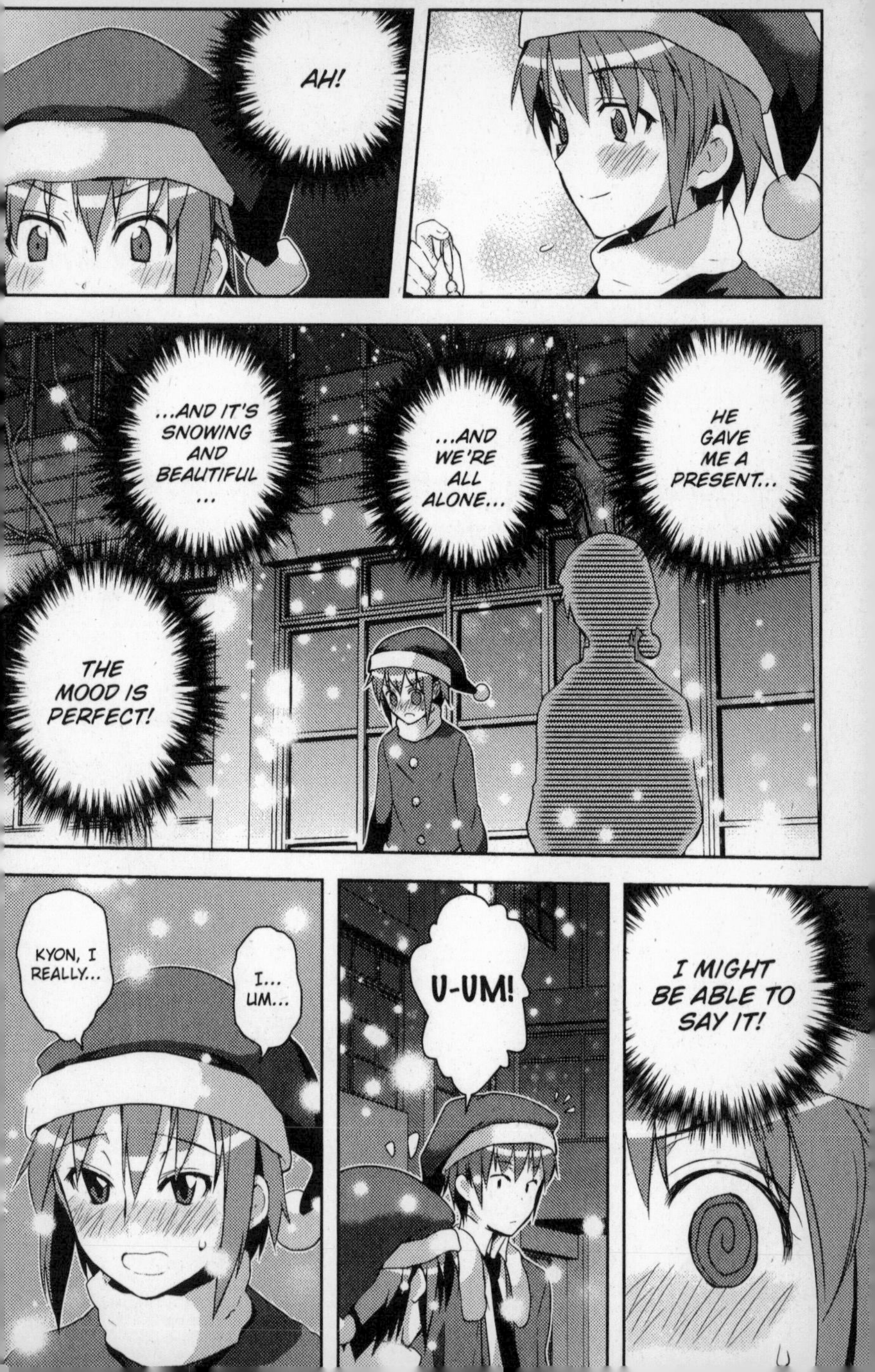
AH!
HE GAVE ME A PRESENT...
...AND WE'RE ALL ALONE...
...AND IT'S SNOWING AND BEAUTIFUL ...
THE MOOD IS PERFECT!
I MIGHT BE ABLE TO SAY IT!
U-UM!
I... UM...
KYON, I REALLY...

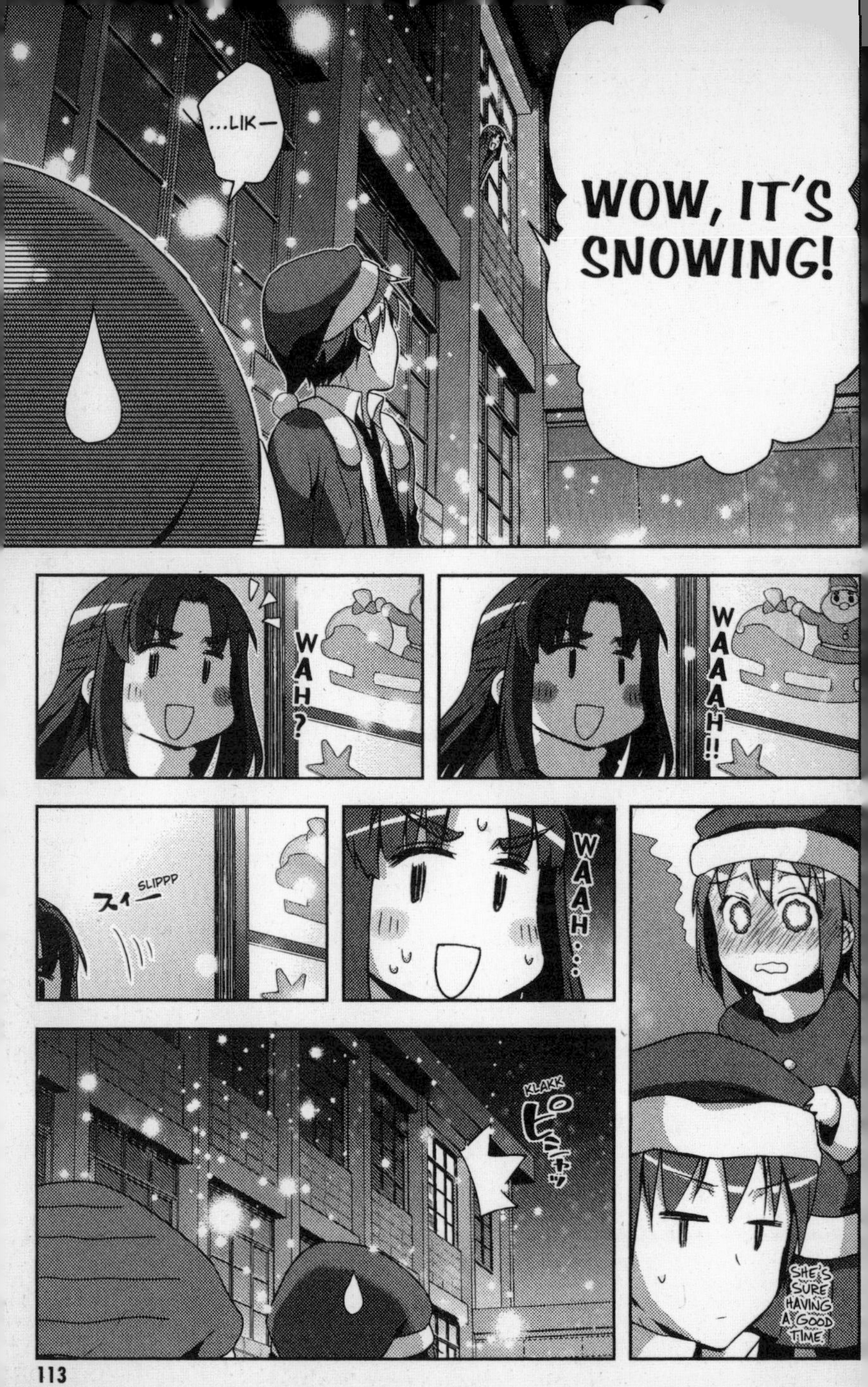

WOW, IT'S SNOWING!
...LIK—
WAAAAH!!
WAH?
SHE'S SURE HAVING A GOOD TIME.
WAAAH...
スィー
SLIPPP
KLAKK
ピョコッ

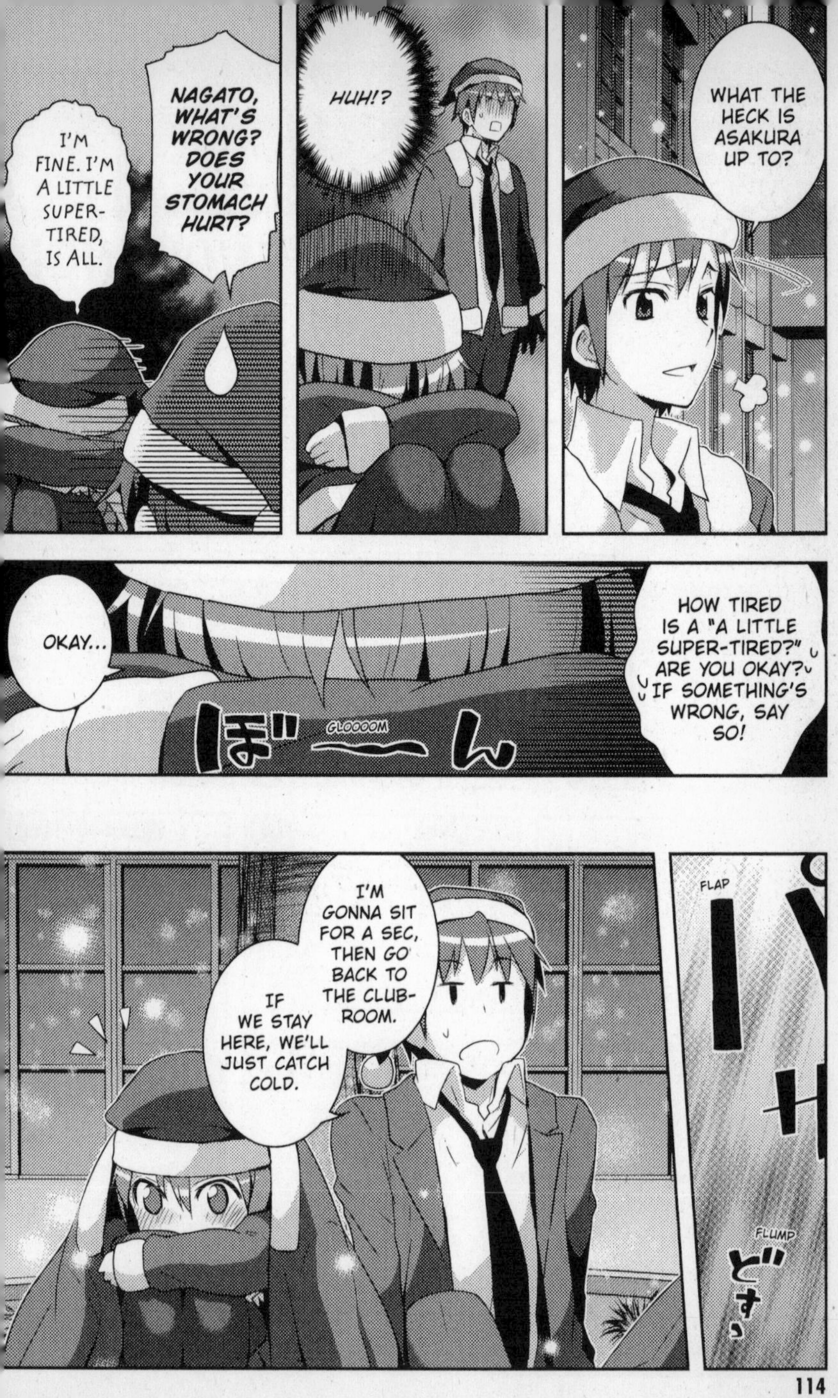
WHAT THE HECK IS ASAKURA UP TO?
HUH!?
NAGATO, WHAT'S WRONG? DOES YOUR STOMACH HURT?
I'M FINE. I'M A LITTLE SUPER-TIRED, IS ALL.
HOW TIRED IS A "A LITTLE SUPER-TIRED?" ARE YOU OKAY? IF SOMETHING'S WRONG, SAY SO!
GLOOOOM
OKAY...
FLAP
FLUMP
I'M GONNA SIT FOR A SEC, THEN GO BACK TO THE CLUB-ROOM.
IF WE STAY HERE, WE'LL JUST CATCH COLD.

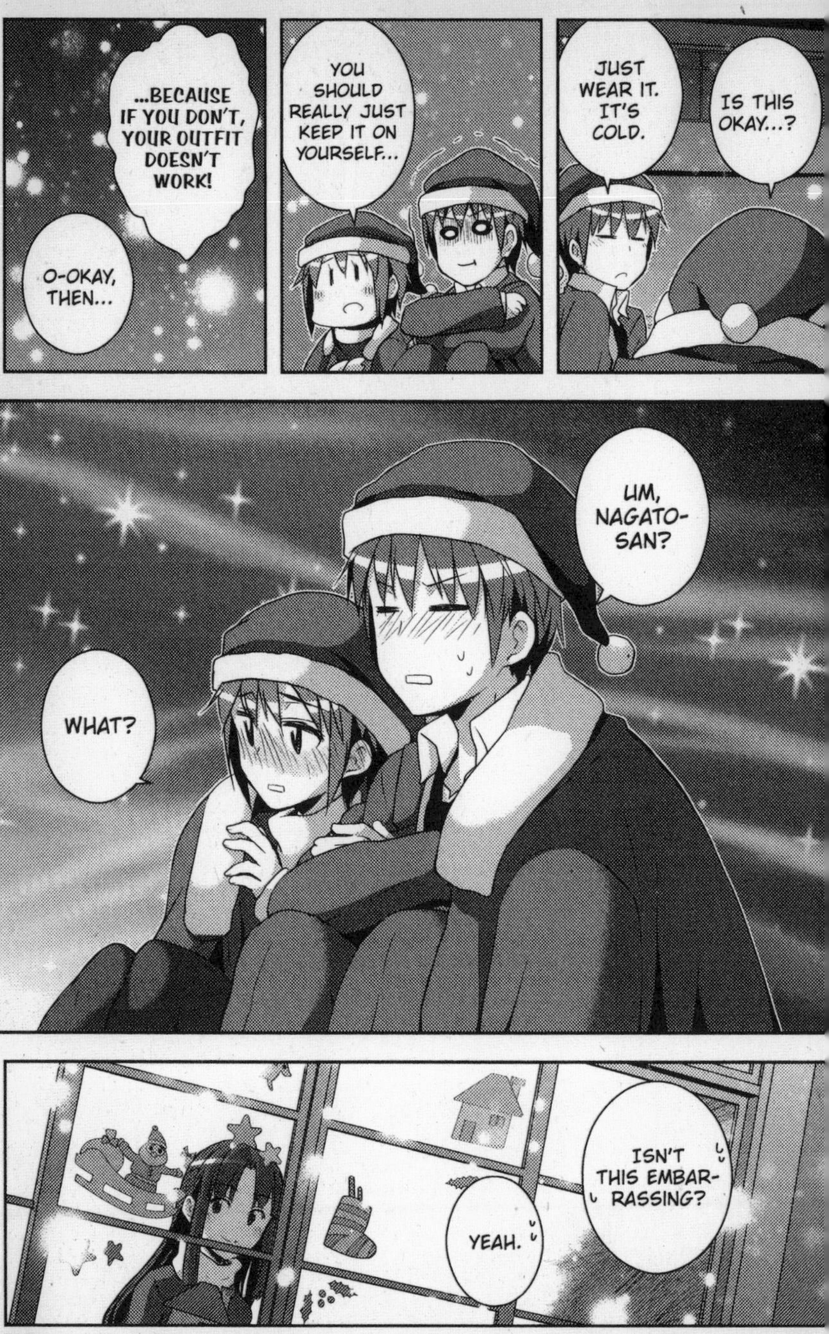
IS THIS OKAY...?
JUST WEAR IT. IT'S COLD.
YOU SHOULD REALLY JUST KEEP IT ON YOURSELF...
...BECAUSE IF YOU DON'T, YOUR OUTFIT DOESN'T WORK!
O-OKAY, THEN...
UM, NAGATO-SAN?
WHAT?
ISN'T THIS EMBARRASSING?
YEAH.

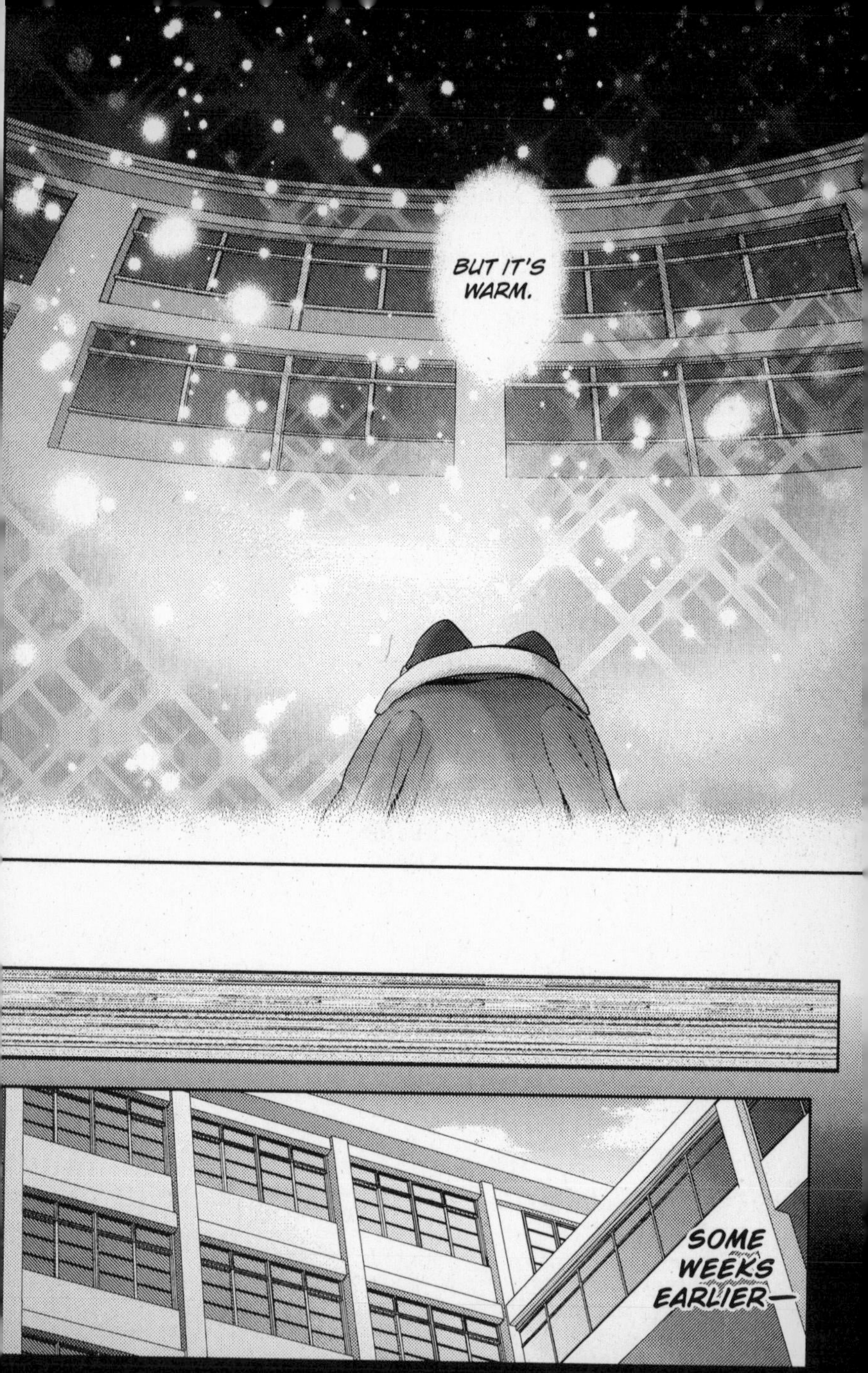
BUT IT'S WARM.
SOME WEEKS EARLIER—

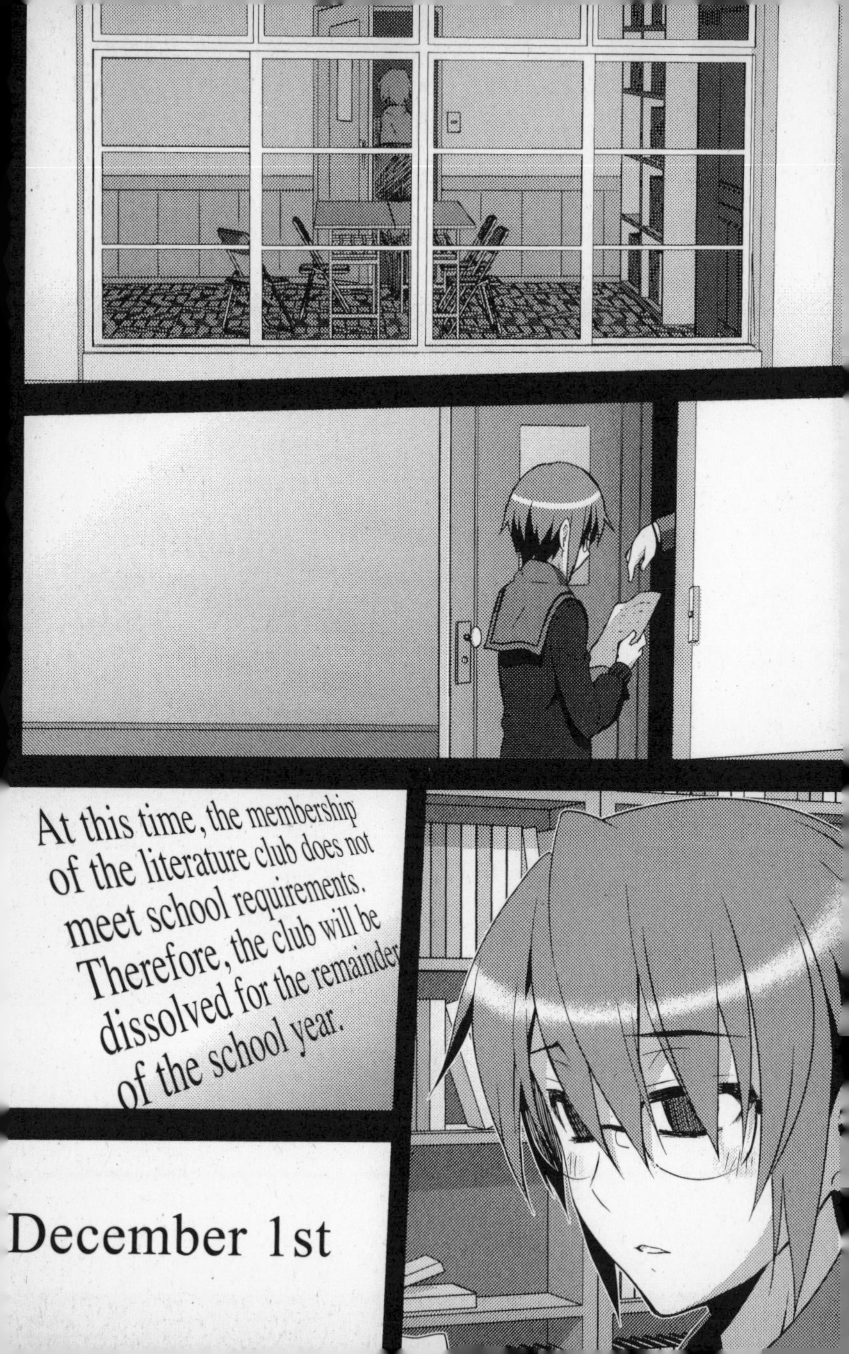
At this time, the membership of the literature club does not meet school requirements. Therefore, the club will be dissolved for the remainder of the school year.
December 1st

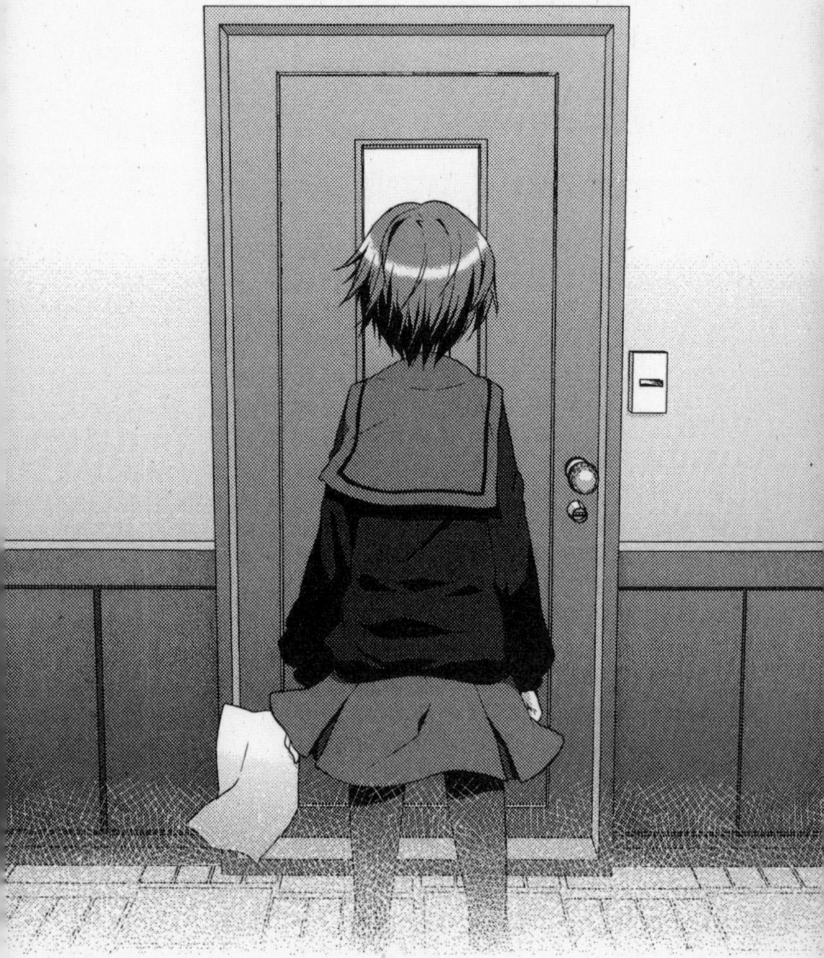

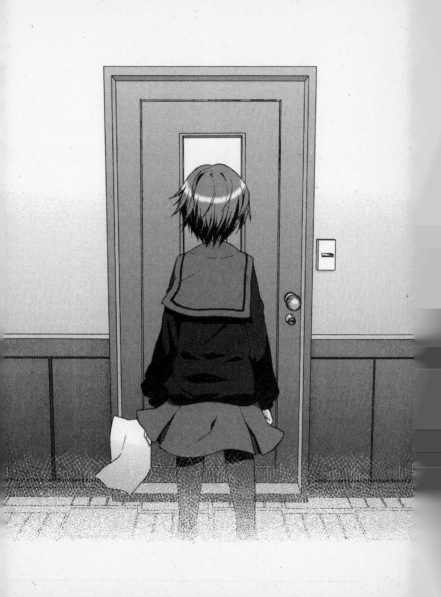

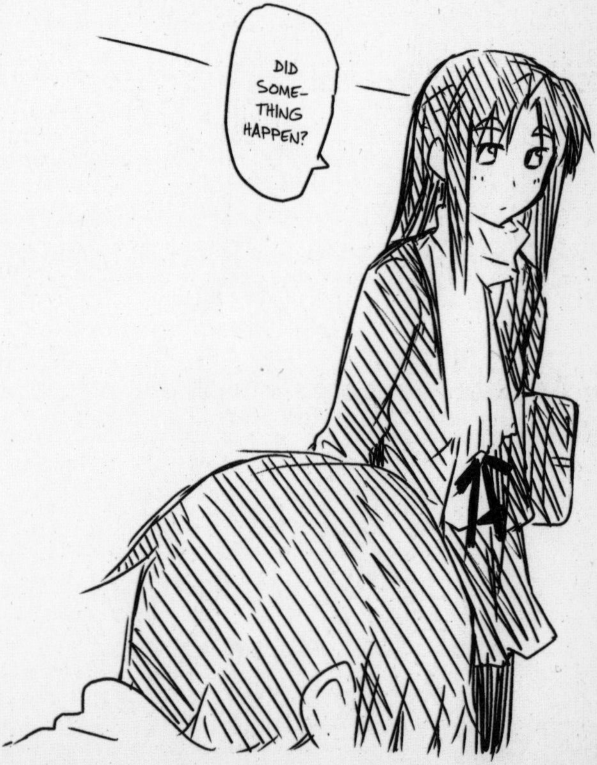
DID SOME-THING HAPPEN?

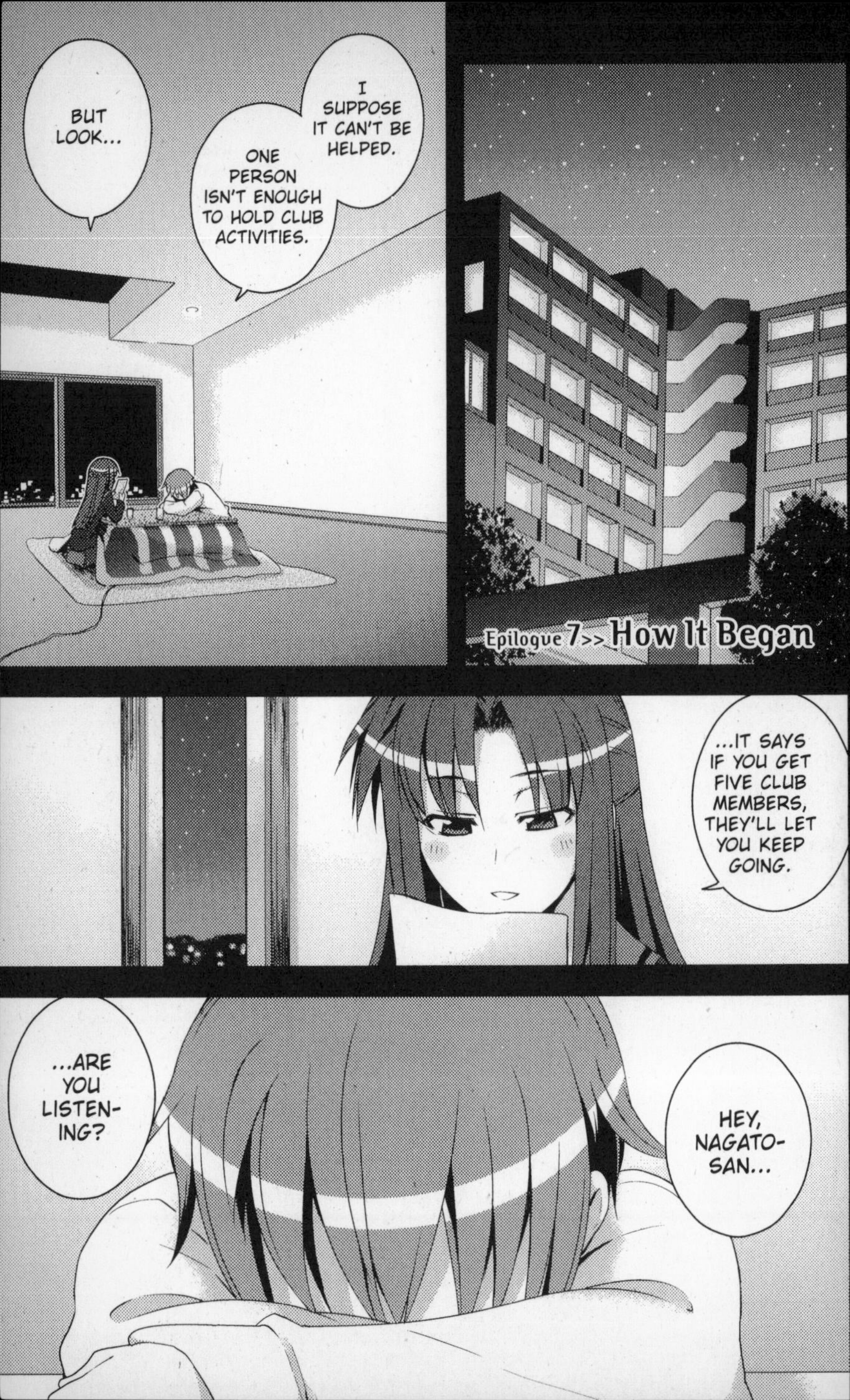
Epilogue 7>> How It Began
I SUPPOSE IT CAN'T BE HELPED.
ONE PERSON ISN'T ENOUGH TO HOLD CLUB ACTIVITIES.
BUT LOOK...
...IT SAYS IF YOU GET FIVE CLUB MEMBERS, THEY'LL LET YOU KEEP GOING.
HEY, NAGATO-SAN...
...ARE YOU LISTENING?

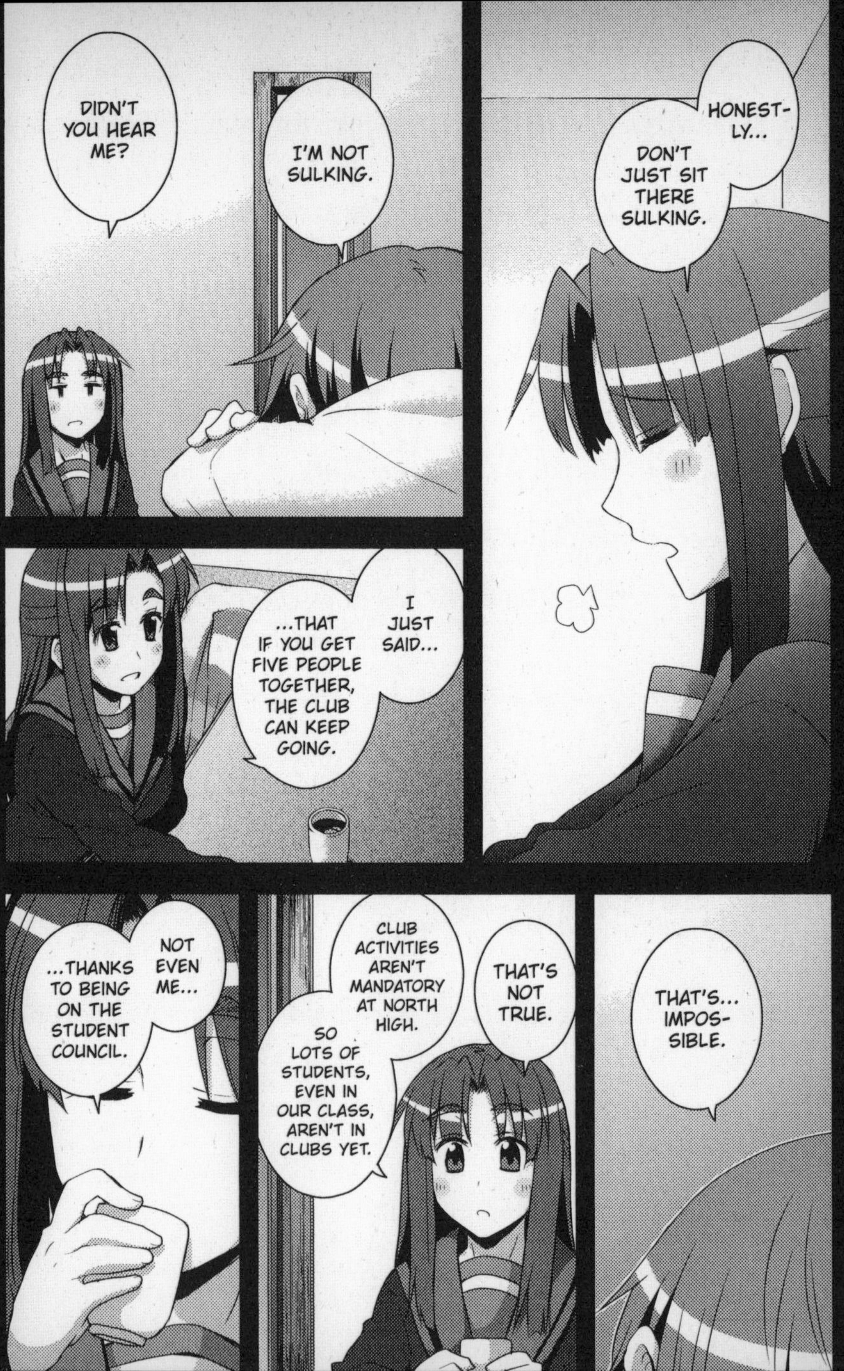
HONESTLY...
DON'T JUST SIT THERE SULKING.
I'M NOT SULKING.
DIDN'T YOU HEAR ME?
I JUST SAID...
...THAT IF YOU GET FIVE PEOPLE TOGETHER, THE CLUB CAN KEEP GOING.
THAT'S... IMPOSSIBLE.
THAT'S NOT TRUE.
CLUB ACTIVITIES AREN'T MANDATORY AT NORTH HIGH.
SO LOTS OF STUDENTS, EVEN IN OUR CLASS, AREN'T IN CLUBS YET.
NOT EVEN ME...
...THANKS TO BEING ON THE STUDENT COUNCIL.

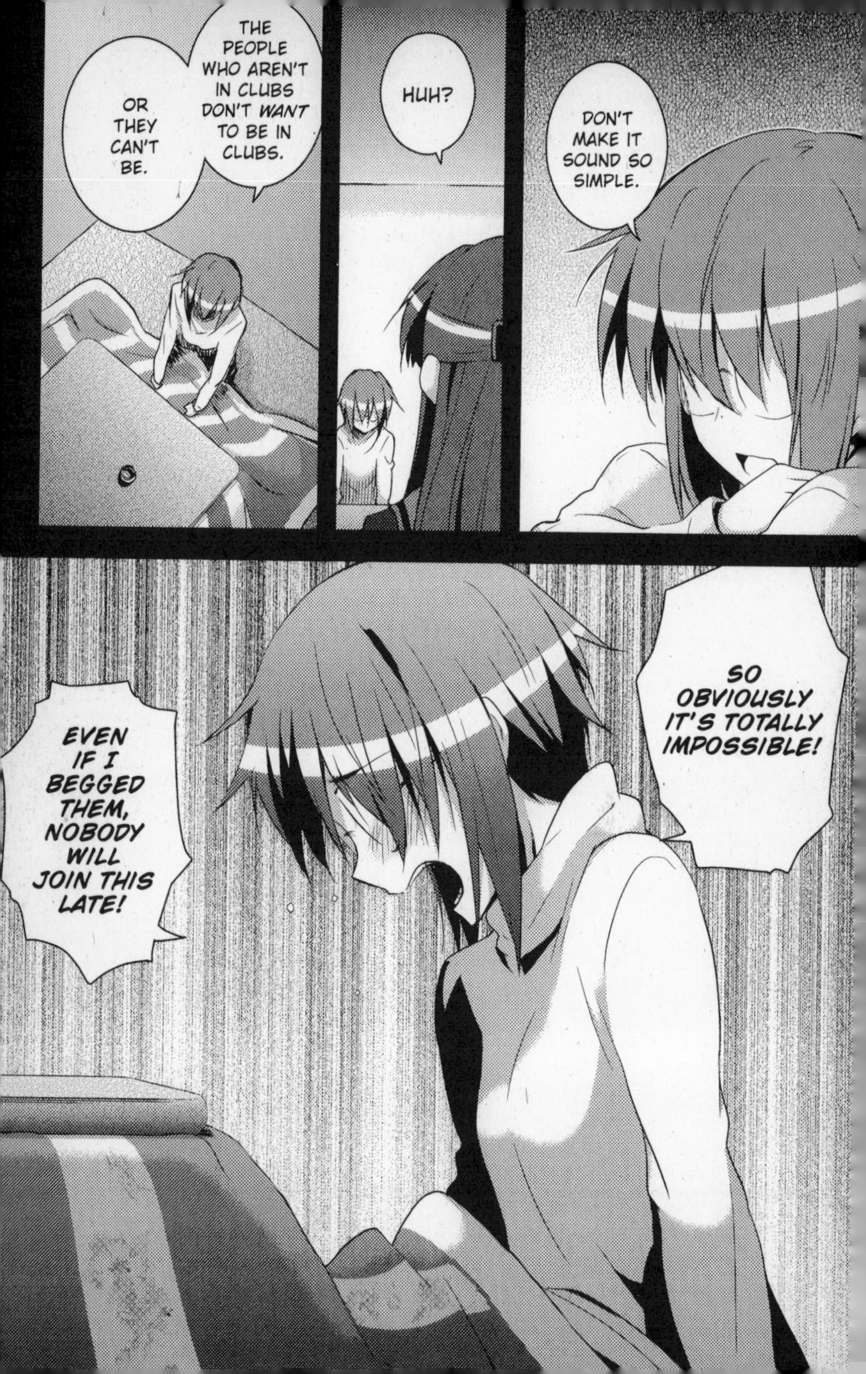
DON'T MAKE IT SOUND SO SIMPLE.
HUH?
THE PEOPLE WHO AREN'T IN CLUBS DON'T *WANT* TO BE IN CLUBS.
OR THEY CAN'T BE.
SO OBVIOUSLY IT'S TOTALLY IMPOSSIBLE!
EVEN IF I BEGGED THEM, NOBODY WILL JOIN THIS LATE!

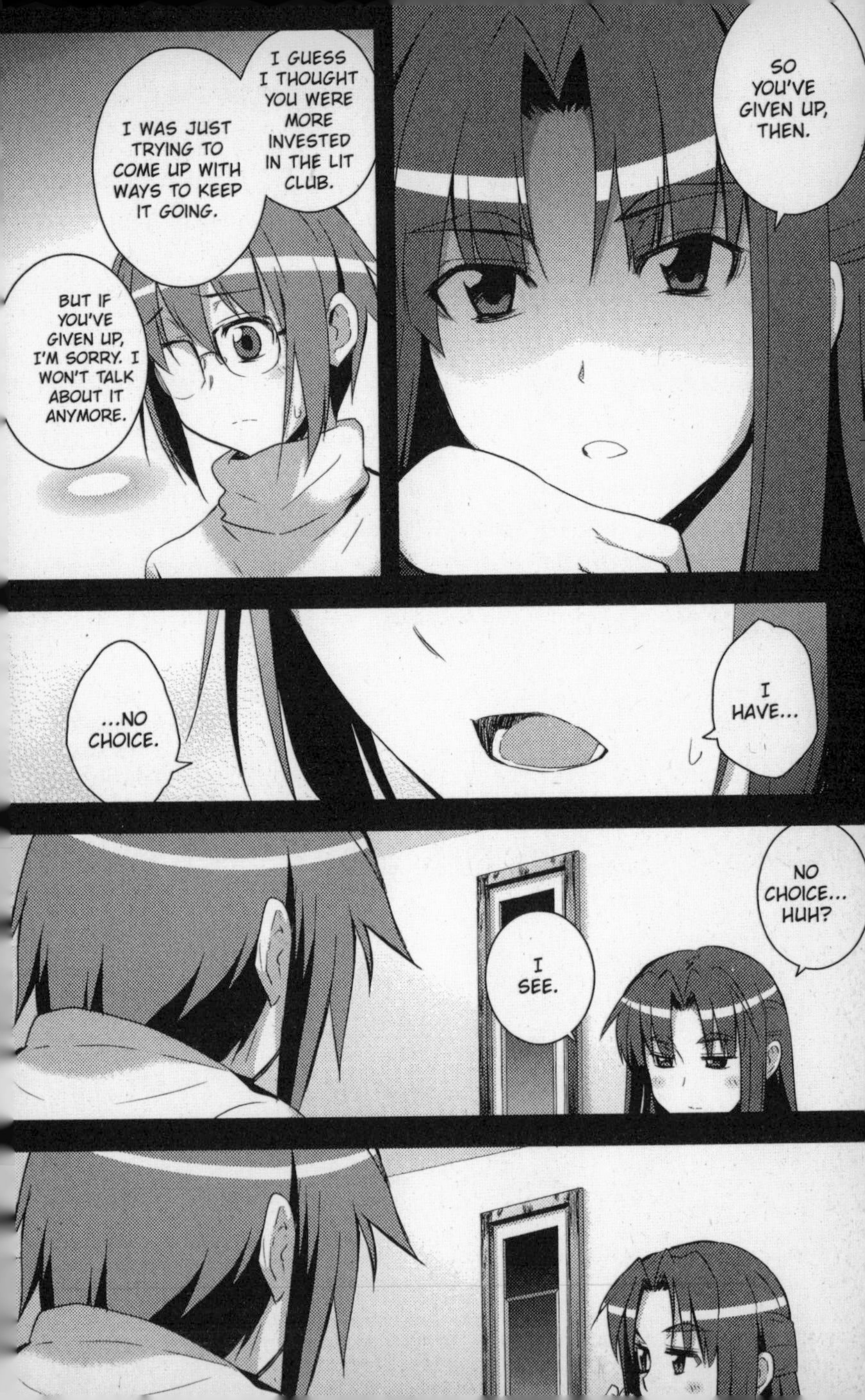
SO YOU'VE GIVEN UP, THEN.
I GUESS I THOUGHT YOU WERE MORE INVESTED IN THE LIT CLUB.
I WAS JUST TRYING TO COME UP WITH WAYS TO KEEP IT GOING.
BUT IF YOU'VE GIVEN UP, I'M SORRY. I WON'T TALK ABOUT IT ANYMORE.
I HAVE...
...NO CHOICE.
NO CHOICE... HUH?
I SEE.

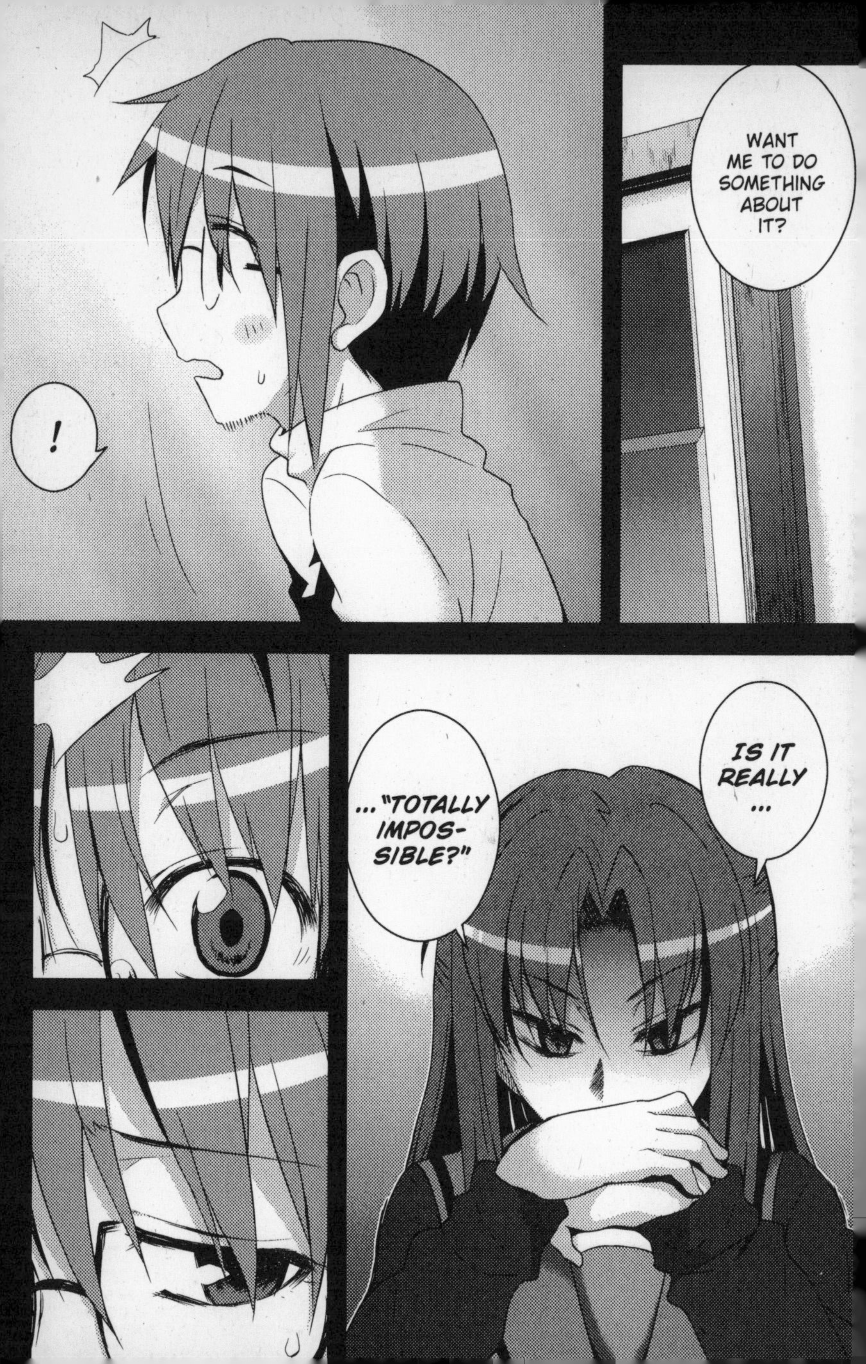
WANT ME TO DO SOMETHING ABOUT IT?
!
IS IT REALLY ...
..."TOTALLY IMPOSSIBLE?"

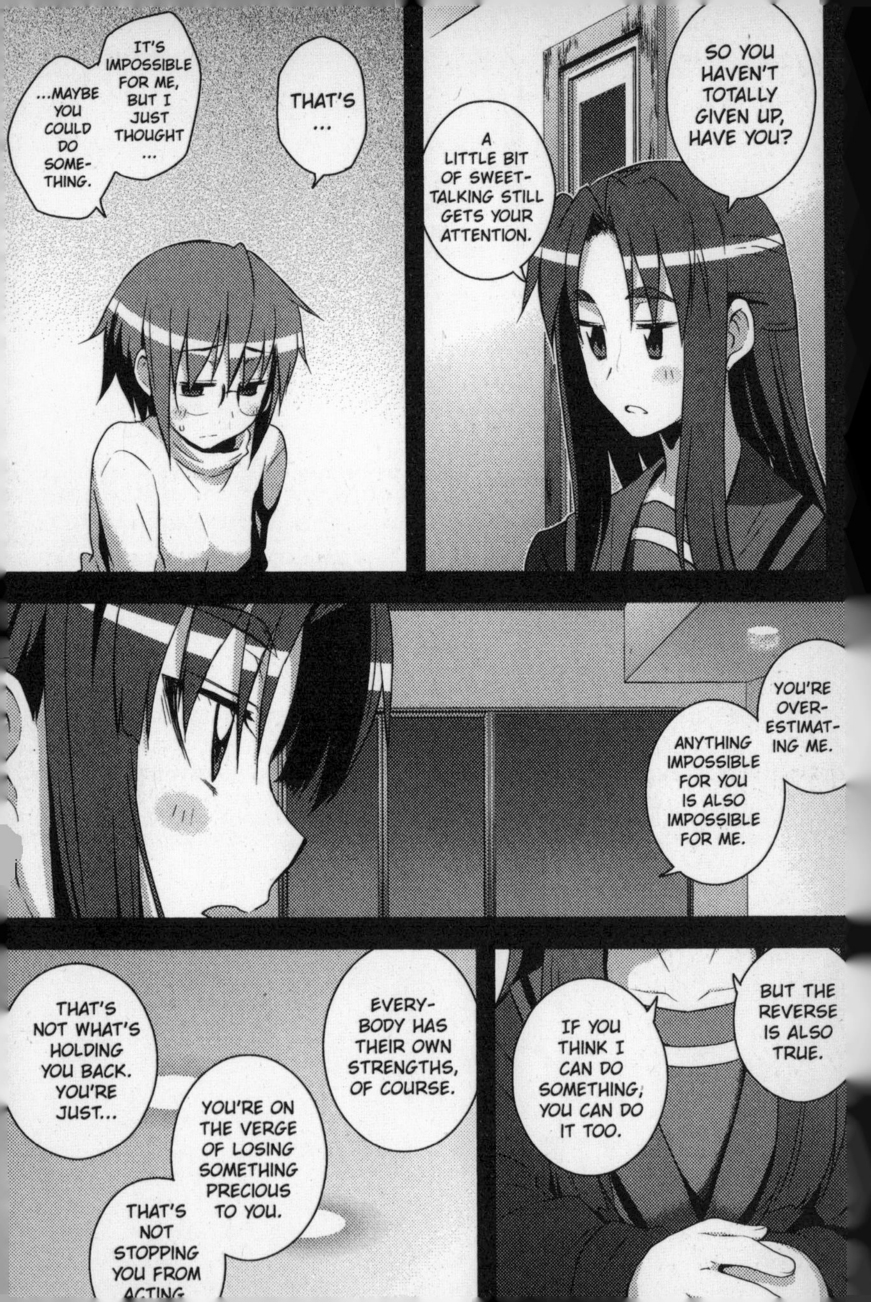
SO YOU HAVEN'T TOTALLY GIVEN UP, HAVE YOU?
A LITTLE BIT OF SWEET-TALKING STILL GETS YOUR ATTENTION.
THAT'S...
IT'S IMPOSSIBLE FOR ME, BUT I JUST THOUGHT...
...MAYBE YOU COULD DO SOME-THING.
YOU'RE OVER-ESTIMAT-ING ME.
ANYTHING IMPOSSIBLE FOR YOU IS ALSO IMPOSSIBLE FOR ME.
BUT THE REVERSE IS ALSO TRUE.
IF YOU THINK I CAN DO SOMETHING, YOU CAN DO IT TOO.
EVERY-BODY HAS THEIR OWN STRENGTHS, OF COURSE.
THAT'S NOT WHAT'S HOLDING YOU BACK. YOU'RE JUST...
YOU'RE ON THE VERGE OF LOSING SOMETHING PRECIOUS TO YOU.
THAT'S NOT STOPPING YOU FROM ACTING

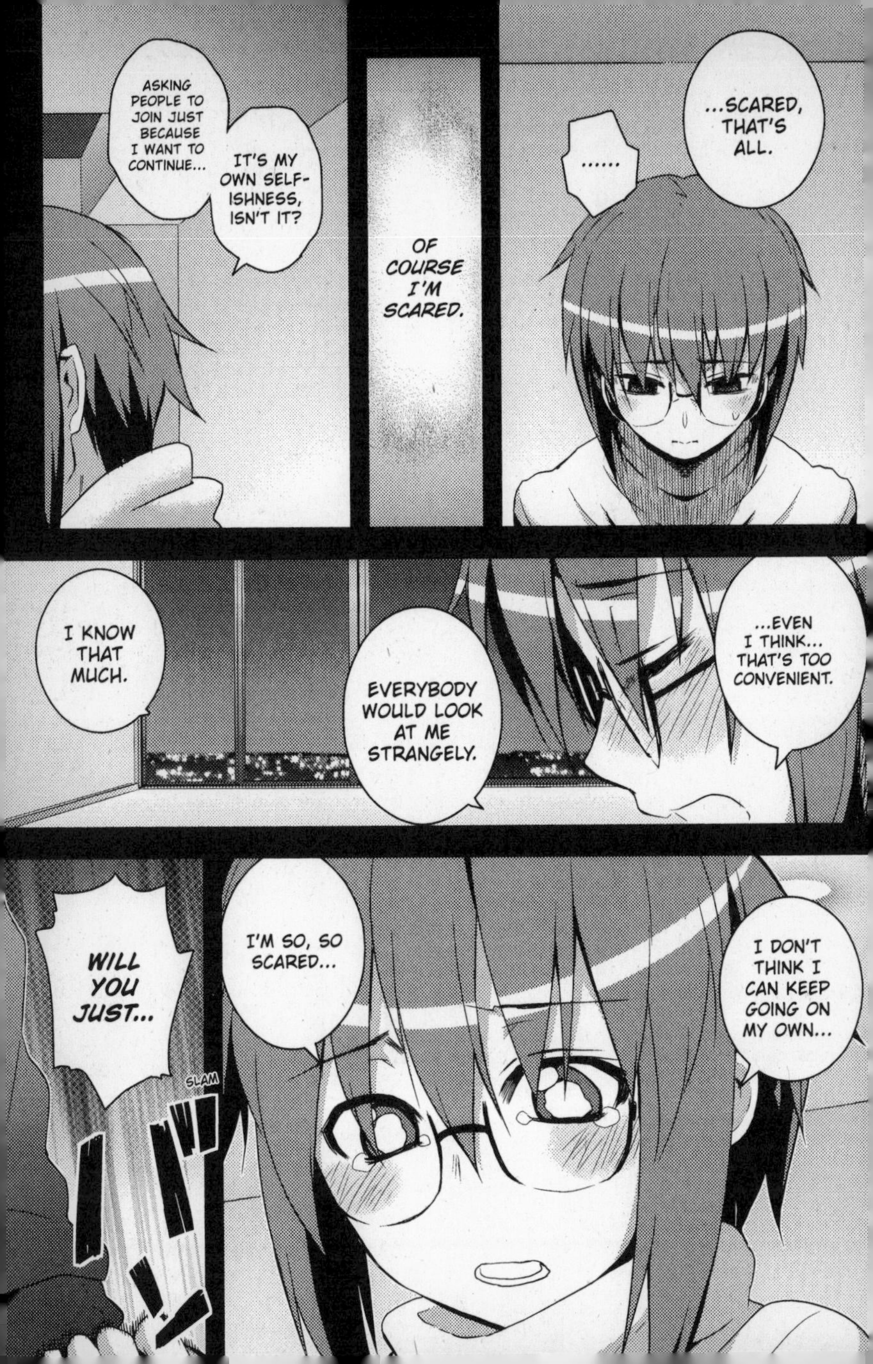
...SCARED, THAT'S ALL.
......
OF COURSE I'M SCARED.
ASKING PEOPLE TO JOIN JUST BECAUSE I WANT TO CONTINUE...
IT'S MY OWN SELF-ISHNESS, ISN'T IT?
...EVEN I THINK... THAT'S TOO CONVENIENT.
EVERYBODY WOULD LOOK AT ME STRANGELY.
I KNOW THAT MUCH.
I DON'T THINK I CAN KEEP GOING ON MY OWN...
I'M SO, SO SCARED...
WILL YOU JUST...
SLAM

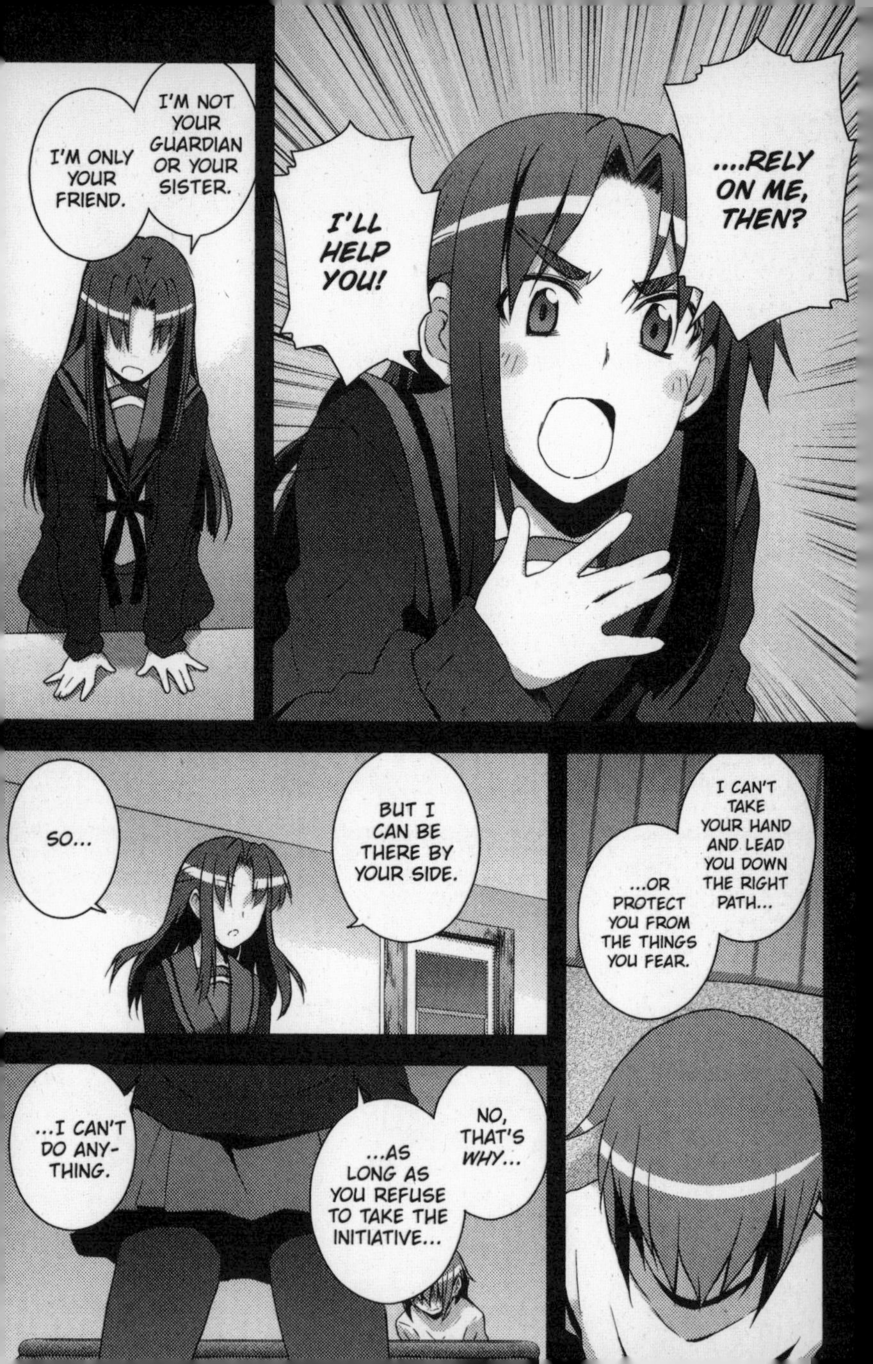
....RELY ON ME, THEN?
I'LL HELP YOU!
I'M NOT YOUR GUARDIAN OR YOUR SISTER.
I'M ONLY YOUR FRIEND.
I CAN'T TAKE YOUR HAND AND LEAD YOU DOWN THE RIGHT PATH...
...OR PROTECT YOU FROM THE THINGS YOU FEAR.
BUT I CAN BE THERE BY YOUR SIDE.
SO...
NO, THAT'S WHY...
...AS LONG AS YOU REFUSE TO TAKE THE INITIATIVE...
...I CAN'T DO ANY-THING.

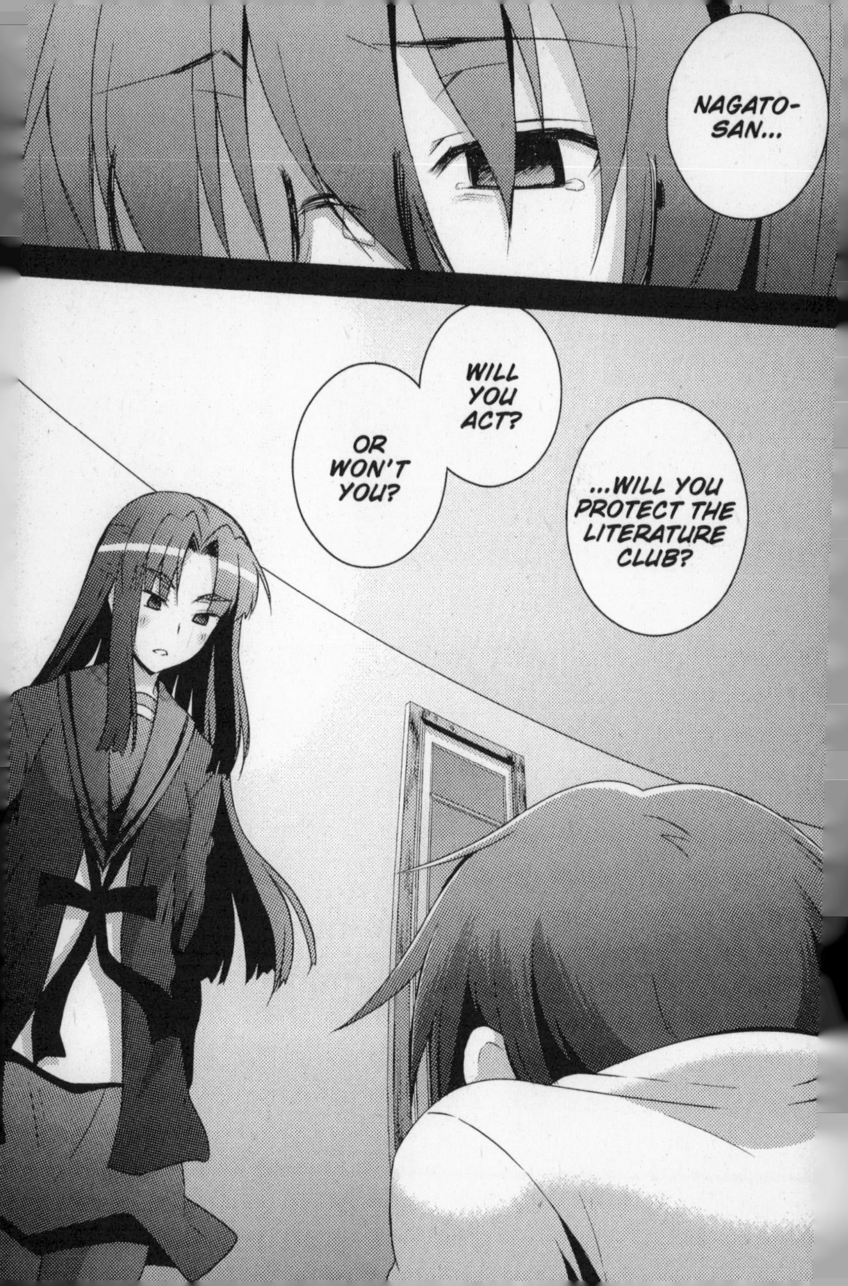
NAGATO-SAN...
WILL YOU ACT?
OR WON'T YOU?
...WILL YOU PROTECT THE LITERATURE CLUB?

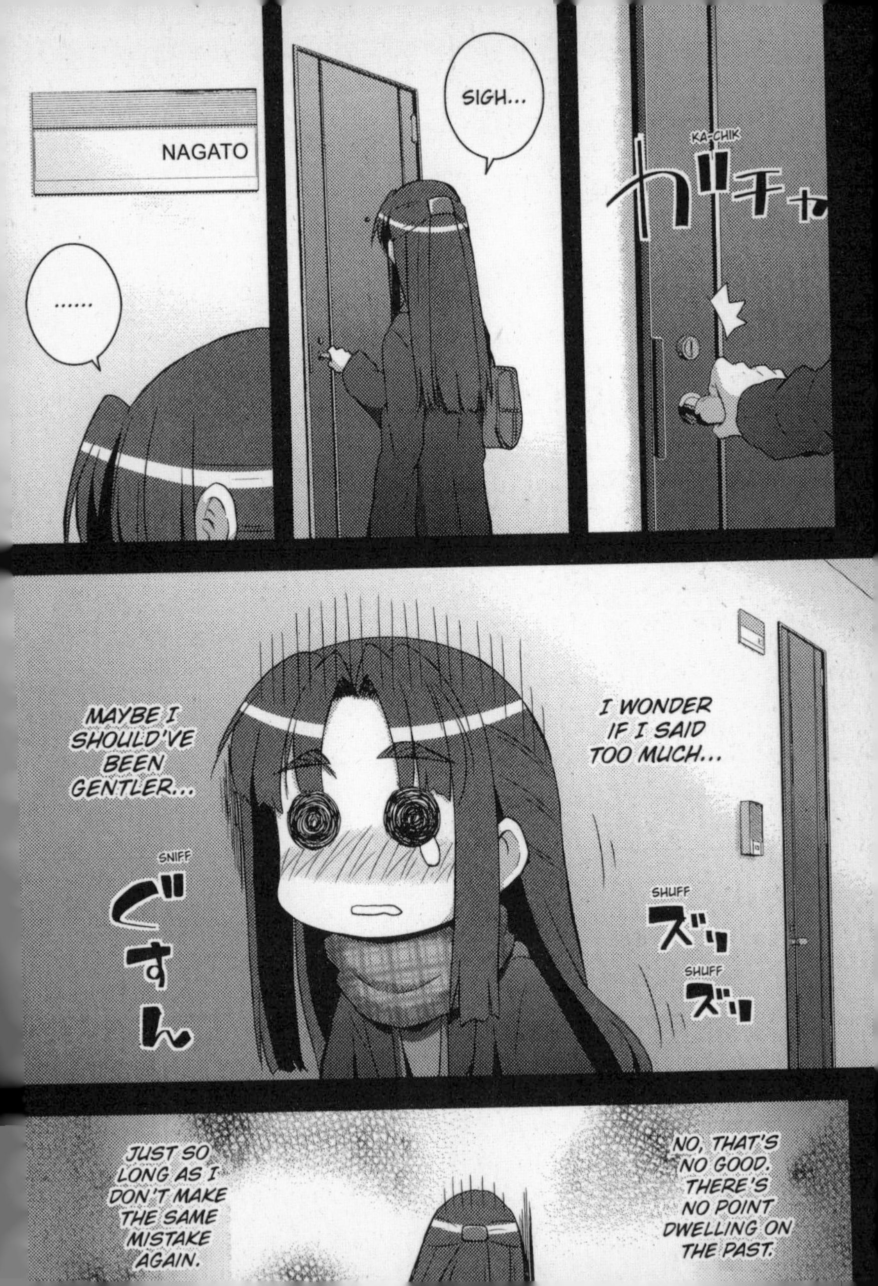
KA-CHIK
カチャ
SIGH...
NAGATO
......
I WONDER IF I SAID TOO MUCH...
SHUFF
ズッ
SHUFF
ズッ
MAYBE I SHOULD'VE BEEN GENTLER...
SNIFF
ぐすん
NO, THAT'S NO GOOD. THERE'S NO POINT DWELLING ON THE PAST.
JUST SO LONG AS I DON'T MAKE THE SAME MISTAKE AGAIN.

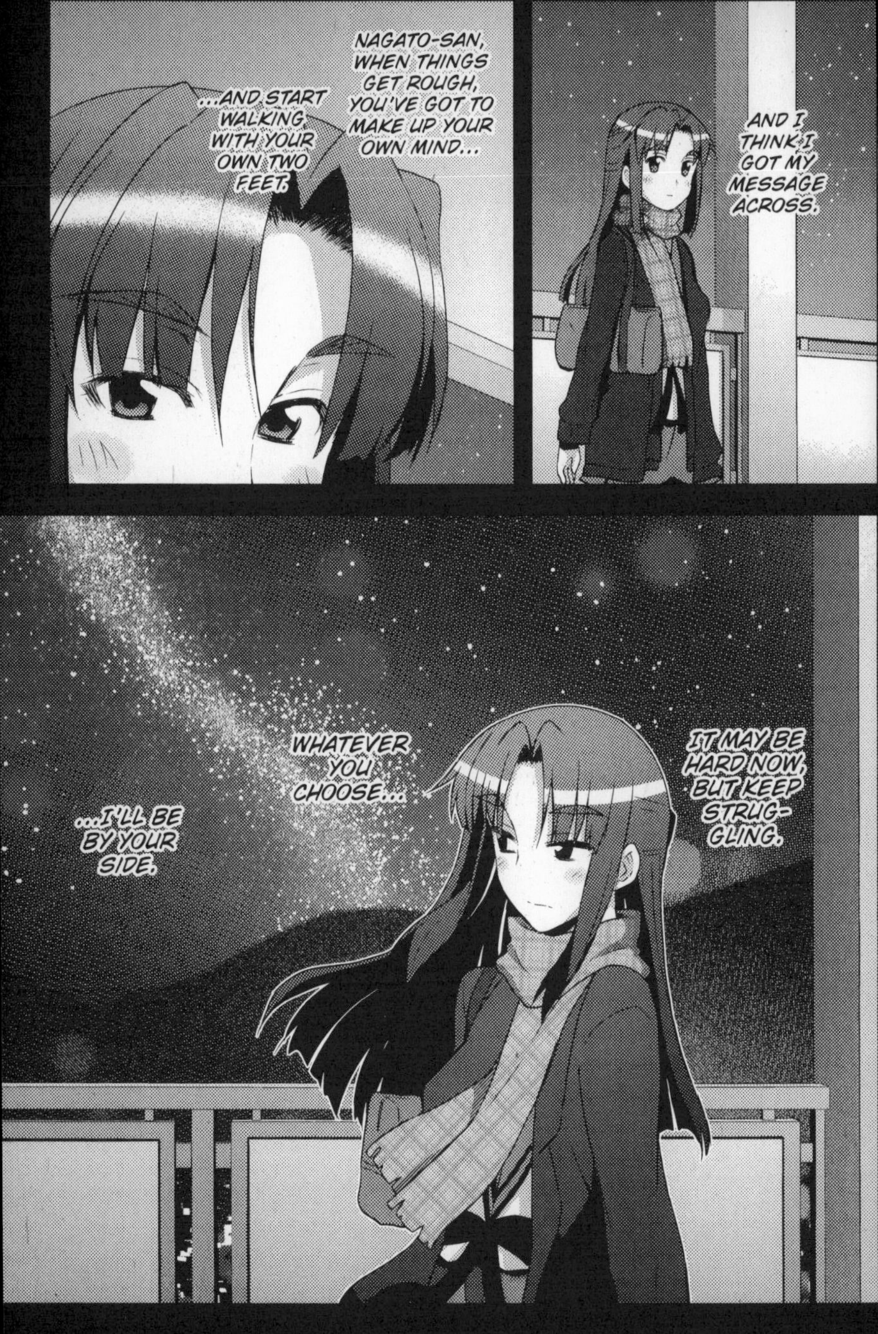
AND I THINK I GOT MY MESSAGE ACROSS.
NAGATO-SAN, WHEN THINGS GET ROUGH, YOU'VE GOT TO MAKE UP YOUR OWN MIND...
...AND START WALKING WITH YOUR OWN TWO FEET.
IT MAY BE HARD NOW, BUT KEEP STRUG-GLING.
WHATEVER YOU CHOOSE...
...I'LL BE BY YOUR SIDE.

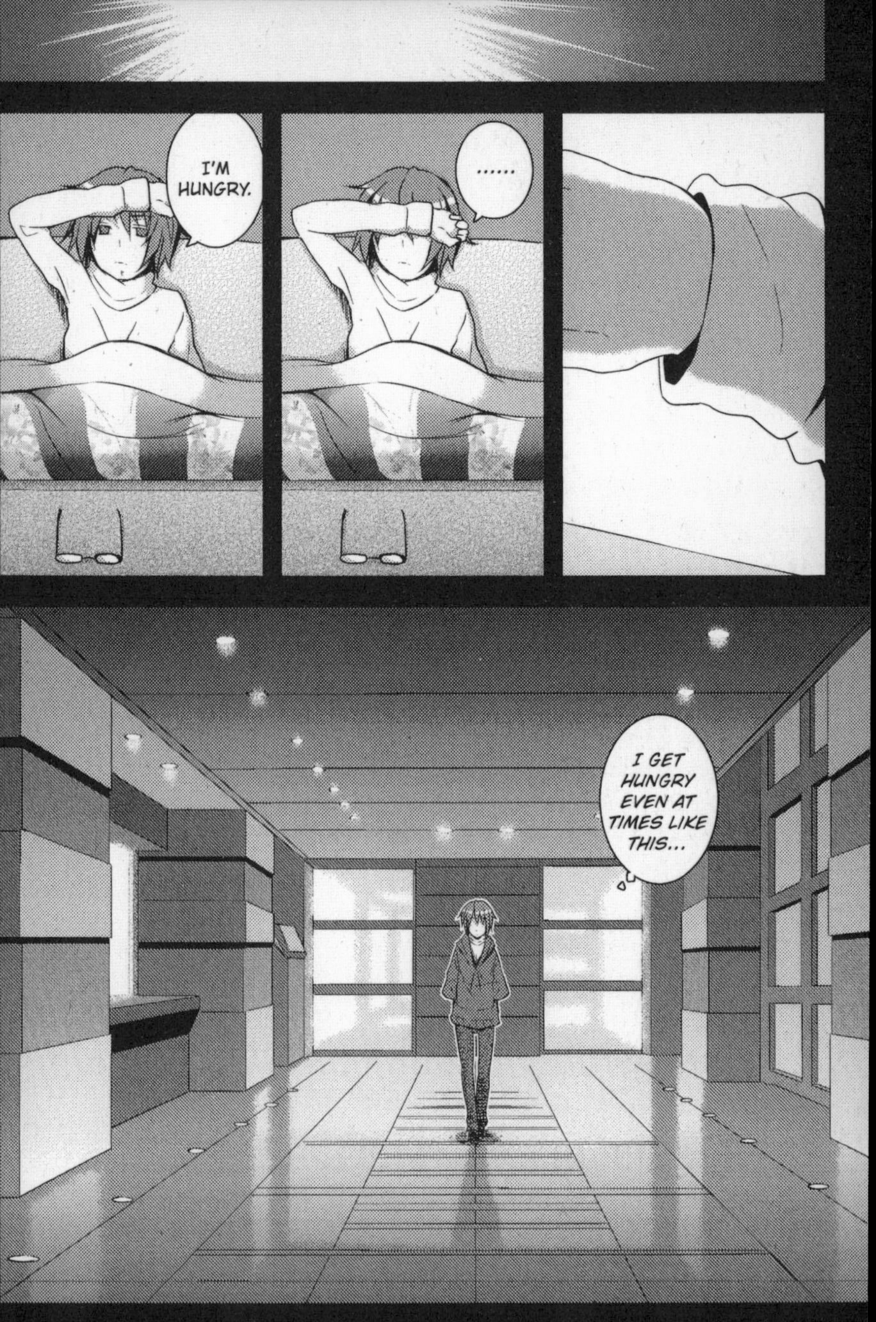
......
I'M HUNGRY.
I GET HUNGRY EVEN AT TIMES LIKE THIS...

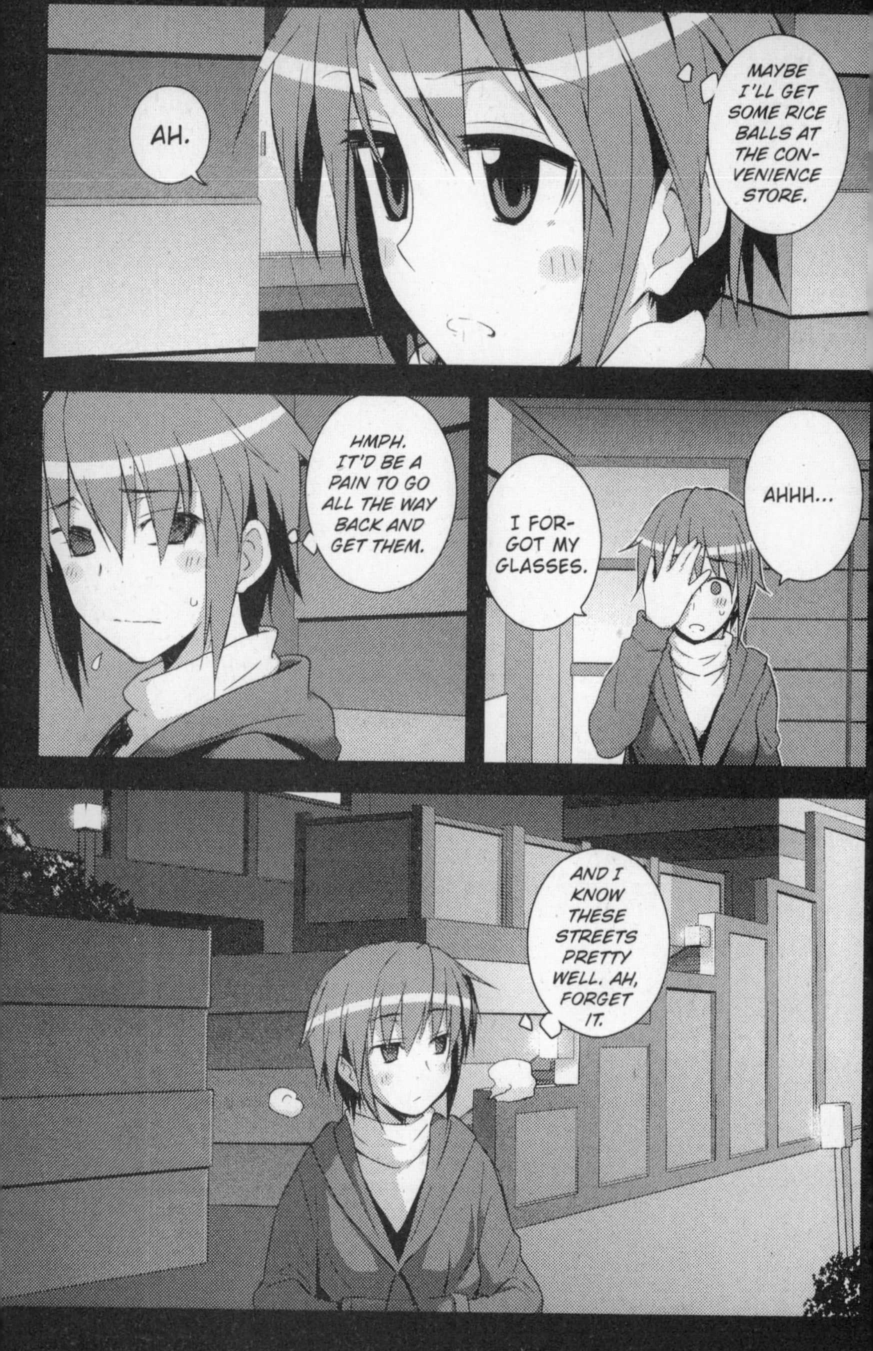
MAYBE I'LL GET SOME RICE BALLS AT THE CON-VENIENCE STORE.
AH.
AHHH...
I FOR-GOT MY GLASSES.
HMPH. IT'D BE A PAIN TO GO ALL THE WAY BACK AND GET THEM.
AND I KNOW THESE STREETS PRETTY WELL. AH, FORGET IT.

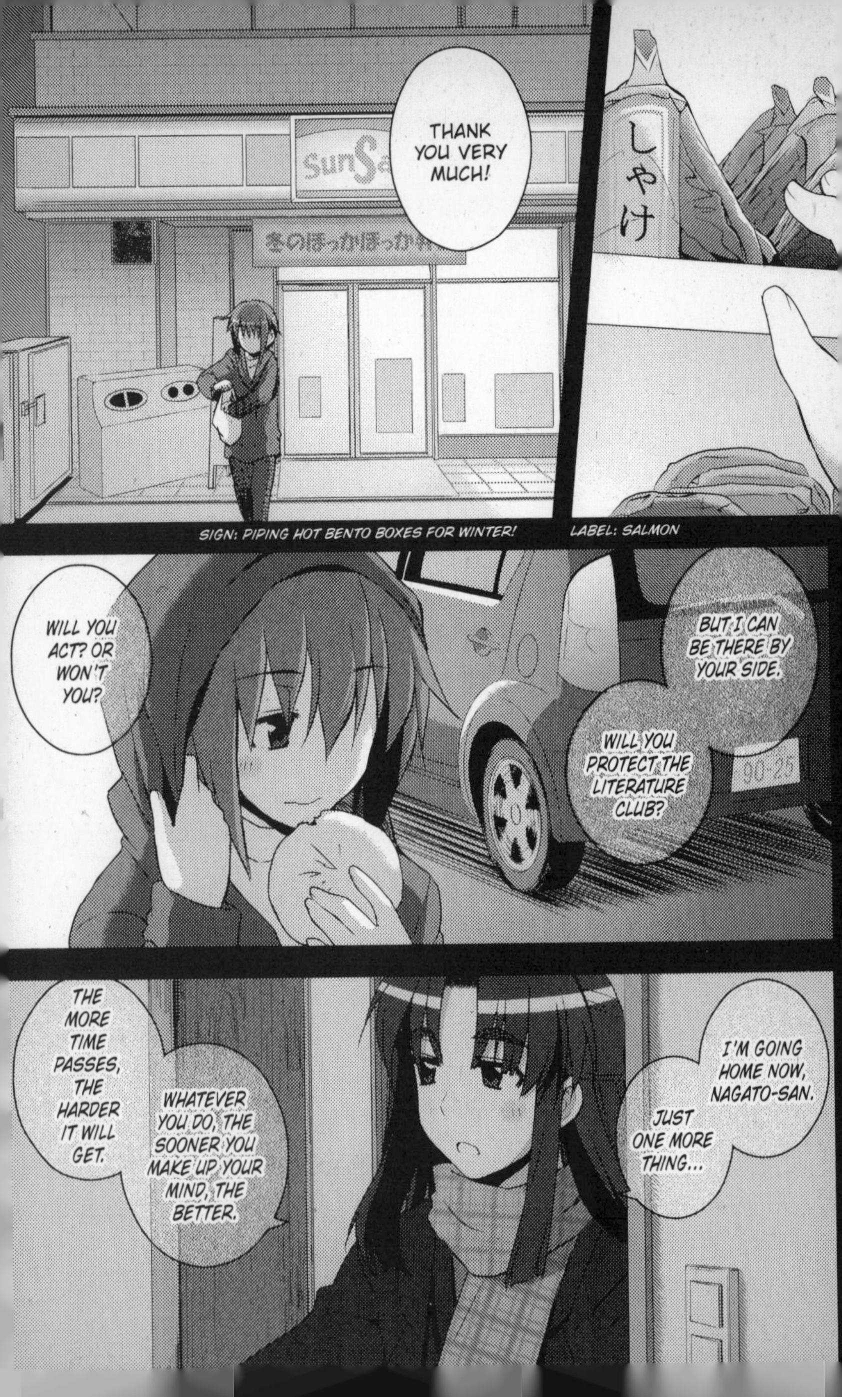
しゃけ
LABEL: SALMON
THANK YOU VERY MUCH!
SIGN: PIPING HOT BENTO BOXES FOR WINTER!
BUT I CAN BE THERE BY YOUR SIDE.
WILL YOU PROTECT THE LITERATURE CLUB?
WILL YOU ACT? OR WON'T YOU?
I'M GOING HOME NOW, NAGATO-SAN.
JUST ONE MORE THING...
WHATEVER YOU DO, THE SOONER YOU MAKE UP YOUR MIND, THE BETTER.
THE MORE TIME PASSES, THE HARDER IT WILL GET.

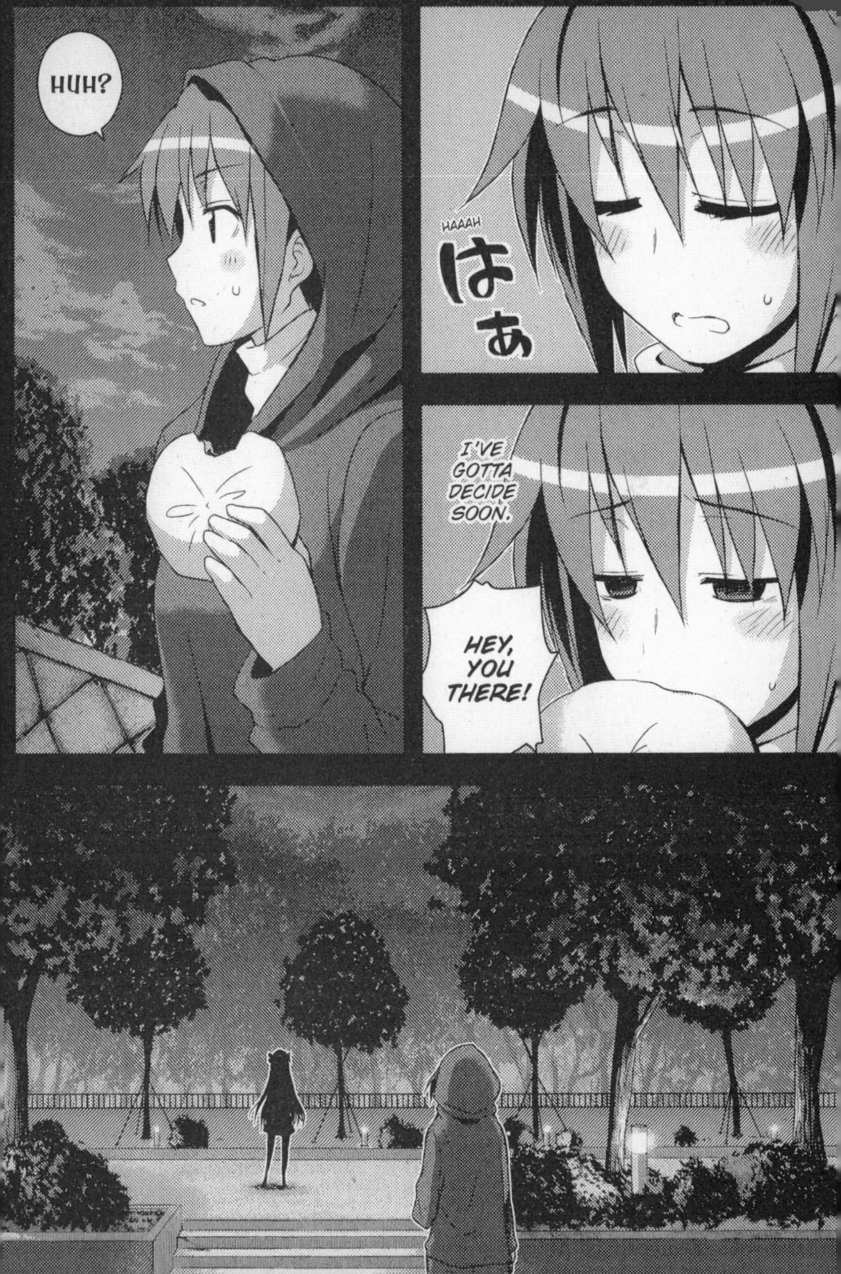
HAAAH
はぁ
I'VE GOTTA DECIDE SOON.
HEY, YOU THERE!
HUH?

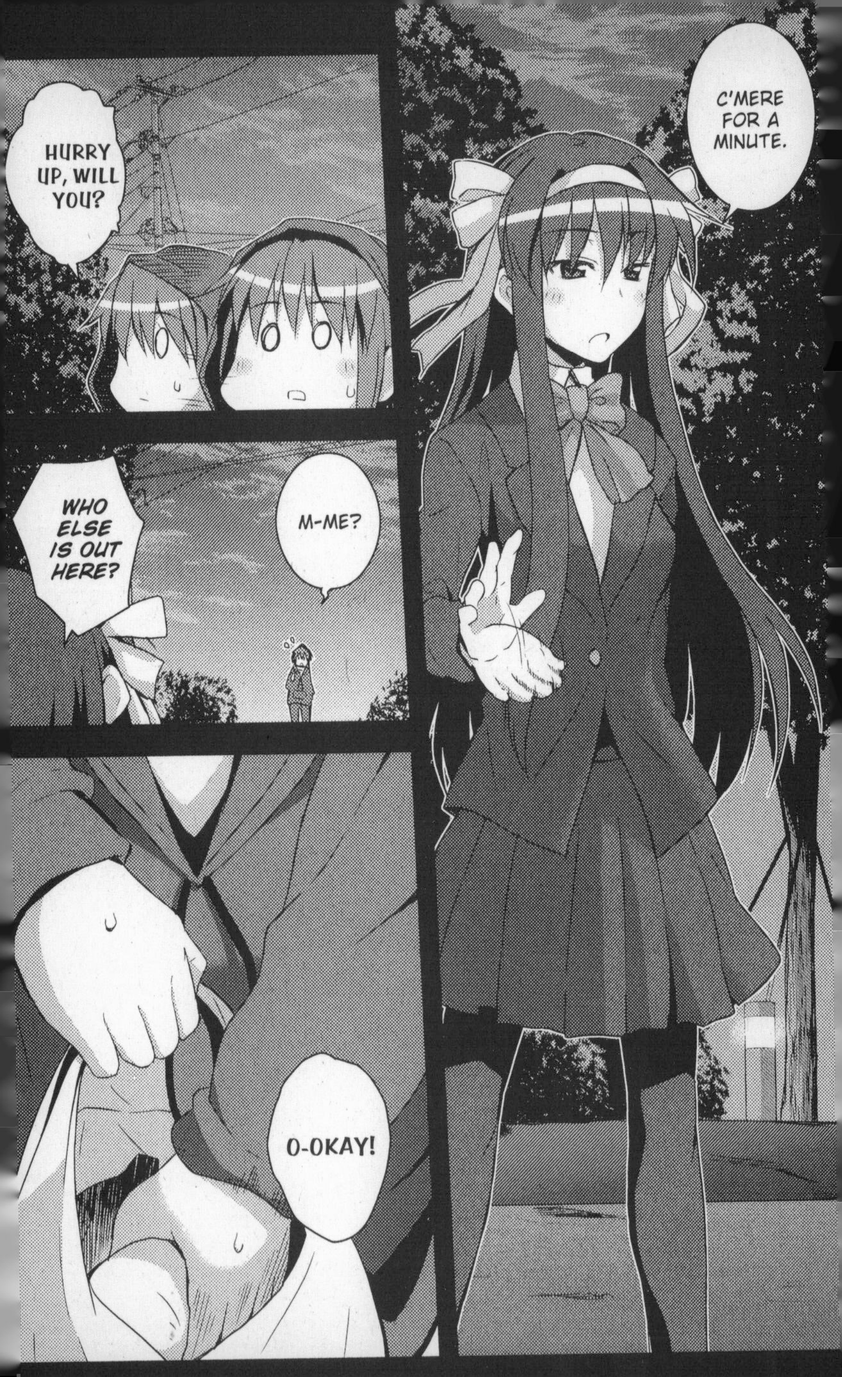
C'MERE FOR A MINUTE.
HURRY UP, WILL YOU?
M-ME?
WHO ELSE IS OUT HERE?
O-OKAY!

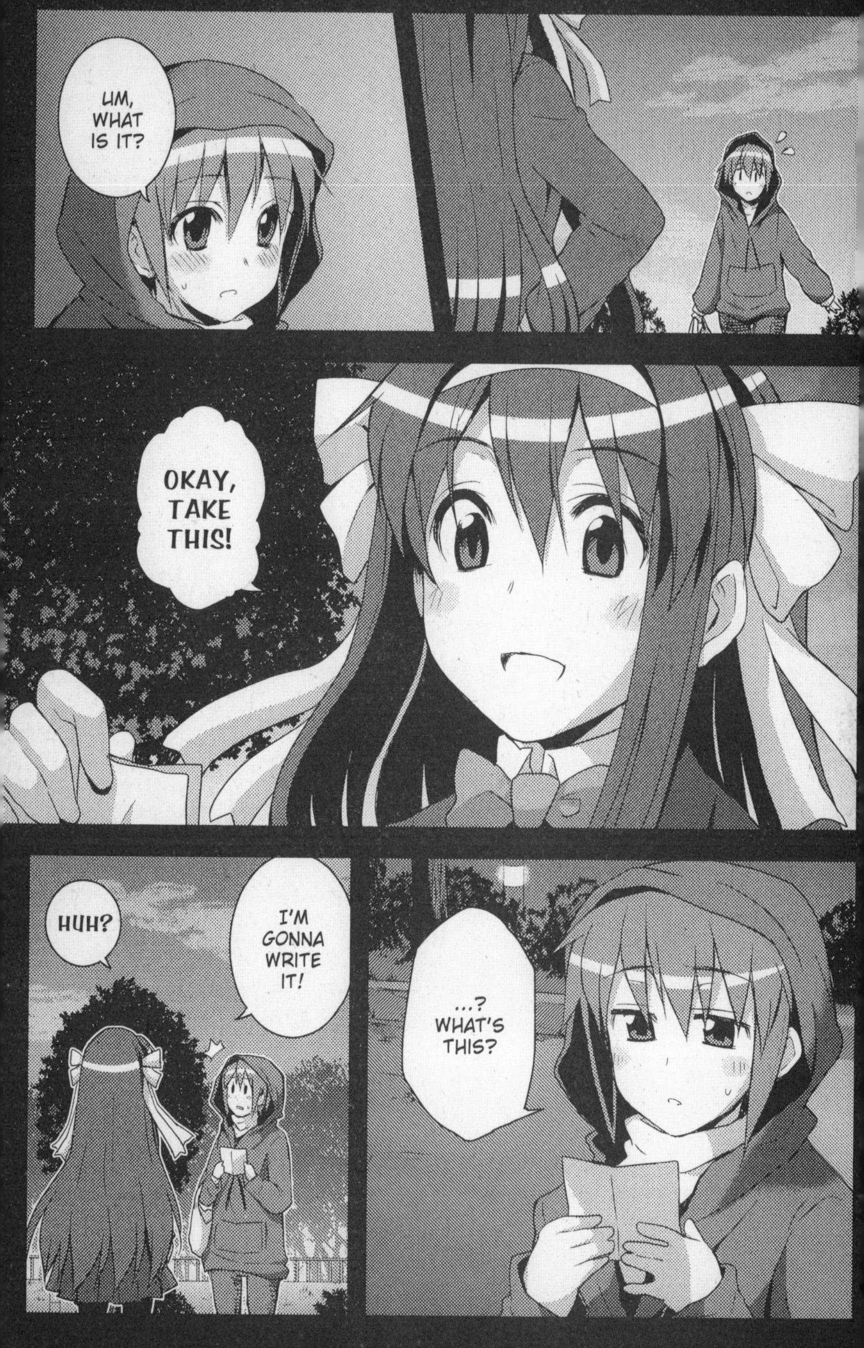
UM, WHAT IS IT?
OKAY, TAKE THIS!
...? WHAT'S THIS?
I'M GONNA WRITE IT!
HUH?

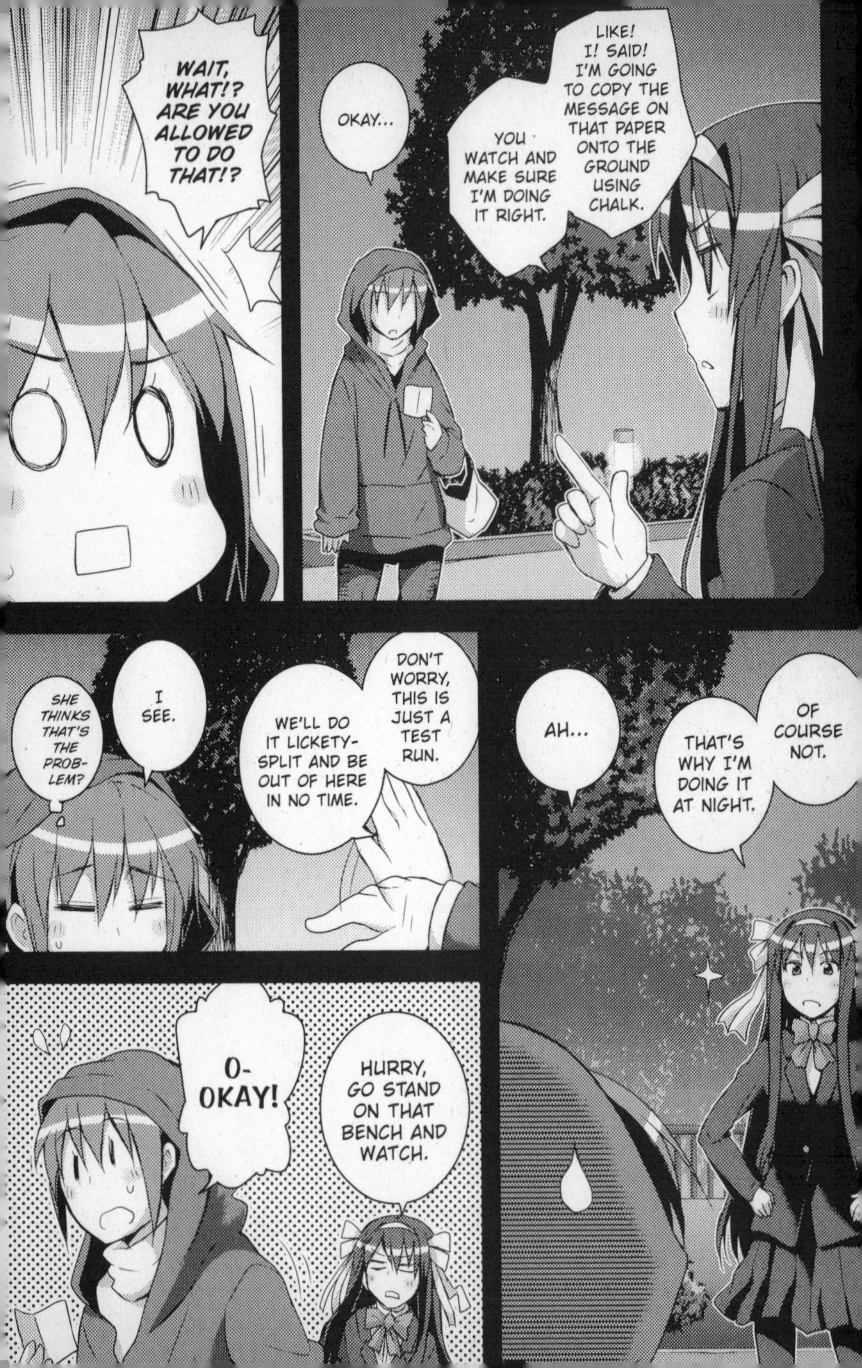
LIKE! I! SAID! I'M GOING TO COPY THE MESSAGE ON THAT PAPER ONTO THE GROUND USING CHALK.
YOU WATCH AND MAKE SURE I'M DOING IT RIGHT.
OKAY...
WAIT, WHAT!? ARE YOU ALLOWED TO DO THAT!?
OF COURSE NOT.
THAT'S WHY I'M DOING IT AT NIGHT.
AH...
DON'T WORRY, THIS IS JUST A TEST RUN.
WE'LL DO IT LICKETY-SPLIT AND BE OUT OF HERE IN NO TIME.
I SEE.
SHE THINKS THAT'S THE PROB-LEM?
HURRY, GO STAND ON THAT BENCH AND WATCH.
O-OKAY!

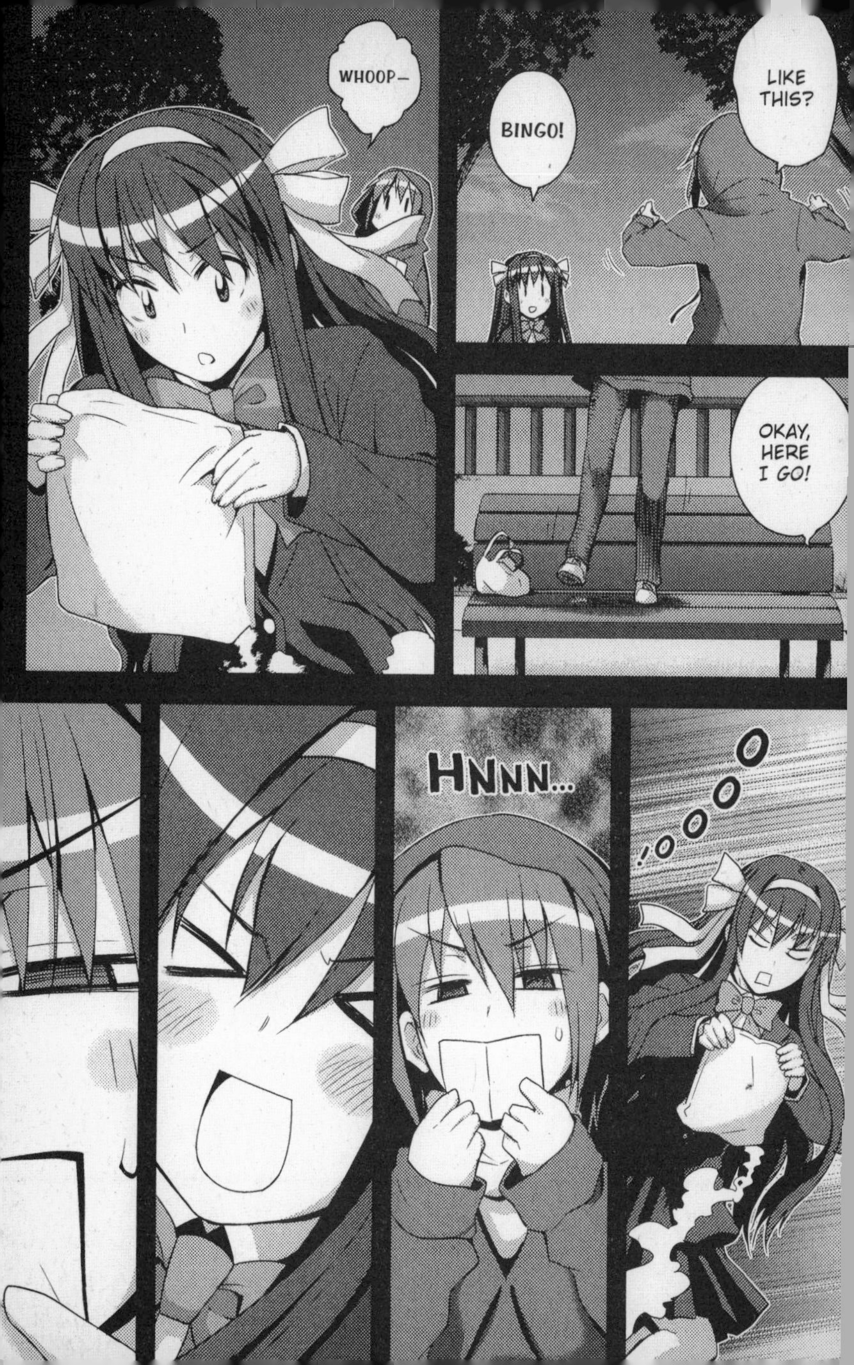
LIKE THIS?
BINGO!
OKAY, HERE I GO!
WHOOP—
HNNN...

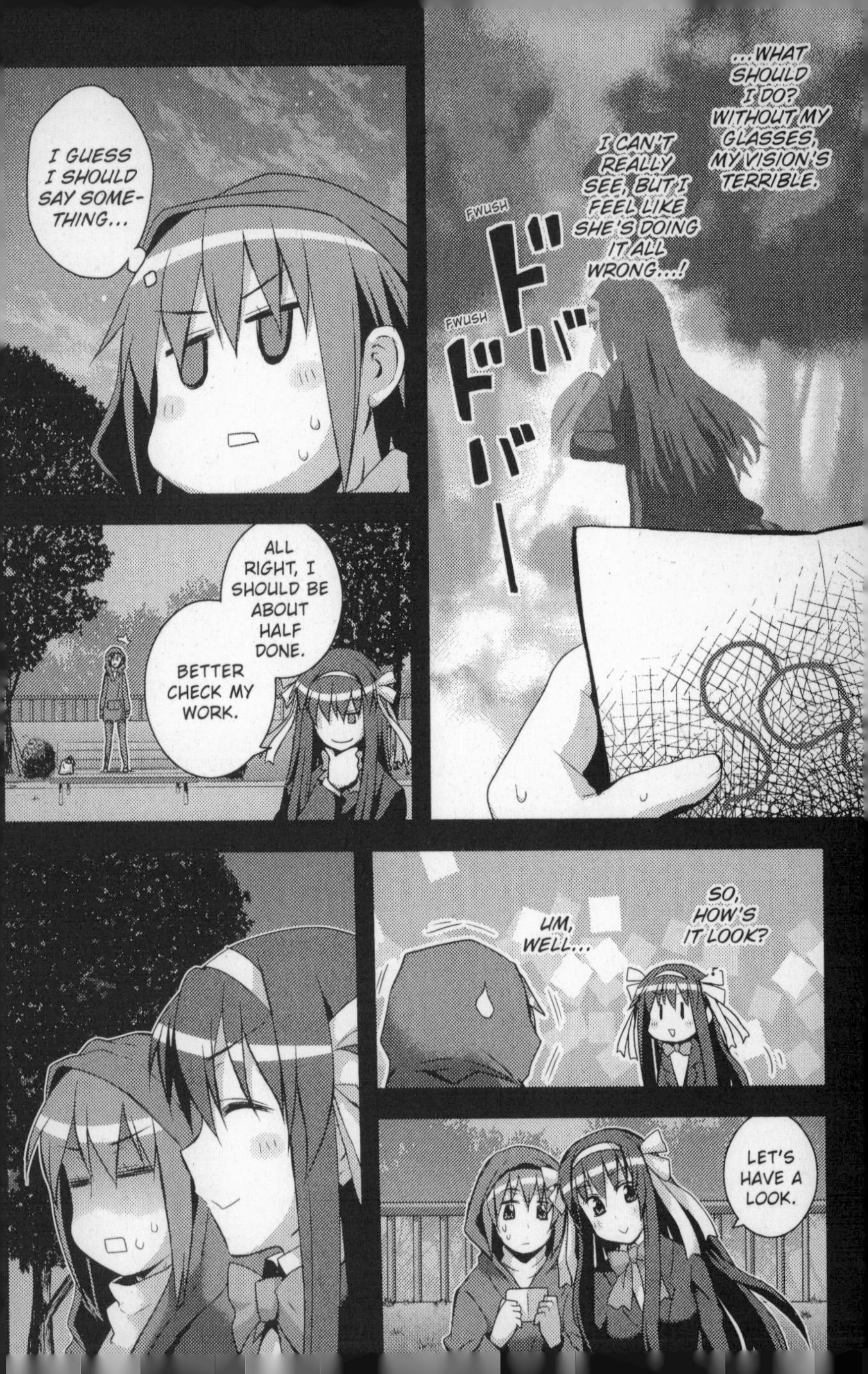
...WHAT SHOULD I DO? WITHOUT MY GLASSES, MY VISION'S TERRIBLE.
I CAN'T REALLY SEE, BUT I FEEL LIKE SHE'S DOING IT ALL WRONG...!
FWUSH
ドバ
FWUSH
ドバー
I GUESS I SHOULD SAY SOME-THING...
ALL RIGHT, I SHOULD BE ABOUT HALF DONE.
BETTER CHECK MY WORK.
SO, HOW'S IT LOOK?
UM, WELL...
LET'S HAVE A LOOK.

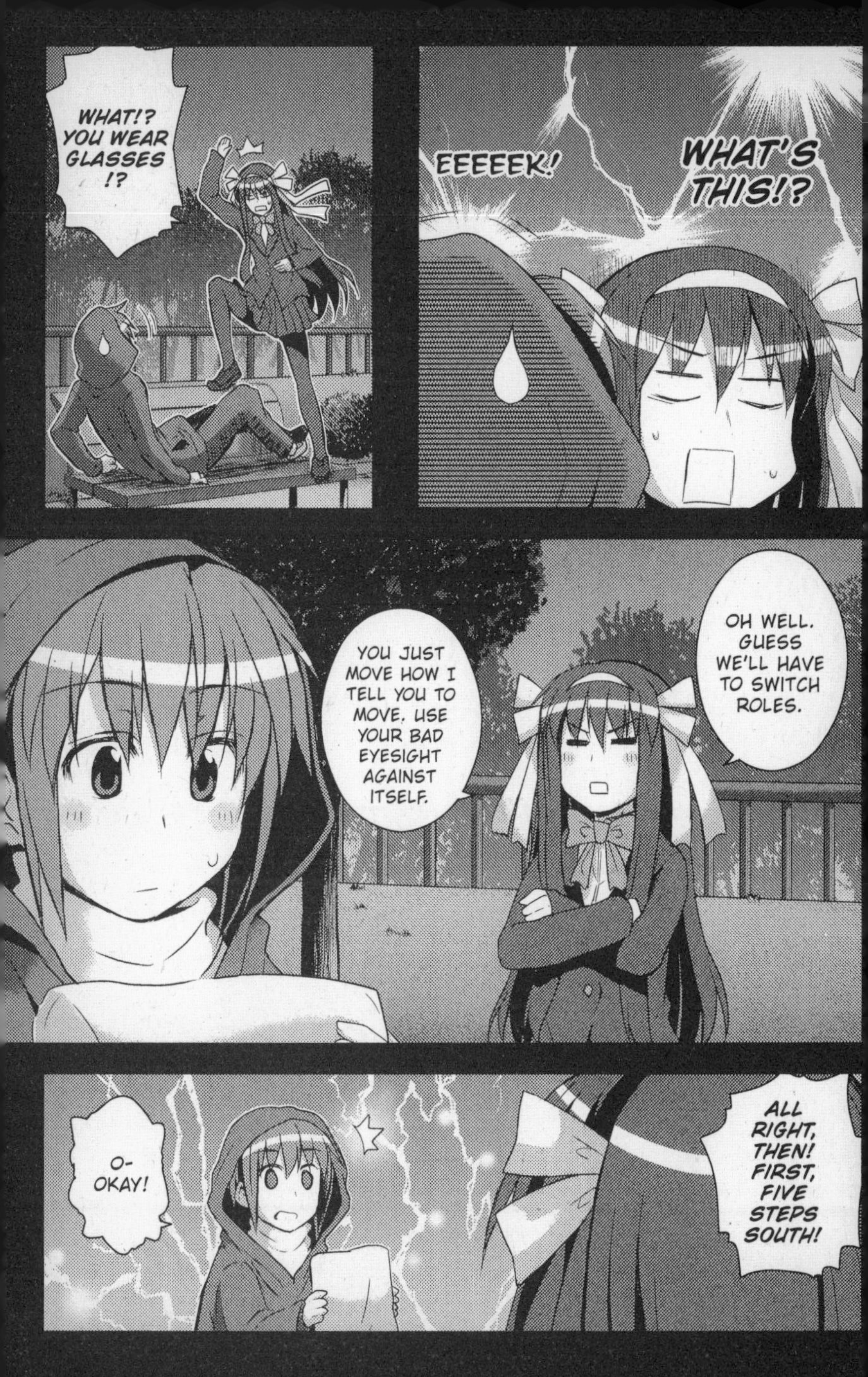
WHAT'S THIS!?
EEEEEK!
WHAT!? YOU WEAR GLASSES!?
OH WELL. GUESS WE'LL HAVE TO SWITCH ROLES.
YOU JUST MOVE HOW I TELL YOU TO MOVE. USE YOUR BAD EYESIGHT AGAINST ITSELF.
ALL RIGHT, THEN! FIRST, FIVE STEPS SOUTH!
O-OKAY!

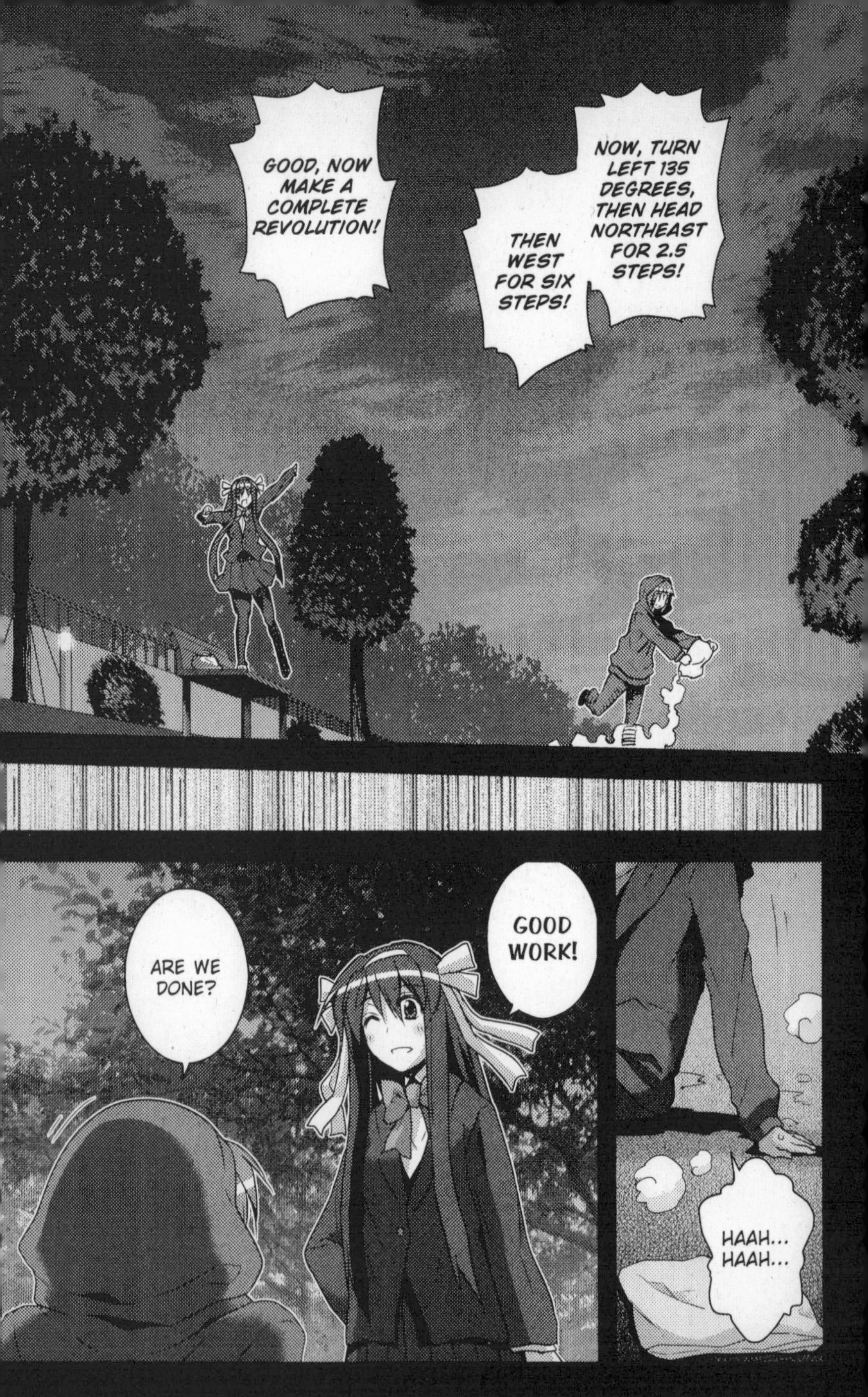
NOW, TURN LEFT 135 DEGREES, THEN HEAD NORTHEAST FOR 2.5 STEPS!
THEN WEST FOR SIX STEPS!
GOOD, NOW MAKE A COMPLETE REVOLUTION!
HAAH... HAAH...
GOOD WORK!
ARE WE DONE?

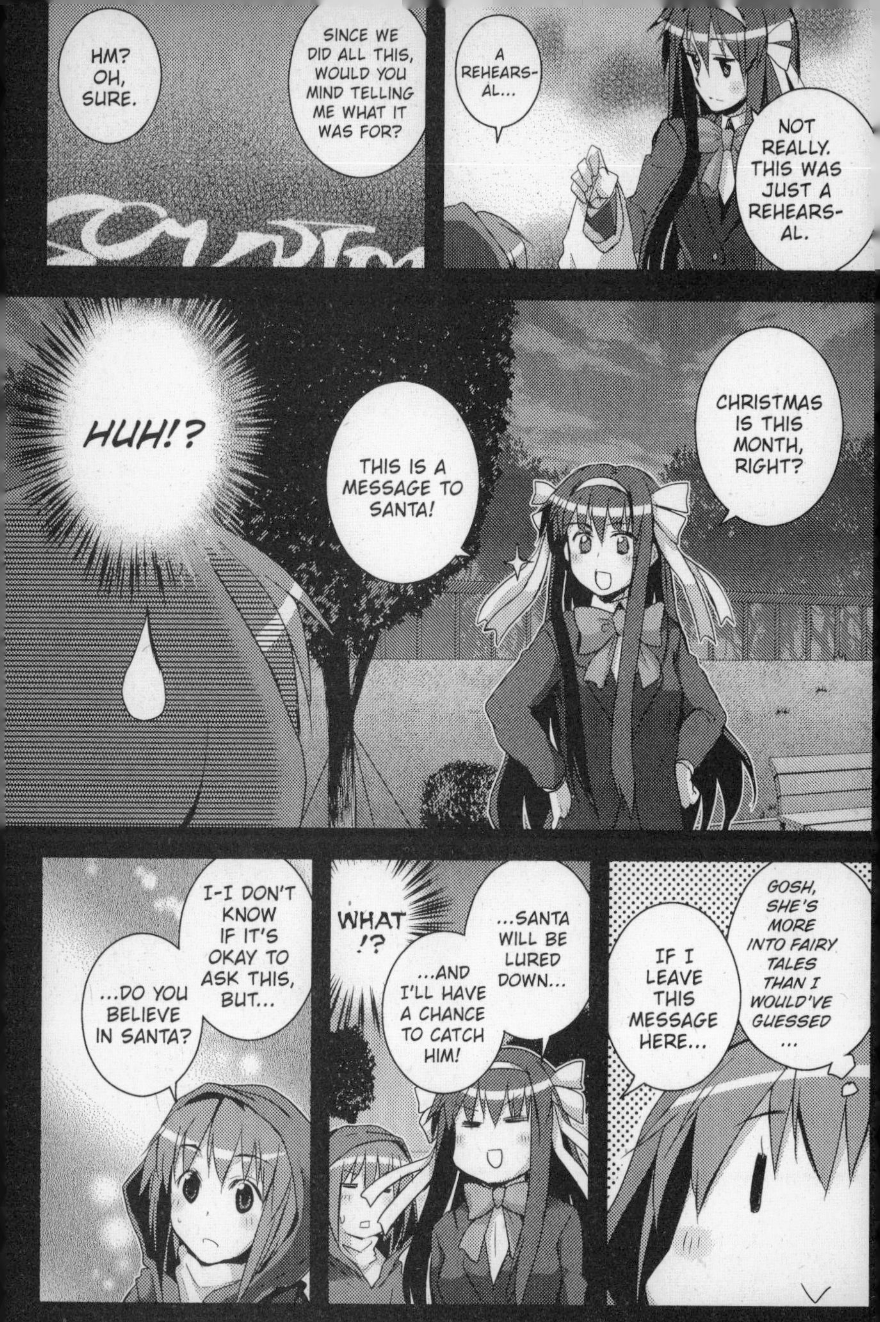
NOT REALLY. THIS WAS JUST A REHEARS-AL.
A REHEARS-AL...
SINCE WE DID ALL THIS, WOULD YOU MIND TELLING ME WHAT IT WAS FOR?
HM? OH, SURE.
CHRISTMAS IS THIS MONTH, RIGHT?
THIS IS A MESSAGE TO SANTA!
HUH!?
GOSH, SHE'S MORE INTO FAIRY TALES THAN I WOULD'VE GUESSED...
IF I LEAVE THIS MESSAGE HERE...
...SANTA WILL BE LURED DOWN...
...AND I'LL HAVE A CHANCE TO CATCH HIM!
WHAT!?
I-I DON'T KNOW IF IT'S OKAY TO ASK THIS, BUT...
...DO YOU BELIEVE IN SANTA?

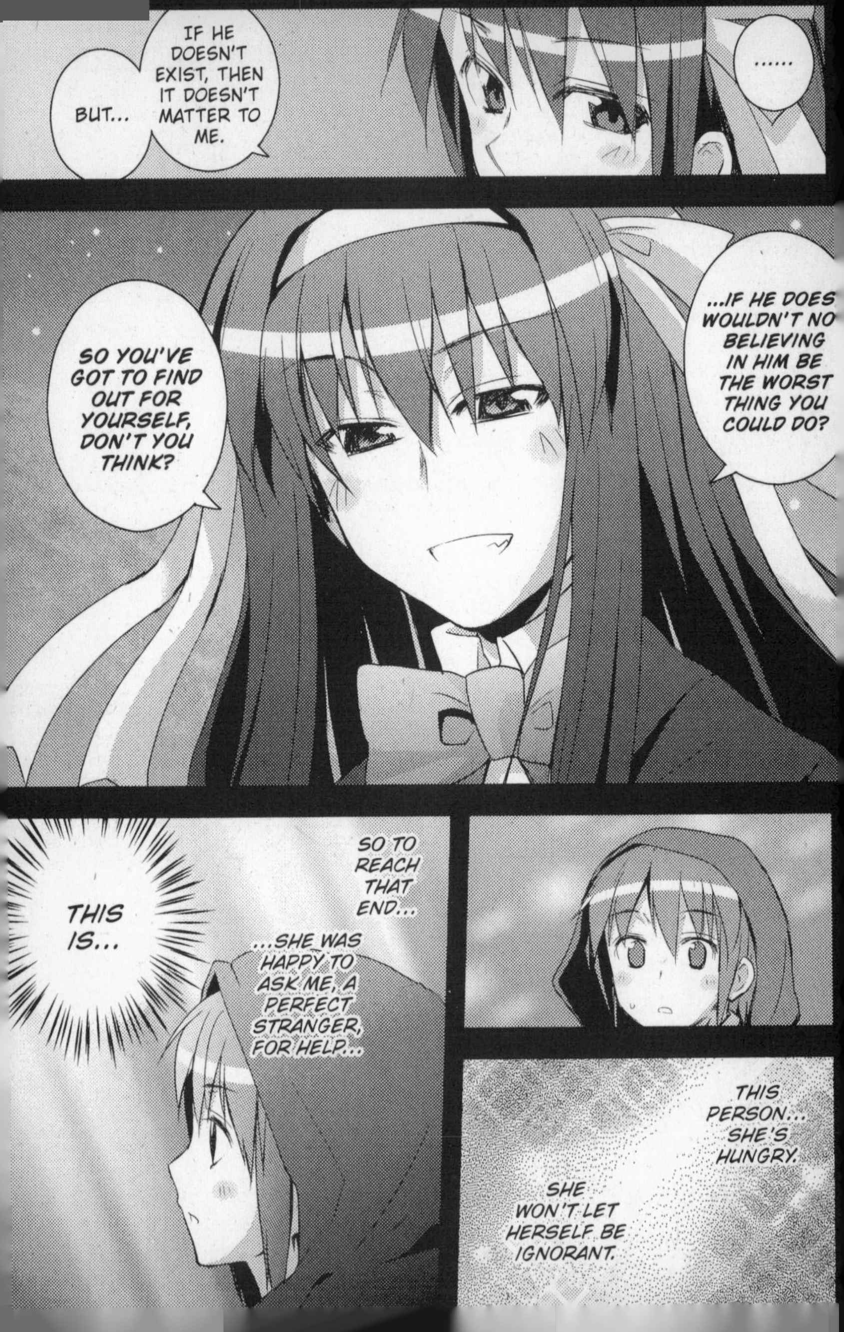
......
IF HE DOESN'T EXIST, THEN IT DOESN'T MATTER TO ME.
BUT...
...IF HE DOES WOULDN'T NO BELIEVING IN HIM BE THE WORST THING YOU COULD DO?
SO YOU'VE GOT TO FIND OUT FOR YOURSELF, DON'T YOU THINK?
THIS PERSON... SHE'S HUNGRY.
SHE WON'T LET HERSELF BE IGNORANT.
SO TO REACH THAT END...
...SHE WAS HAPPY TO ASK ME, A PERFECT STRANGER, FOR HELP...
THIS IS...

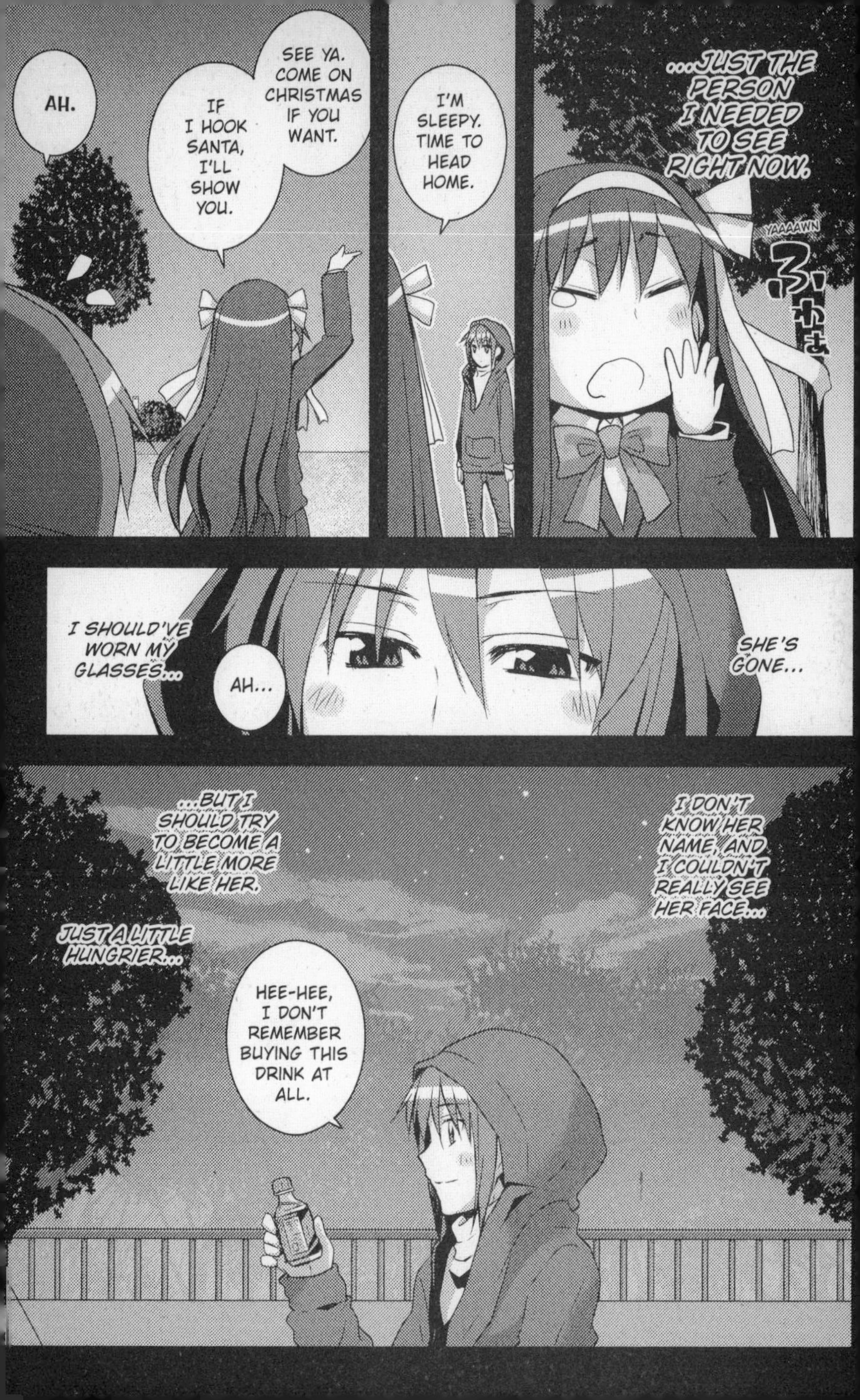
...JUST THE PERSON I NEEDED TO SEE RIGHT NOW.
YAAAAWN
I'M SLEEPY. TIME TO HEAD HOME.
SEE YA. COME ON CHRISTMAS IF YOU WANT.
IF I HOOK SANTA, I'LL SHOW YOU.
AH.
SHE'S GONE...
AH...
I SHOULD'VE WORN MY GLASSES...
I DON'T KNOW HER NAME, AND I COULDN'T REALLY SEE HER FACE...
...BUT I SHOULD TRY TO BECOME A LITTLE MORE LIKE HER.
JUST A LITTLE HUNGRIER...
HEE-HEE, I DON'T REMEMBER BUYING THIS DRINK AT ALL.

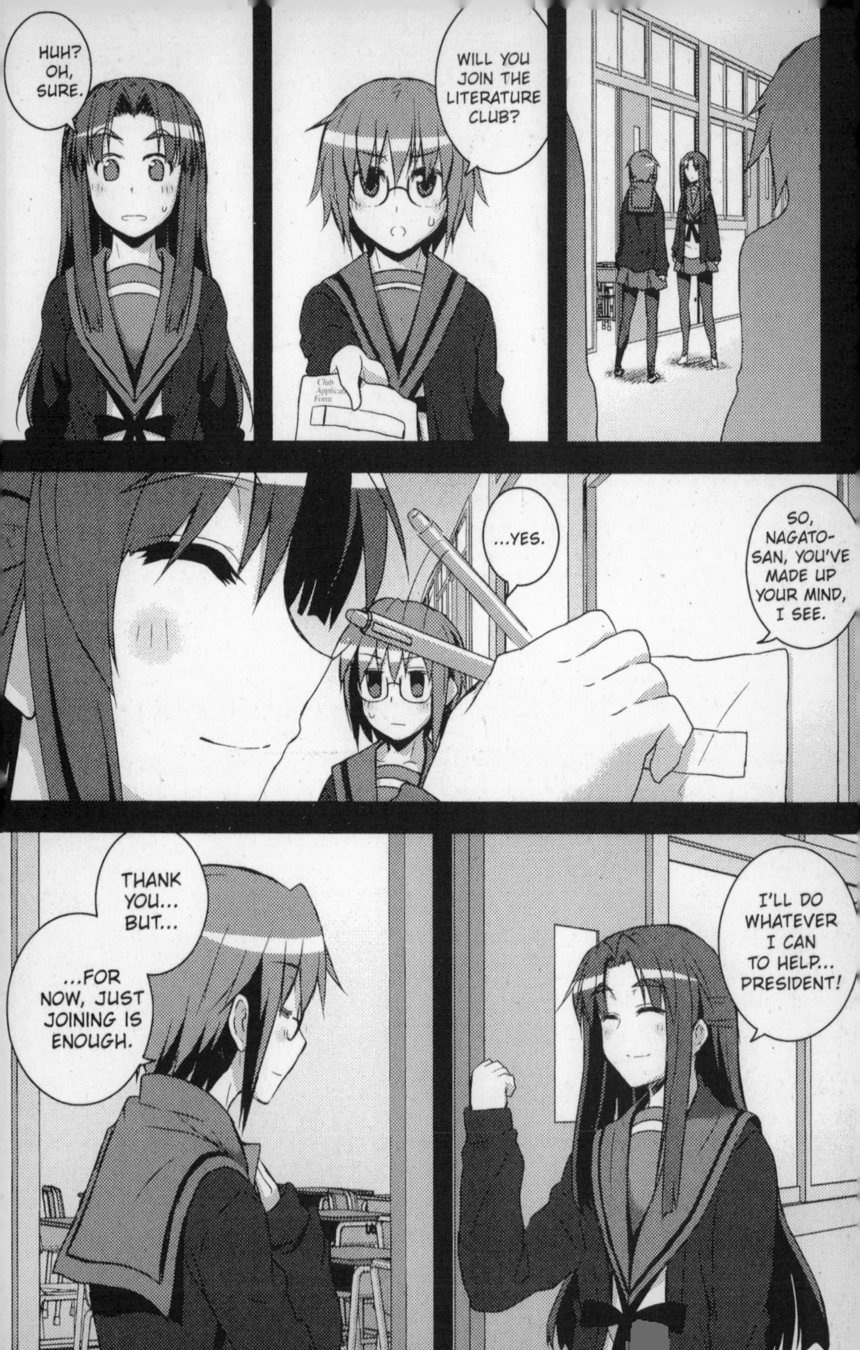
WILL YOU JOIN THE LITERATURE CLUB?
HUH? OH, SURE.
SO, NAGATO-SAN, YOU'VE MADE UP YOUR MIND, I SEE.
...YES.
I'LL DO WHATEVER I CAN TO HELP... PRESIDENT!
THANK YOU... BUT...
...FOR NOW, JUST JOINING IS ENOUGH.

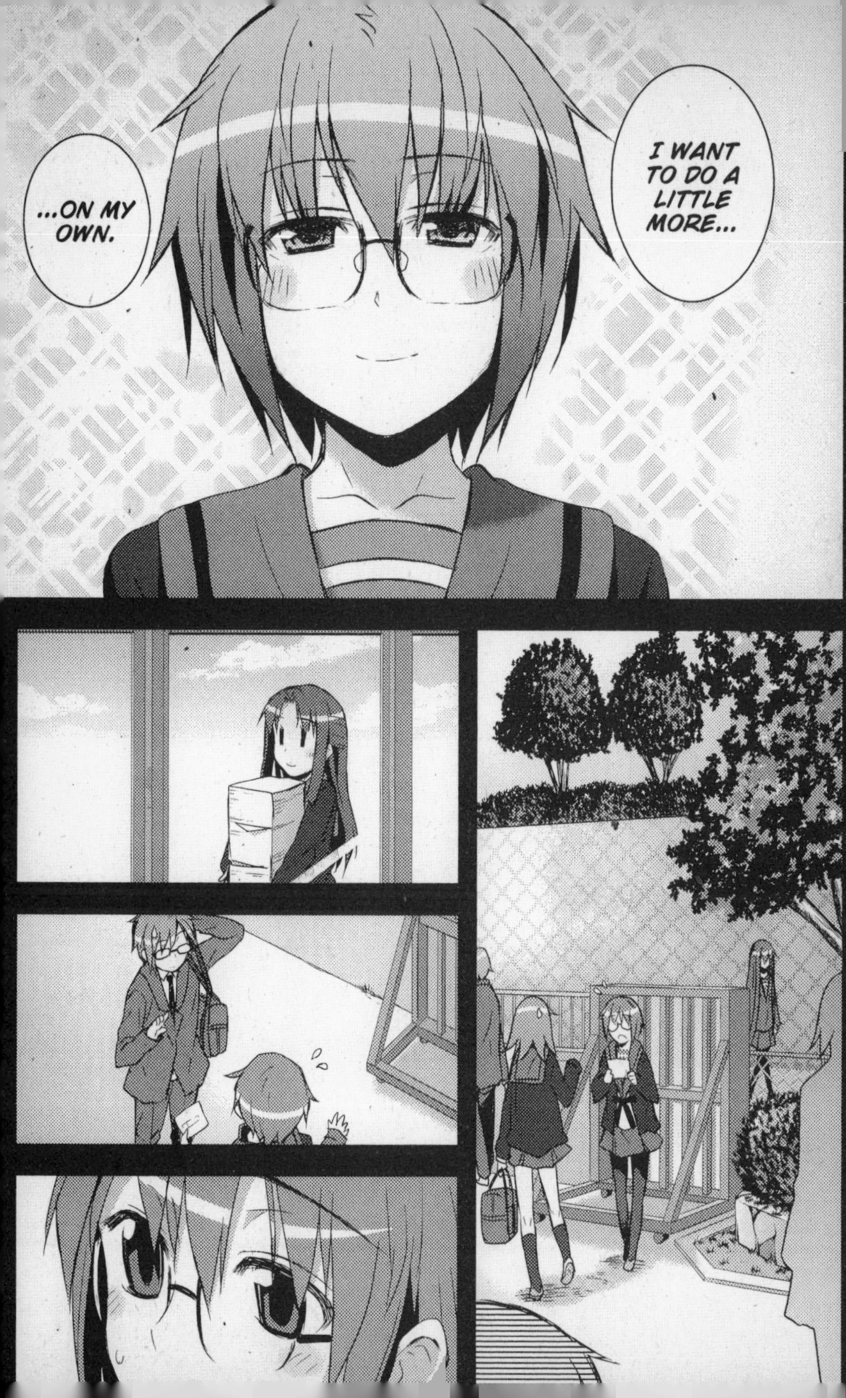
I WANT TO DO A LITTLE MORE...
...ON MY OWN.

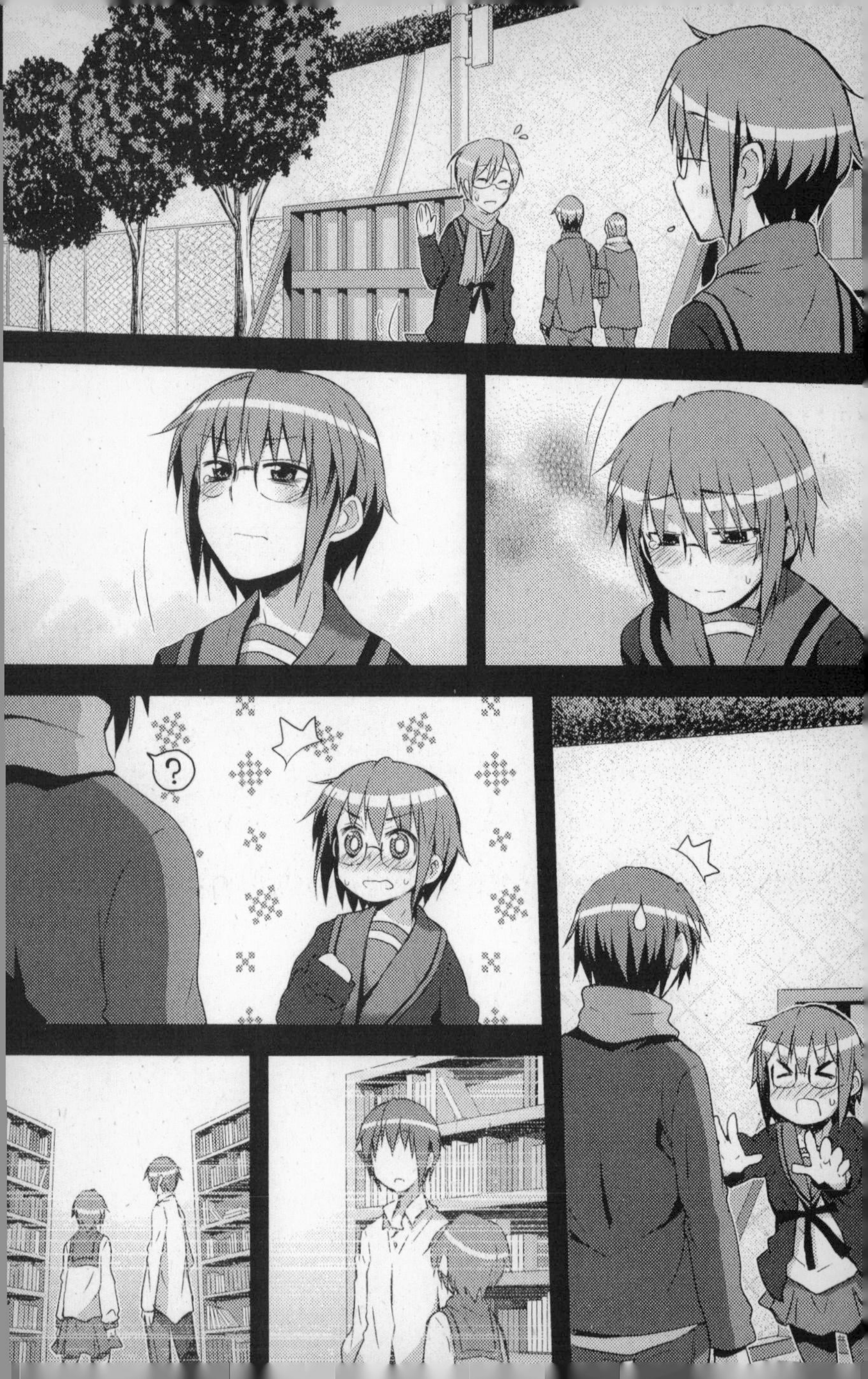
?

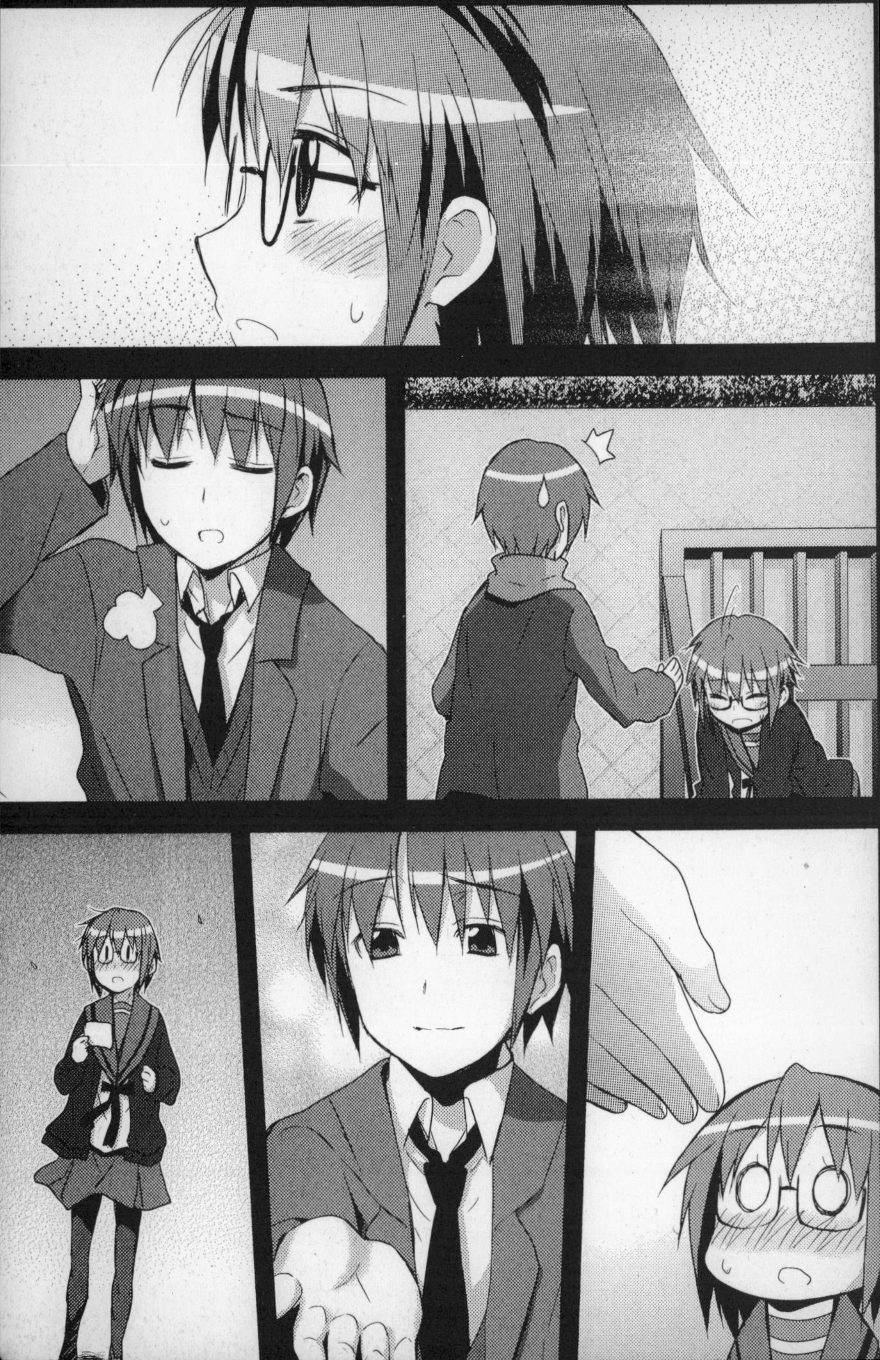

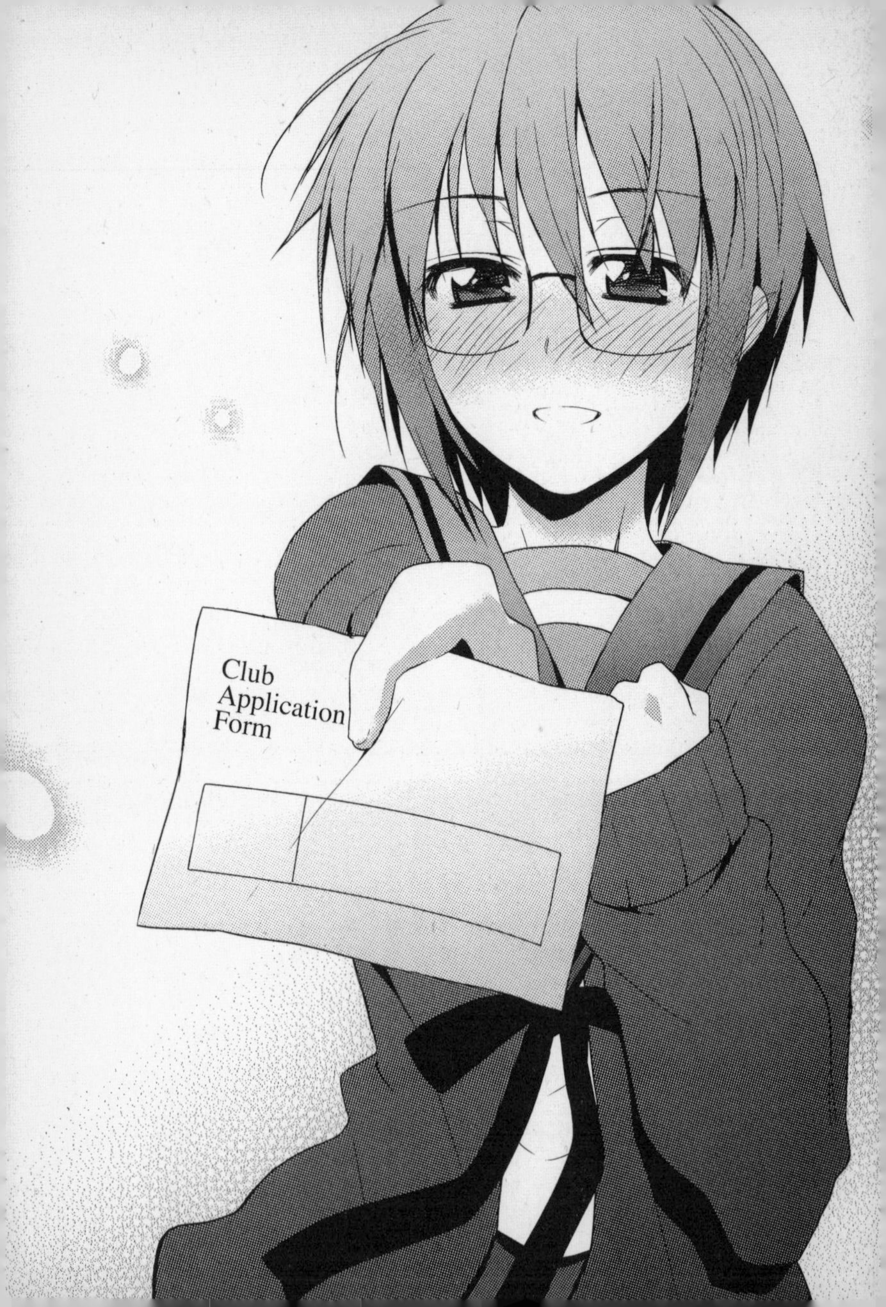
Club
Application
Form

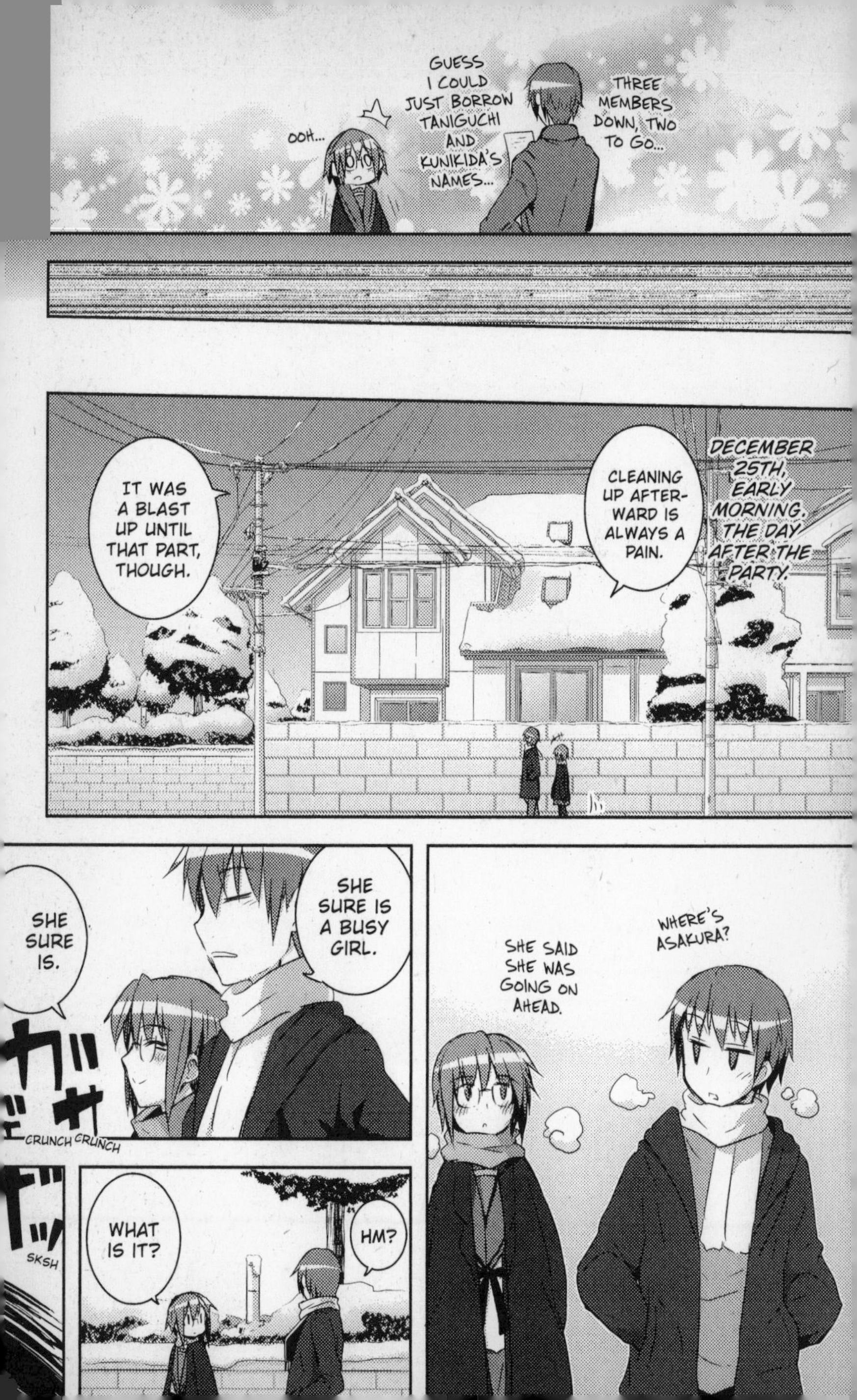
THREE MEMBERS DOWN, TWO TO GO...
GUESS I COULD JUST BORROW TANIGUCHI AND KUNIKIDA'S NAMES...
OOH...
DECEMBER 25TH, EARLY MORNING. THE DAY AFTER THE PARTY.
CLEANING UP AFTER-WARD IS ALWAYS A PAIN.
IT WAS A BLAST UP UNTIL THAT PART, THOUGH.
WHERE'S ASAKURA?
SHE SAID SHE WAS GOING ON AHEAD.
SHE SURE IS A BUSY GIRL.
SHE SURE IS.
CRUNCH CRUNCH
HM?
WHAT IS IT?
SKSH

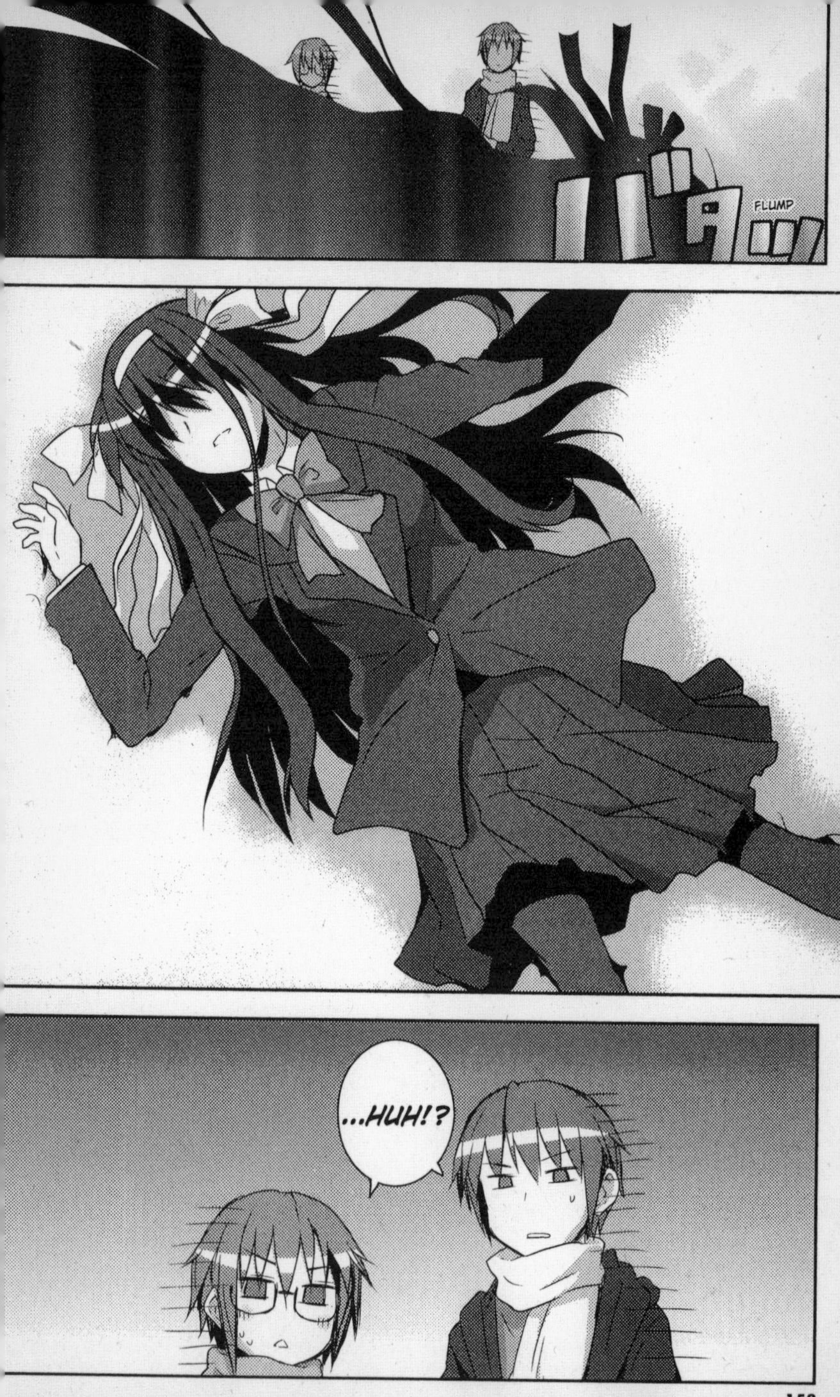
FLUMP
...HUH!?

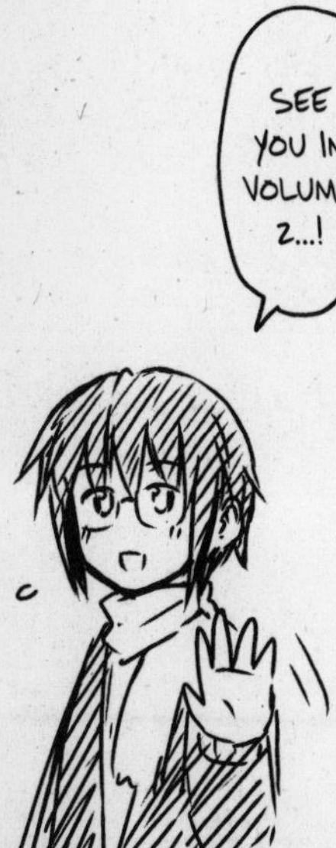
SEE YOU IN VOLUME 2...!

The Disappearance of Nagato Yuki-chan BONUS MATERIAL

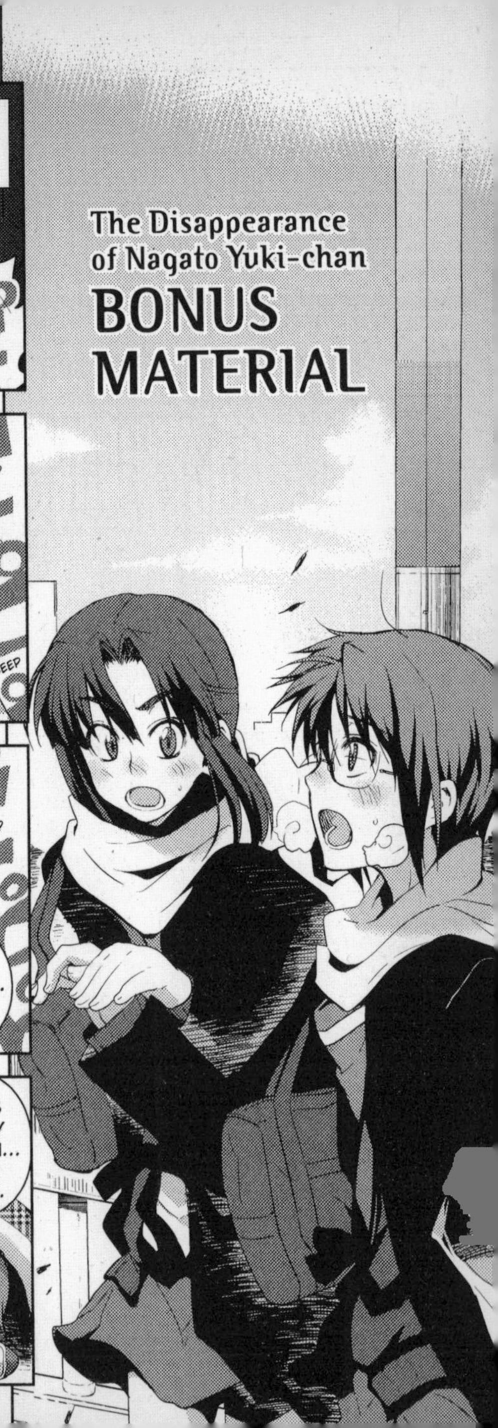

NAKED EYE

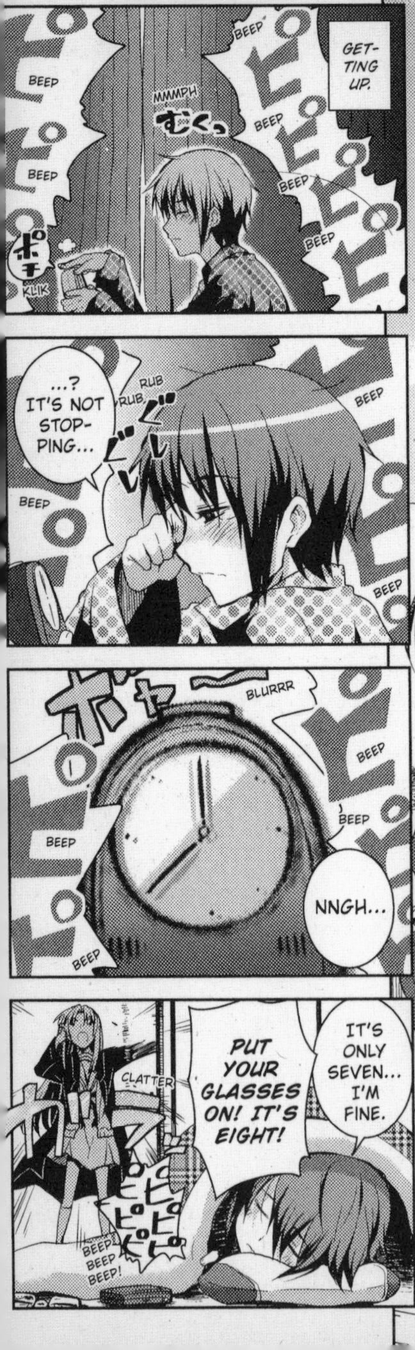
GET-TING UP.
BEEP
MMMPH
むくっ
BEEP
BEEP
BEEP
BEEP
BEEP
ポチ
KLIK
BEEP
RUB RUB
...? IT'S NOT STOP-PING...
BEEP
BEEP
BLURRR
BEEP
BEEP
BEEP
NNGH...
BEEP
IT'S ONLY SEVEN... I'M FINE.
PUT YOUR GLASSES ON! IT'S EIGHT!
CLATTER
BEEP! BEEP! BEEP!

FORGOTTEN ITEMS

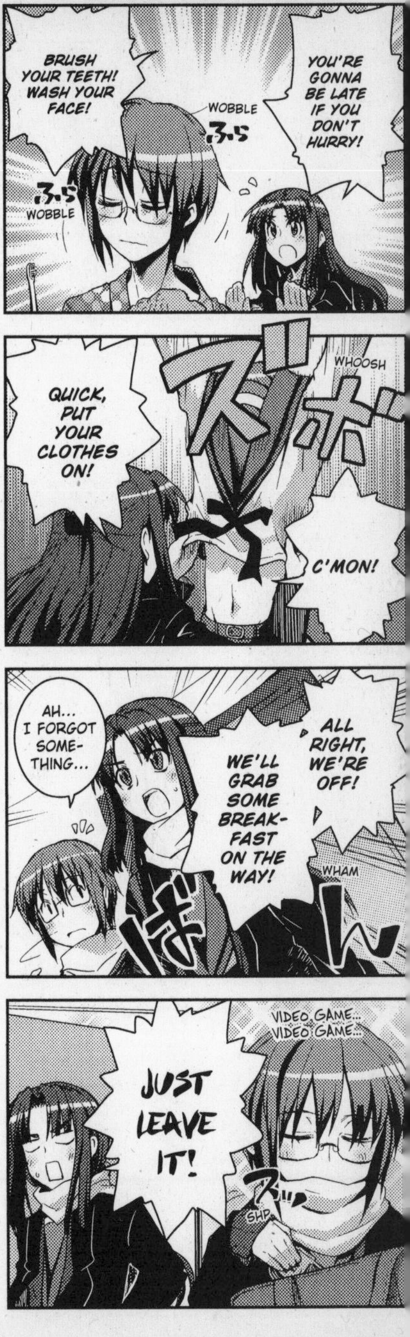
YOU'RE GONNA BE LATE IF YOU DON'T HURRY!
BRUSH YOUR TEETH! WASH YOUR FACE!
WOBBLE
WOBBLE
WHOOSH
QUICK, PUT YOUR CLOTHES ON!
C'MON!
ALL RIGHT, WE'RE OFF!
WE'LL GRAB SOME BREAKFAST ON THE WAY!
AH... I FORGOT SOMETHING...
WHAM
VIDEO GAME... VIDEO GAME...
JUST LEAVE IT!
SHP

PARENT

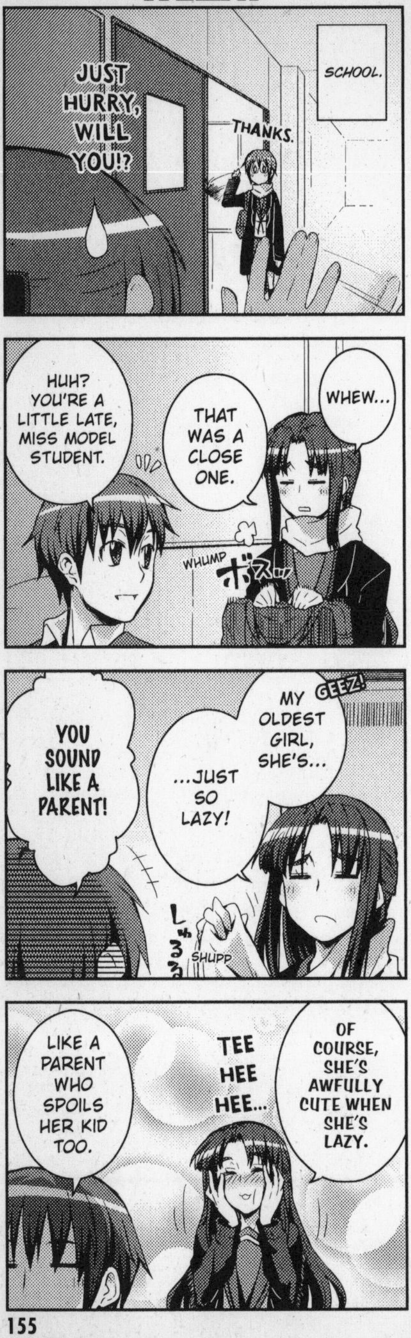
SCHOOL.
THANKS.
JUST HURRY, WILL YOU!?
WHEW...
THAT WAS A CLOSE ONE.
HUH? YOU'RE A LITTLE LATE, MISS MODEL STUDENT.
WHUMP
GEEZ!
MY OLDEST GIRL, SHE'S...
...JUST SO LAZY!
YOU SOUND LIKE A PARENT!
SHUPP
OF COURSE, SHE'S AWFULLY CUTE WHEN SHE'S LAZY.
TEE HEE HEE...
LIKE A PARENT WHO SPOILS HER KID TOO.

HARUHI-CHAN'S BUTLER

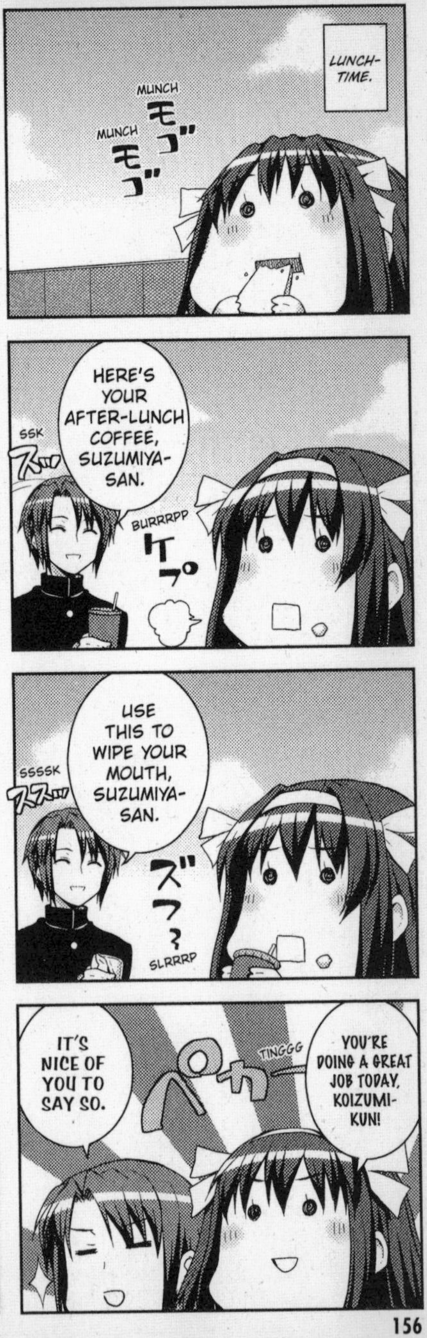
LUNCH-TIME.
MUNCH
MUNCH
HERE'S YOUR AFTER-LUNCH COFFEE, SUZUMIYA-SAN.
SSK
BURRRPP
USE THIS TO WIPE YOUR MOUTH, SUZUMIYA-SAN.
SSSSK
SLRRRP
YOU'RE DOING A GREAT JOB TODAY, KOIZUMI-KUN!
TINGGG
IT'S NICE OF YOU TO SAY SO.

MIKURU-CHAN'S BODYGUARD

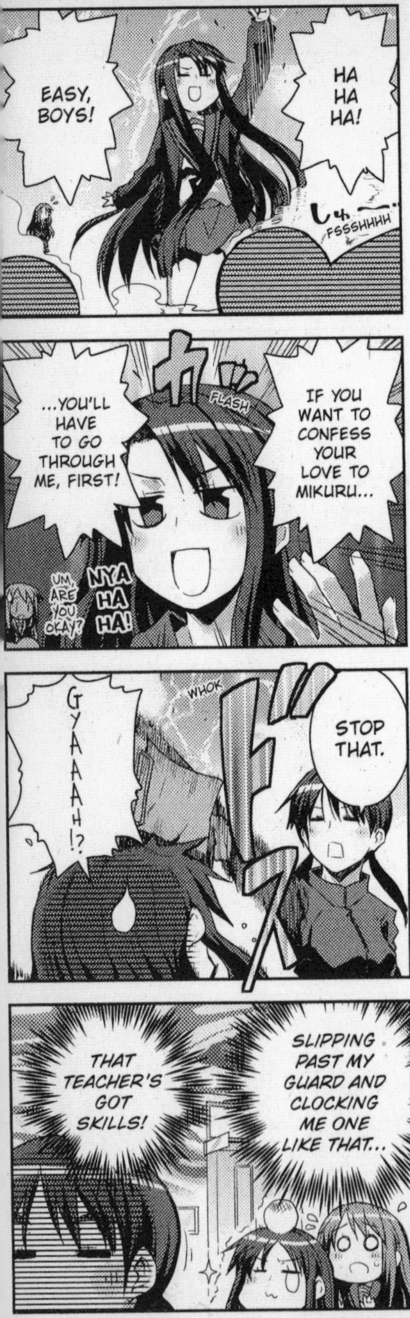
HA HA HA!
FSSSHHHH
EASY, BOYS!
IF YOU WANT TO CONFESS YOUR LOVE TO MIKURU...
FLASH
...YOU'LL HAVE TO GO THROUGH ME, FIRST!
NYA HA HA!
UM, ARE YOU OKAY?
STOP THAT.
WHOK
GYAAAAH!?
SLIPPING PAST MY GUARD AND CLOCKING ME ONE LIKE THAT...
THAT TEACHER'S GOT SKILLS!

CONVERSATION

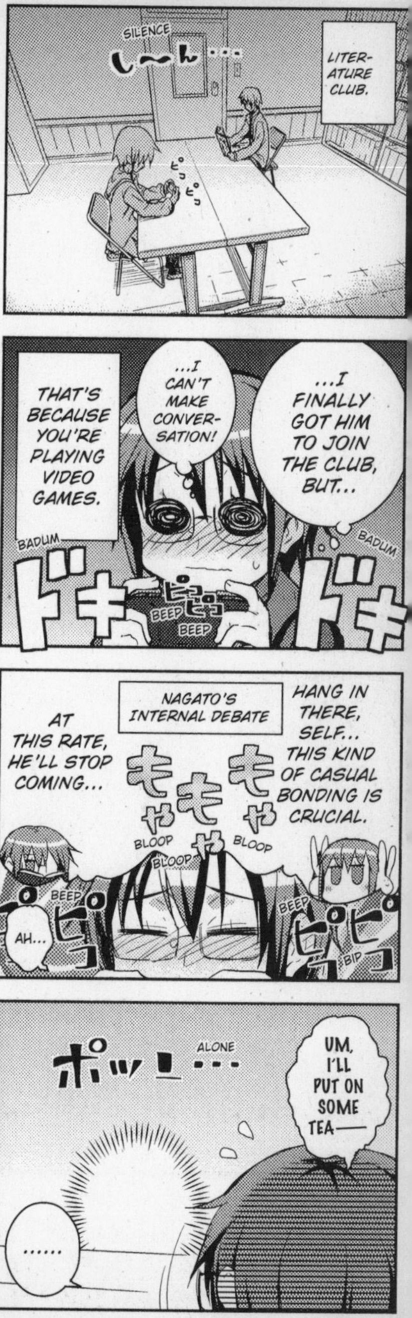
LITER-ATURE CLUB.
SILENCE
...I FINALLY GOT HIM TO JOIN THE CLUB, BUT...
...I CAN'T MAKE CONVER-SATION!
THAT'S BECAUSE YOU'RE PLAYING VIDEO GAMES.
BADUM
BADUM
BEEP
BEEP
HANG IN THERE, SELF... THIS KIND OF CASUAL BONDING IS CRUCIAL.
NAGATO'S INTERNAL DEBATE
AT THIS RATE, HE'LL STOP COMING...
BLOOP
BLOOP
BLOOP
BEEP
BEEP
BIP
AH...
UM, I'LL PUT ON SOME TEA—
ALONE
......

TEA

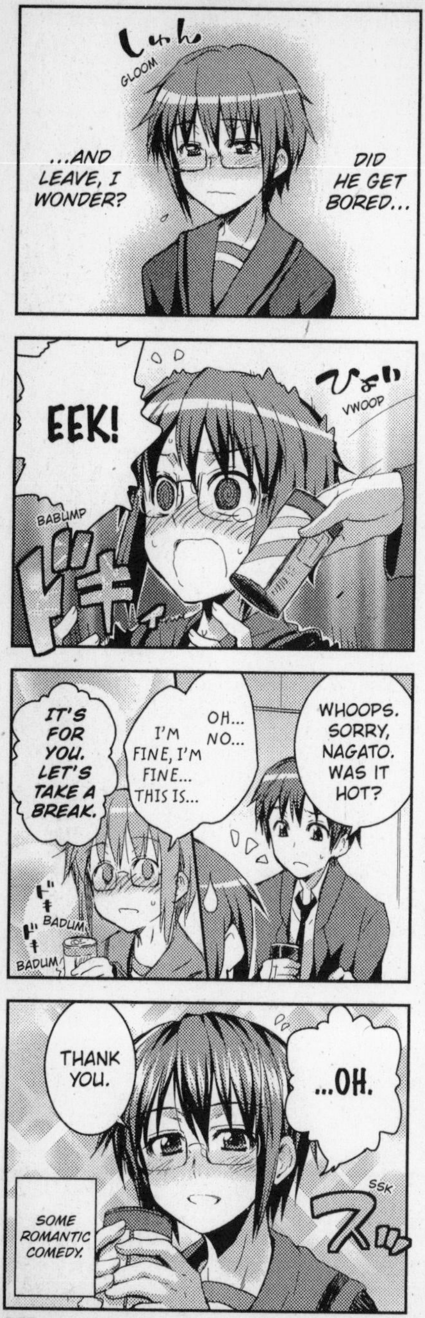
DID HE GET BORED...
...AND LEAVE, I WONDER?
GLOOM
VWOOP
EEK!
BABUMP
WHOOPS. SORRY, NAGATO. WAS IT HOT?
OH... NO...
I'M FINE, I'M FINE... THIS IS...
IT'S FOR YOU. LET'S TAKE A BREAK.
BADUM
BADUM
...OH.
THANK YOU.
SSK
SOME ROMANTIC COMEDY.

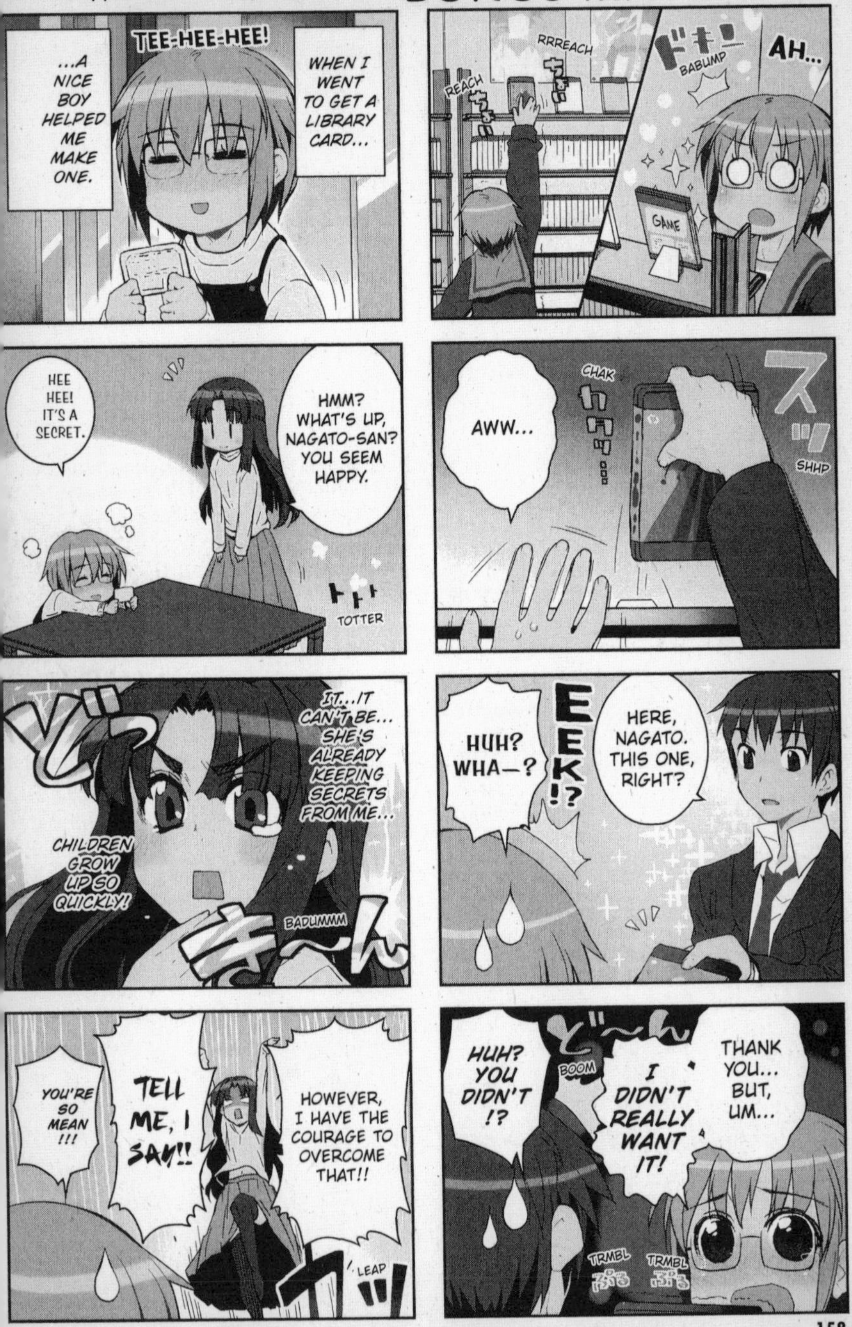
AH...
BABUMP
RRREACH
REACH
GAME
CHAK
AWW...
SHHP
HERE, NAGATO. THIS ONE, RIGHT?
EEK!?
HUH? WHA—?
THANK YOU... BUT, UM...
I DIDN'T REALLY WANT IT!
BOOM
HUH? YOU DIDN'T !?
TRMBL
TRMBL
WHEN I WENT TO GET A LIBRARY CARD...
TEE-HEE-HEE!
...A NICE BOY HELPED ME MAKE ONE.
HMM? WHAT'S UP, NAGATO-SAN? YOU SEEM HAPPY.
HEE HEE! IT'S A SECRET.
TOTTER
IT...IT CAN'T BE... SHE'S ALREADY KEEPING SECRETS FROM ME...
CHILDREN GROW UP SO QUICKLY!
BADUMMM
HOWEVER, I HAVE THE COURAGE TO OVERCOME THAT!!
TELL ME, I SAY!!
YOU'RE SO MEAN !!!
LEAP

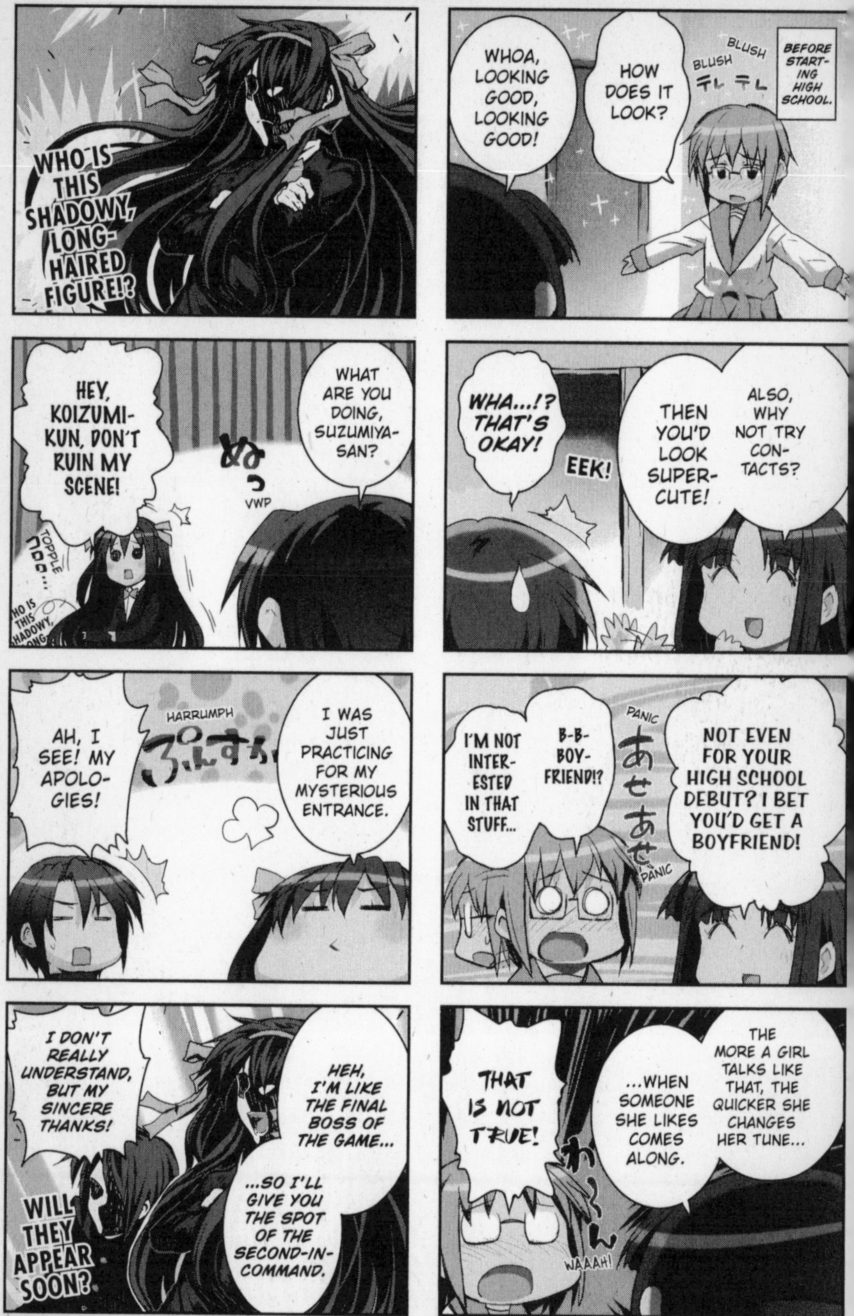
BEFORE STARTING HIGH SCHOOL.
BLUSH BLUSH テレ テレ
HOW DOES IT LOOK?
WHOA, LOOKING GOOD, LOOKING GOOD!
ALSO, WHY NOT TRY CONTACTS?
THEN YOU'D LOOK SUPERCUTE!
EEK!
WHA...!? THAT'S OKAY!
NOT EVEN FOR YOUR HIGH SCHOOL DEBUT? I BET YOU'D GET A BOYFRIEND!
PANIC あせあせ PANIC
B-B-BOYFRIEND!?
I'M NOT INTERESTED IN THAT STUFF...
THE MORE A GIRL TALKS LIKE THAT, THE QUICKER SHE CHANGES HER TUNE...
...WHEN SOMEONE SHE LIKES COMES ALONG.
わーん WAAAH!
THAT IS NOT TRUE!
WHO IS THIS SHADOWY, LONG-HAIRED FIGURE!?
WHAT ARE YOU DOING, SUZUMIYA-SAN?
ぬっ VWP
HEY, KOIZUMI-KUN, DON'T RUIN MY SCENE!
TOPPLE コロロ...
I WAS JUST PRACTICING FOR MY MYSTERIOUS ENTRANCE.
HARRUMPH ぷんすか
AH, I SEE! MY APOLOGIES!
HEH, I'M LIKE THE FINAL BOSS OF THE GAME...
...SO I'LL GIVE YOU THE SPOT OF THE SECOND-IN-COMMAND.
I DON'T REALLY UNDERSTAND, BUT MY SINCERE THANKS!
WILL THEY APPEAR SOON?

WE'RE GONNA BE ALL OVER THE NEXT VOLUME!

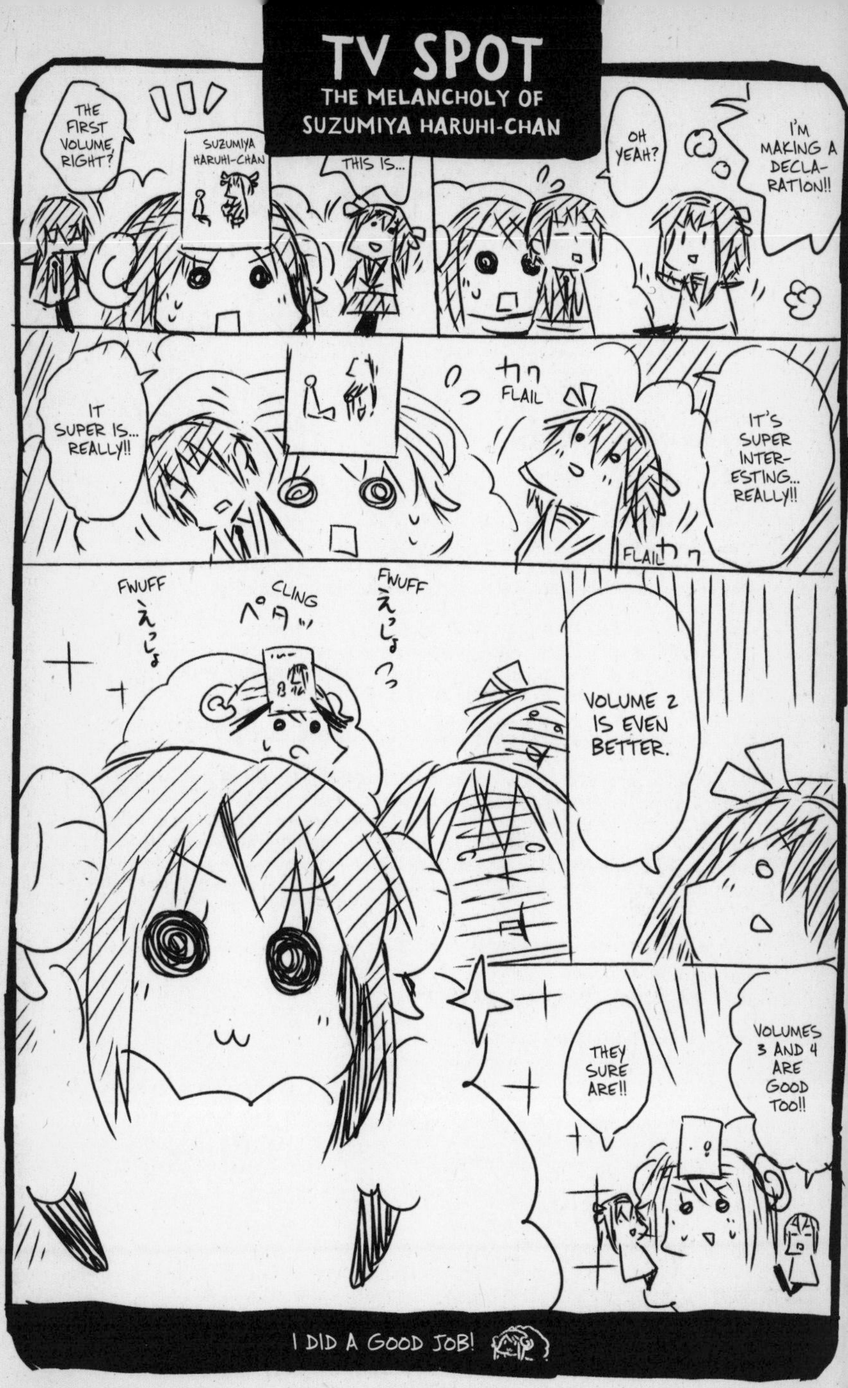
TV SPOT
THE MELANCHOLY OF SUZUMIYA HARUHI-CHAN
I'M MAKING A DECLARATION!!
OH YEAH?
THIS IS...
SUZUMIYA HARUHI-CHAN
THE FIRST VOLUME, RIGHT?
IT'S SUPER INTERESTING... REALLY!!
FLAIL
FLAIL
IT SUPER IS... REALLY!!
VOLUME 2 IS EVEN BETTER.
VOLUMES 3 AND 4 ARE GOOD TOO!!
THEY SURE ARE!!
FWUFF
CLING
FWUFF
I DID A GOOD JOB!

THE DISAPPEARANCE OF NAGATO
YUKI-CHAN
❶

Original Story: Nagaru Tanigawa
Manga: PUYO
Character Design: Noizi Ito

Translation: Paul Starr
Lettering: Jennifer Skarupa

NAGATO YUKI CHAN NO SHOSHITSU Volume 1 © Nagaru TANIGAWA • Noizi ITO 2010 © PUYO 2010. First published in Japan in 2010 by KADOKAWA SHOTEN Co., Ltd., Tokyo. English translation rights arranged with KADOKAWA SHOTEN Co., Ltd., Tokyo through TUTTLE-MORI AGENCY, INC., Tokyo.

English translation © 2012 by Hachette Book Group, Inc.

Yen Press
Hachette Book Group
237 Park Avenue, New York, NY 10017

www.HachetteBookGroup.com
www.YenPress.com

Yen Press is an imprint of Hachette Book Group, Inc.
The Yen Press name and logo are trademarks of Hachette Book Group, Inc.

First Yen Press Edition: July 2012

ISBN: 978-0-316-21712-5

10 9 8 7 6 5 4

BVG

Printed in the United States of America